POLITICAL APOCALYPSE

POLITICAL APOCALYPSE

A Study of Dostoevsky's Grand Inquisitor

ELLIS SANDOZ

LOUISIANA STATE UNIVERSITY PRESS • BATON ROUGE

72-14894

ISBN 0–8071–0936–3
Library of Congress Catalog Card Number: 77–152707
Copyright © 1971 by Louisiana State University Press
All rights reserved
Manufactured in the United States of America
Printed by The TJM Corporation, Baton Rouge, Louisiana
Designed by J. Barney McKee

To my mother
and the
memory of my father

Man is broad, even too broad. I'd have him narrower. . . . God and the devil are fighting there and the battlefield is the hearts of men.

 DOSTOEVSKY, *The Brothers Karamazov*

PREFACE

The secularization of existence marks the modern age. It has occurred, not only at the expense of the Christian tradition and the transcendentalist understanding of himself held by man since Moses and Plato, but also at the expense of common sense in politics and of rationality in philosophy through the disordering infusion of temporality with an ultimacy formerly reserved for the eternal beyond. This has, in turn, fostered the rise of ideological mass movements whose key experiential ingredient is political apocalypse—visions which penetrate present agony, misery, and injustice to perceive their end in the radical transformation of man and history into the perfect existence of peace, plenty, justice, happiness, and a "Final Harmony" of one description or another. The great diagnostician of the quest for succor and bliss by mankind in its peculiarly modern guise is the novelist Fyodor M. Dostoevsky, and the present essay addresses this political dimension of his thought and work as it reaches a climax in the "Legend of the Grand Inquisitor."

If "relevance" is a desideratum in what we think and do to understand and resolve the deepening crisis of the world today, then Dostoevsky is more than merely apposite; he is required reading. For almost all of the vexed problems which characterize the anguished plight of contemporary alienated men and women were illuminatingly inventoried and sympathetically explored by him a century ago, not in the didactic and sometimes moralizing manner of theology, philosophy, political science, and sociology, but in the existentially immediate modalities of creative artistry and poetry. Prophet, mystic, and philosopher though he was, these were but dimensions of Dostoevsky the tragic artist, the poet whose true predecessors were Aeschylus, Dante, Cervantes, Shakespeare, and Goethe.

Dostoevsky's work, as has often been asserted, is highly philosophical and so lends itself to the kind of theoretical analysis attempted herein. It is pervaded by a love of beauty and of the good which is the preeminent mark of philosophy (the love of the divine Wisdom) from Plato onward. Dostoevsky read Pascal during his youth, and from him derived an impression which profoundly shaped his comprehensive view of man and being. This view depends upon the early awareness of the essential rationality of Christian revelation and mystical intuition no less than of discursive, or instrumental, "Euclidian" reasoning—the distinction approximately signified in ancient philosophy by noetic and dianoetic reason and very largely lost from view after Bacon and Descartes, to be revived in the present century by Bergson. This does not suggest that Dostoevsky spoke in terms of philosophical doctrines or religious dogmas, for he, of course, did nothing of the kind; but it is to say that the intellectual content of his work is informed by a sophisticated theoretical literacy that finds expression in the existentially analytical dramaturgy of tragic-epics in the major novels. Not only does Dostoevsky tell a good story; his astonishing artistic creativity is matched by the acuteness of a great and educated mind.

The purpose of this book is to present in a fairly full and explicit way the meaning of the Grand Inquisitor. Because that passage is the author's valedictory, the task entailed the study of most of his writings and a sizable fraction of the critical literature as well. The present author is not a professional student of literature, his Russian is at best primitive, and the account given makes no claim to be exhaustive. The range of problems raised is encyclopedic, and not every source meaningful for Dostoevsky has been discussed or even identified. The approach here is from the side of political science, and it is hoped that at least the major political questions posed by the Legend have been cogently elucidated. The book began as a paper in a doctoral seminar in 1959 and is a revision of the writer's dissertation for the *Dr. oec. publ.* at the University of Munich.

Two previously published articles have, with permission, been incorporated into this volume: "The Problem of Good and Evil in Dostoevsky's 'Legend of the Grand Inquisitor,'" *Proceedings*, Louisiana Academy of Sciences, XXV (1961), 126–34; and "Philosophical Anthropology and Dostoevsky's 'Legend of the Grand Inquisitor,'" *The Review of Politics*, XXVI (1964), 353–77. The dissertation was privately printed in Germany under the title *The Grand Inquisitor: A Study in Political Apocalypse* (1967).

The pleasure remains to thank, without attributing to them responsibility for any errors or shortcomings, the many people who rendered a wide variety of assistance to the book's author over the decade of its germination. To all of them I extend sincere thanks. Especially do I wish to single out Eric Voegelin and to thank him for patient encouragement given at each step of the way in the metamorphosis of a seminar paper into a doctoral dissertation and, finally, into the form in which it now appears. Special gratitude also is due to Gregor Sebba, Manfred Henningsen, Rudolph Fiehler, Nikolai Naidenko, Avrahm Yarmolinsky, Georges Florovsky, John H. Kendrick, Charles E. Smith, Steve Rodakis, John F. Leich, Abraham Attrep, Sammy A. Dyson, Miroslav J. Hanak and Clyde E. Fant, Jr. My mother and my late father gave unfailing support in this as in every other endeavor of mine. My students over the years have been a continual source of stimulation and a sounding board for ideas that find expression in these pages. To the Fulbright Commission, the Germanistic Society of America, the Relm Foundation, the Earhart Foundation, and the Division of Organized Research of East Texas State University, I am grateful for a variety of financial support which at various stages aided the research and writing of this study. Finally, with utter equanimity and devotion, my wife Alverne has borne the many domestic duties I have shirked and even more of the brunt of care for our four children—who have grown up with the book and given encouragement in their unique ways—than was at all her share. To her I owe the especial gratitude due a prejudiced but perceptive reader whose confidence never flagged and who never once doubted the worth of the enterprise.

INTRODUCTION

The political thought of Fyodor Dostoevsky arises from opposition
to nihilism, atheistic humanism, and socialism in much the same
way as the philosophy of Plato arose from opposition to the Sophists.
Indeed, without necessarily meaning to suggest dependence or similarity in detail, the parallel of Dostoevsky's thought with that of
Plato can be seen in some further aspects of this fundamental opposition. Both the Russian master of the novel and the Hellenic founder
of political science confronted adversaries for whom "Man is the
measure of all things"; and each based his opposition on the principle, "God is the Measure"—to use Plato's formulation.[1] And this
declaration, echoing like a thunderclap across more than twenty
centuries of history, found consummate expression in the last great
work of each writer, the *Laws* and *The Brothers Karamazov*.

This book offers reflections on the political aspects of Dostoevsky's

---

[1] "No it is God who is, for you and me, of a truth the 'measure of all things,'
much more truly than, as they say, 'man.' So he who would be loved by such a being
must himself become such to the utmost of his might, and so, by this argument, he
that is temperate among us is loved by God, for he is like God, whereas he that
is not temperate is unlike God and at variance with him; so also it is with the un-
just, and the same rule holds in all else." Plato, *Laws* 716c–d, trans. A. E. Taylor
(London: Dent, 1960), 100–101. See, for a discussion of this opposition, Werner
Jaeger, *Humanism and Theology* (Milwaukee: Marquette University Press, 1943),
passim.

philosophical anthropology and upon the "Legend of the Grand
Inquisitor" considered as political apocalypse. By way of introduction, it will be appropriate to recall the pertinence of anthropology
and ethics to political theory. The basic connection is of the utmost
simplicity. Because political science is a search (*zetema*) for the truth
of things political,[2] it is of necessity concerned with man as human
and as citizen (*polites*) and with the axiological factors which give
order and cohesion to the lives of individuals and communities. The
science of man is anthropology, and the science of the goods which
order human existence is ethics.

The unity of the sciences of anthropology, ethics, and politics in
Classical political philosophy is well known. Anyone concerned with
these subjects will be interested to read, for instance, Aristotle's
treatise on political science, the *Nicomachean Ethics* and the *Politics*.
In a celebrated formula, Plato put man at the center of the science of
politics: society is man written in large letters (*Republic*, 368d). This
formulation, stating what Eric Voegelin calls the "anthropological
principle," [3] occurs in what is, next to the *Laws*, Plato's most important political dialogue. The substantial identity of the central
problems of ethics and politics, of man and society, is thereby postulated. The inquiry of the *Republic* into the nature of Justice (*Dike*)
is conducted as a political and ethical exploration simultaneously.
Moreover, the philosophical anthropology which Plato develops in
Book IV (435c), leads to the bifurcation at the beginning of Book
V (449a). The central passage of the dialogue unfolds the anthropology and theory of politics to climax in the Myth of the Cave and
the vision of the Good (*Agathon*). The analysis at the lower level is
directly resumed beginning with Book VIII (544), where the account of the four declining constitutional forms and the cycle of
history are presented strictly on the basis of the theory of the nature
of man and on a diagnosis of the political consequences of the various
disordering diseases of the soul. "The anthropological principle in

---

2 Leo Strauss, *What is Political Philosophy?* (Glencoe, Ill.: The Free Press,
1959) 10ff.

3 Eric Voegelin, *Plato and Aristotle* (Baton Rouge: Louisiana State University
Press, 1957), Vol. III of Voegelin, *Order and History* (3 vols. to date; Baton Rouge:
Louisiana State University Press, 1956——), 69.

politics as established by Plato requires that the idea of the perfect polis expresses (or that the standards developed by a political science are based on) the nature of man. We must have a systematic understanding of the nature of man if we want to have a systematic political science." And, again: "... the substance of society is psyche. Society can destroy a man's soul because the disorder of society is a disease in the psyche of its members." [4] The emphasis in Aristotle is similar. His philosophical anthropology is given in outline in *Ethics* I.

The centrality of the anthropological problem has not been lost on modern thinkers. Kant, in commenting on the import of his Fourth Question, "What is man?," stated that it encompassed all the other fundamental questions of philosophy. The three prior questions of philosophy in the universal sense—that is, What can I know? (answered by metaphysics), What ought I do? (answered by ethics), What may I hope? (answered by religion)—"could be reckoned as anthropology, since the first three questions are related to the last." [5] In French and German positivism, idealism, and materialism, the anthropological question assumed overwhelming proportions. French social thought moved from Fourier through Saint-Simon to Comte and the religion of Humanity, *le grand être*, the Great Being. The Hegelian Identities opened the way for Feuerbach's anthropological reduction and the final destruction of the idea of man in Marxian sociology. It is, therefore, in a sense true that "Marx's concept of socialism follows from his concept of man." [6] At this point Dostoevsky makes his entrance. And there simultaneously occurs the Nietzschean apotheosis of man and the transvaluation of values heralding the onset of the Age of Nihilism.

Dostoevsky pitted his conception of man against the anthropology of atheistic humanism. The anthropological question was of foremost importance to him. As a young man of nineteen he wrote: "Man is a mystery. It must be unravelled, and if you give your life to the task, do not think that you wasted it; I devote myself to this mystery

---

[4] *Ibid.*, 296, 69.

[5] From Kant's *Handbook* to the lectures in logic as quoted in Martin Buber, *Between Man and Man*, trans. R. G. Smith (Boston: Beacon Press, 1947), 119.

[6] Erich Fromm, *Marx's Concept of Man* (New York: Frederick Ungar Publ. Co., 1961), 58.

because I wish to be a man." [7] He remained true to this task throughout his days and in all of his art.

The present essay traces the effort of Dostoevsky to unravel the
mystery of man as this climaxes in the Legend of the Grand Inquisitor. The presentation is divided into three parts. The first attempts a sketch of the spiritual and intellectual background of the
novelist's work which makes explicit the conception of faith implicit in *The Brothers Karamazov*. The second—the principal part of
the book—is a meditative analysis of the Legend regarded as political apocalypse in the light of its context, structure, and sources. A
brief third part considers certain matters peripheral to the foregoing parts and brings the study to a conclusion by drawing the
major consequences of the analysis for the theory of politics.

---

[7] As quoted in Avrahm Yarmolinsky, *Dostoevsky: His Life and Art* (2nd ed.;
New York: Grove Press, Inc., 1960), 28.

CONTENTS

POLITICAL APOCALYPSE

PART ONE

MAJOR FORMATIVE FACTORS: A SKETCH

CHAPTER I

ROOTS OF RUSSIAN REVOLUTIONISM

Any attempt to reduce the pattern of Dostoevsky's thought to a single literary or philosophical source is doomed at the outset by the breadth of the author's reading and experience and the depth of his creative sensibility. It is of interest and importance, however, to establish the contours of the major forces which shaped his mind and art. Despite what is often written (with, however, considerable justification) about his erratic behavior, the shattering experiences of the epileptic fits, the gambling mania of his middle years, and the dark suspicions of unspeakable debauchery, the evidence on balance testifies to the abiding presence in Dostoevsky of a scholarly temperament, orderly work habits, and a sustained concern with the fundamental problems of human existence. While the excesses, disruptions, and vicissitudes of this ardent soul are not to be unduly minimized, neither should they be so exaggerated as to mislead us into supposing that Dostoevsky's life was one long chaotic binge. Dostoevsky's biography testifies not only to his intellectual and imaginative genius, but also to his constancy to obligations assumed, perseverance in tasks undertaken, systematic literary production under the most trying circumstances, and a high courage in facing and overcoming the most staggering adversities.[1] What at first appears in-

---

1 On the work habits of Dostoevsky, see, for example, the "Notes Made by Anna Grigorievna to Fyodor Mikhailovich's Letters to Her During 1874," in Fyodor M. Dostoevsky, *The Letters of Dostoevsky to His Wife*, trans. E. Hill and D. Mudie (New York: Richard R. Smith Co., 1930), especially 357ff.

choate and disorderly in his art is shown through the careful analyses of modern criticism to be a polyphonic technique of composition in which form and contents, elaborate symbolism, multiple levels of meaning, and an astonishing diversity of thematic elements are superbly combined into unified works. The achievement is the more impressive in view of the pressure under which he habitually worked, the swiftness with which he was compelled to write, and the necessity of publishing incomplete works in serial installments. The content and meaning of Dostoevsky's works are as little the result of chance and whim as is their form. It is necessary, therefore, briefly to notice the milieu in which he lived and wrote. This will be done by first considering the impact of various philosophical movements (and especially of Hegelianism) on nineteenth century Russia, the surge of Western revolutionary thought into the country after 1800, and the profoundly important and complex texture of the Russian religious experience and its symbolization. Then will follow an analysis of the problem of faith as it is represented in Russian Orthodoxy and, specifically, in Dostoevsky's work and will conclude part 1.

1. INTELLECTUAL CURRENTS: HEGELIANISM à la Russe

The philosophy of German idealism—that of Kant and Baader, but particularly of Schelling and Hegel—dominated the nineteenth century, both in western Europe and in Russia. While it cannot be proved that Dostoevsky ever read even so much as one word written by Hegel, Hegelianism à la Russe and the Hegelians of the left wing supplied the intellectual grist of Russian life from about 1835 until the end of Dostoevsky's life.[2] Dostoevsky was thoroughly immersed

---

[2] The influence of Hegel in Russia has received thorough study by Dmitri Chizhevski, *Hegel bei den Slaven* (Reichenberg: Stiepel, 1934), 145–396. Chizhevski divides the principal intellectual influences in Russia from the time of Peter the Great through the nineteenth century into the French and the German: "On the side of French culture stands the Enlightenment, Rationalism, and political Radicalism; on the German side—mysticism, speculative philosophy, Romanticism." *Ibid.*, 145. A revised edition of this work appeared in Paris in 1939 under the title *Gegel v Rossii*. For a less specialized survey of philosophical influences in Russia, see Thomas G. Masaryk, *The Spirit of Russia: Studies in History, Literature and Philosophy*, Vols. I and II, trans. Eden and Cedar Paul (2nd ed.; New York: Macmillan Co., 1955); Vol. III, ed. George Gibian, trans. Robert Bass (New York: Barnes and Noble, Inc., 1967).

in the intellectual life of Russia, not to say that of all western Europe. He refers directly to Hegel in the long letter written to his brother, Michael, from exile in Siberia immediately after release from prison saying, "if you have the chance of sending anything *not* officially, then be sure to send Hegel—but particularly Hegel's *History of Philosophy*. Upon that depends my whole future." Whether Dostoevsky ever actually read this book has not been established.[3] But given Dostoevsky's tenacity, it is improbable that a literary source important to his "whole future" should have permanently escaped scrutiny. The interest in Hegel unquestionably continued for at least the next two years, and there is evidence which is sufficient to establish that Dostoevsky probably had read something of Hegel during the exile portion of the Siberian period. Baron Alexander Vrangel in 1856 wrote from Semipalatinsk that "destiny has brought me into contact with a man of rare intellect and disposition—the gifted young author Dostoevsky. . . . I work daily with him; at the moment we think of translating Hegel's 'Philosophy' [*sic*] and the 'Psyche' of Carus." [4] One of Dostoevsky's biographers, E. H. Carr, has seen "clear traces of Hegel" in the author's art and laments the fact that this philosopher's "influence on nearly every branch of thought during the middle years of the last century has never been fully assessed." The particular point influenced by Hegel was the notion of the duality of human nature, borrowed from the French romantics by Dostoevsky in Carr's view, but transformed into the formula of the "double" as presented in the pre-Siberian work *The Double* (1846) and continued as a permanent element of his art. The point in which Dostoevsky may claim originality is the identification of this "lower" element (called the "double") with the unconscious or the subconscious in man.[5]

---

3 Fyodor M. Dostoevsky to his brother, Michael, February 22, 1854, in E. C. Mayne (trans.), *Letters of F. M. Dostoevsky to His Family and Friends* (New York: Horizon Press, 1961), 67. N. N. Strakhov reported Hegel's book was received but never read, and Dostoevsky presented it to him as a gift shortly after their first meeting. See Robert Louis Jackson, *Dostoevsky's Quest for Form: A Study of His Philosophy of Art* (New Haven: Yale University Press, 1966), 185.

4 Mayne (trans.), *Letters of Dostoevsky*, 298.

5 E. H. Carr, *Dostoevsky (1821–1881): A New Biography* (London: Allen and Unwin, 1949), 255–56. The deficiency Carr notes has been relieved by Chizhevski.

The pervasiveness of Hegelian influence in Russia at the time is vividly described by Alexander Herzen after 1840, when he returned to Moscow from exile. Particularly the *Phenomenology* and *Logic* reigned supreme.

> They discussed [them] incessantly; there was not a paragraph . . . which had not been the subject of furious battles for several nights together. People who loved each other were parted for weeks at a time because they disagreed about the definition of "transcendent spirit," or had taken as a personal insult an opinion on "the absolute personality and its existence in itself." Every insignificant treatise published in Berlin or other provincial or district towns of German philosophy was ordered and read into tatters, so that the spattered leaves fell out in a few days, if only there was a mention of Hegel in it.[6]

The center of these philosophical discussions was the Moscow circles at first, the influence radiating to St. Petersburg somewhat later. Herzen, who was Dostoevsky's friend in the sixties and a contributor to *Vremia,* spoke of the University of Moscow as "the University of secret Hegelism." One of the most important of these circles was that of Herzen himself; another that of N. V. Stankevich, who was succeeded as leader by M. Bakunin. Vissarion G. Belinsky, who went to St. Petersburg in 1839, was one of the members of the latter circle.

Dostoevsky's personal contact with Herzen in the sixties is well known, as is also his intimate friendship with N. N. Strakhov from the beginning of the sixties until the end of his life. For this late period, Strakov—a self-designated Hegelian and the leading popularizer of Hegelianism in Russia—was Dostoevsky's principal "philosophical authority." [7] Less well known is that as late as 1872 Dostoevsky spoke of two essays by Herzen on the central theme of Hegel (the relation between Reality and Thought and the problem of the

---

6 Alexander I. Herzen, *My Past and Thoughts,* trans. Constance Garnett (6 vols.; New York: Alfred A. Knopf, Inc., 1924–28), II, 115.

7 Chizhevski, *Hegel bei den Slaven,* 245, 312–13. It is all the more ironic that he became Dostoevsky's most savage posthumous calumniator. Cf. the celebrated accusation lodged by Strakhov against Dostoevsky in a letter to Tolstoy and Anna Grigorievna's reply to it in A. G. Dostoevsky, *Dostoevsky Portrayed by His Wife: The Diary and Reminiscences of Mme. Dostoevsky,* ed. and trans. S. S. Koteliansky (New York: E. P. Dutton and Co., 1926).

Identities) as the "best philosophy not only in Russia—in Europe." [8]
These essays are regarded by Chizhevski as "the most important literary products of Russian Hegelianism of the forties."

Bakunin was the dominant figure of the Stankevich circle. It was
he who educated Belinsky philosophically, introducing him to Schelling, Fichte, and in 1847 to the thought of Hegel. Herzen encouraged
him to study Feuerbach and the other writers of the Hegelian Left.
By 1842 Belinsky was acquainted with French socialism and by 1846
with the positivism of Comte and Littré. He regarded the latter as
the "richer nature" of the two.[9] Like so many other Russian pro-
gressives of the period, Belinsky passed in his metaphysics from German idealism and romanticism "to positivism, materialism, and
atheism." Bakunin and Herzen remained his close literary and
philosophical associates. Bakunin, in particular, Belinsky referred
to as his "spiritual father." [10] Herzen once remarked that, in his life,
he had met only two people who really understood Hegel and neither
of these could read a word of German: one was Proudhon and the
other Belinsky.[11]

Dostoevsky first met Belinsky on the occasion of his triumph in
the spring of 1845. The then leading critic of Petersburg hailed the
young (twenty-four years old) author of *Poor Folk* as "a new Gogol."
Dostoevsky became (in a rather irregular way, it is true) a member
of Belinsky's circle from that time until the final rupture of their
friendship in the spring of 1847. Belinsky died in the following year.
During those two years, Dostoevsky associated with the literary lions
of the day and, as he himself tells us, was immersed in the ideological
world of the "Furious Vissarion." He became a member of the

8 See Chizhevski, *Hegel bei den Slaven*, 266–67. Cf. the discussion of Dostoevsky's
relation to Herzen, for whom Hegel is "the greatest thinker," in the note of N.
Belchikov in Dostoevsky, *The Letters of Dostoevsky to His Wife*, 333–34. For the
quoted expression, see Herzen, *My Past and Thoughts*, VI, 224.

9 Vissarion G. Belinsky to V. P. Botkin, February 17, 1847, in Belinsky, *Selected
Philosophical Works* (Moscow: Foreign Languages Publishing House, 1956), 523.

10 Masaryk, *The Spirit of Russia*, I, 350–78, 434–35. Cf. Chizhevski, *Hegel bei den
Slaven*, 164ff. M. Yovchuk, in his "A Great Russian Thinker: Introductory Essay,"
criticizes this periodization of Belinsky's development and attributes it to Ple-
khanov in Belinsky, *Selected Philosophical Works*, xv.

11 Evgueny Lampert, *Studies in Rebellion* (New York: Frederick A. Praeger, Inc.,
1957), 68–69. D. Chizhevski is less enthusiastic.

Petrashevsky circle where the socialism of Fourier was a principal topic of conversation. But it is little appreciated that Petrashevsky was himself a member of the Hegelian Left who opposed the "abstract speculation" of Hegel and was concerned about the "difficult problems of the working class," about "living human life." Petrashevsky's *Conversational Dictionary* is the very "voice of the Hegelian Left." [12] Moreover, Y. Pokrovskaya has shown that his dissatisfaction with the passivity of the Petrashevists led young Dostoevsky to join the more radical circle of Sergei Durov.[13] It was, primarily, for his reading of Belinsky's *Letter to Gogol* to the Petrashevsky circle that Dostoevsky was arrested and sent to Siberia for ten years.[14] Dostoevsky continued his friendship, gained through Belinsky, with the erudite Schellingian and *Dekabrist* Prince V. F. Odoevsky up until the time of his imprisonment in April, 1849. Odoevsky, Goncharov, and Turgenev regarded Belinsky as the "most educated man in Russia of his time"—although Goncharov would add, "with the exception of Herzen." [15] The contempt in which he later held Belinsky was not the view of the young Dostoevsky of the period of *Poor Folk* and *The Double*. On the contrary, that he was profoundly under the influence of Belinsky at this time he himself later acknowledged.

Belinsky introduced the young prodigy of the forties into the intellectual and literary elite of St. Petersburg, and from this initiation Dostoevsky moved toward the radical Left in his associations and in the vagaries of his curiosity and political allegiances. The experiences and impressions of the last three pre-Siberian years were decisive for the content of Dostoevsky's late work. To a reader of *The Diary of a Writer* (published sporadically from 1873 until 1881), Belinsky ap-

---

12 Chizhevski, *Hegel bei den Slaven*, 288.

13 Cf. Vladimir Seduro, *Dostoevsky in Russian Literary Criticism, 1846–1956* (New York: Columbia University Press, 1957), 100, 321. Durov was one of the six (including Petrashevsky and Dostoevsky) taken to the Semionov Square for execution by a firing squad for their revolutionary activities on December 22, 1849, only to have their sentences commuted at the last minute. For the full account by Dostoevsky, see the letter to his brother, Michael, of that day in S. S. Koteliansky and J. Middleton Murry (trans.), *Dostoevsky: Letters and Reminiscences* (New York: Alfred A. Knopf, Inc., 1923), 5–13.

14 An English translation of the letter is to be found in Belinsky, *Selected Philosophical Works*, 536–46.

15 Lampert, *Studies in Rebellion*, 28.

pears as the very *bête noire* of Dostoevsky. He is execrated with virtually every reference to his name. But the enmity expressed is that of the disillusioned lover: fascination has given way to the discovery that a hideous flaw lies beneath the beautiful exterior—yet something of the old love still lingers.

The stimulus of these associations helped to educate Dostoevsky and also led him to isolate and reject the central metaphysical tenet of positivism, materialism, and radical socialism: namely, atheism. The positive aspect of Hegelianism, from the perspective of Dostoevsky's art, included the Identities and pantheism. Both his theism and romanticism found an enduring merit and luminosity in these elements. And there is, indeed, a sense in which Hegel does not depart far from the metaphysical conceptions of Fichte and Schelling, even though he was attacked by their authors. They are alike in professing a monistic metaphysics which asserts that the universe is a single whole embracing all that occurs in nature as well as in history and that this whole manifests an ultimate reality called the "Absolute." This Absolute takes the form of experience in the finite human mind.[16] In the intellectual and spiritual biography of Dostoevsky, this monistic metaphysical doctrine is then connected with the pantheism of Spinoza through the mediation of Vladimir Solovyov's avowedly gnostic panentheism and theosophical mysticism.

The importance of the youthful Solovyov to Dostoevsky, in the period beginning in 1873 when they first became friends, while unquestionably great, is difficult to assay with precision. Dostoevsky attended his young friend's "Lectures on Godmanhood" in the spring of 1878. Perhaps the chief significance of Solovyov for Dostoevsky is that he formulates in philosophical language much that the novelist presents through mythopoesis. But that Solovyov goes far beyond Dostoevsky in the direction of gnosticism seems certain. While Dostoevsky is sure to have drawn from Solovyov, the principal current of influence runs in the opposite direction. Solovyov's influence complements and gives metaphysical support to views and convictions which derive from a much earlier period, more specifically from Dostoevsky's considered opposition to the atheistic idea and the

---

16 Cf. *ibid.*, 69.

metaphysical rebellion founded upon it. But in the God-man and the man-god antinomy as well as in the cosmic mysticism of *The Brothers Karamazov*, the influence of Solovyov can be traced.[17] His significance for the Legend of the Grand Inquisitor must later concern us in some detail.

The negative aspect of the Belinsky legacy (if it may be so designated) is that it is in terms of the Feuerbachian-Comtean socialism of the later Belinsky that Dostoevsky defines the enemy. To be sure, Dostoevsky is eclectic in his extensive portraiture of socialism. But the thrust of his politics is delineated in the first issue of *Grazhdanin*.

Some two years ago, the International prefaced one of its proclamations with this straightforward, meaningful statement: "Above all, we are an atheistic society"—that is, they started with the very essence of the matter.[18] Such was also Belinsky's prelude.

Treasuring above everything reason, science and realism, at the same time he comprehended more keenly than anyone that reason, science and realism alone can merely produce an ant's nest, and not social "harmony" within which man can organize his life. He knew that moral principles are the basis of all things. He believed, to the degree of delusion and without any reflex, in the new moral foundations of socialism (which, however, up to the present revealed none but abominable perversions of nature and common sense). Here was nothing but rapture. Still, as a socialist, he had to destroy Christianity in the first place. He knew that the revolution must necessarily begin with atheism. He had to dethrone that religion whence the moral foundations of the society rejected by him had sprung up. Family, property, personal moral responsibility—these he denied radically. . . . Doubtless, he understood that by denying the moral responsibility of man, he thereby denied also his freedom; yet, he believed with all his being . . . that socialism not only does not destroy the freedom of man, but, on the contrary, restores it in a form of unheard-of majesty, only on a new and adamantine foundation.

---

[17] See V. V. Zenkovsky, *A History of Russian Philosophy*, trans. George L. Kline (2 vols.; New York: Columbia University Press, 1953), I, 425–26; II, 469ff; Vladimir S. Solovyov, *Lectures On Godmanhood*, trans. Peter Zouboff (London: Dennis Dobson, 1948); Solovyov, *A Solovyov Anthology*, ed. and with an intro. by S. L. Frank, trans. N. Duddington (London: S. C. M. Press, 1950).

[18] The precise wording of the slogan (actually the opening words of the *Programme*) read as follows: "The Alliance proclaims itself atheist: it stands for the abolition of cults, the substitution of science for faith, and of human for divine justice." See G. D. H. Cole, *A History of Socialist Thought* (5 vols.; London: Macmillan Co., 1957), II, 232.

At this juncture, however, there remained the radiant personality of Christ himself to contend with, which was the most difficult problem. As a socialist, he was duty bound to destroy the teaching of Christ, to call it fallacious and ignorant philanthropy doomed by modern science and economic tenets. Even so, there remained the beatific image of God-man, its moral inaccessibility, its wonderful and miraculous beauty. But in his incessant, unquenchable transport, Belinsky did not stop even before this insurmountable obstacle, as did Renan, who proclaimed in his *La Vie de Jésus*—a book permeated with incredulity—that Christ nevertheless is the ideal of human beauty, an inaccessible type which cannot be repeated even in the future.

"But do you know," he screamed one evening (sometimes in a state of great excitement he used to scream), "do you know it is impossible to charge man with sins, to burden him with debts and turning the other cheek, when society is organized so meanly that man cannot help but perpetrate villainies; when, economically, he has been brought to villainy, and that it is silly and cruel to demand from man that which, by the very laws of nature, he is impotent to perform even if he wished to . . . ?

"Oh, no! If Christ were to appear in our day, He would join the movement and head it. . . . Precisely, He would join the socialists and follow them."

These propellers of mankind, whom Christ was designed to join, were then the French: George Sand, the now altogether forgotten Cabet, Pierre Leroux and Proudhon who was then only beginning his activities. As far as I remember, at that time Belinsky respected these four.—Fourier had already lost much of his prestige. [N.B.]—They were being discussed through whole evenings.

There was also a German before whom Belinsky bowed with great deference, namely, Feuerbach. (Belinsky, who all his life was unable to master any foreign language, pronounced the name of Feuerbach as Fierbach.) Strauss was spoken of with reverence.

With this warm faith in his idea, Belinsky was, of course, the happiest of human beings.

Even so, this most blessed human being endowed with such a remarkably serene conscience, would sometimes become very sad; but this melancholy was of a special kind—resulting not from doubts, not from disillusions—oh, no—but from the query: why, indeed, not today, but tomorrow?

During the last year of his life I did not visit him. He took a dislike to me, *but then I had passionately embraced his teaching.*[19]

---

[19] Fyodor M. Dostoevsky, *The Diary of a Writer*, trans. Boris Brasol (2 vols.; New York: Charles Scribner's Sons, 1949); (*The Citizen*, 1873, No. 1), I, 6–9, hereinafter cited as Dostoevsky, *Diary*. Italics mine.

The thought and intention of the man whose teaching Dostoevsky had "passionately embraced" might detain us at length. Belinsky's revolutionism had, properly speaking, only one opponent: the Russian theocracy and its ecclesiastical religion. It was directed against the superstition and the mysticism of the established church. His invocation of Hegel, Feuerbach, Comte, and their enlightened rationalism was meant to scare away superstition and mysticism. As Masaryk remarks, Belinsky knew Russia and knew himself.[20] Dostoevsky's judgment—that Belinsky was essentially a revolutionist and that his revolutionism had as a cardinal presupposition the opinion that the realm of transcendent being is chimerical—seems well founded. The perspicacity of Dostoevsky in this regard is suggested by the laudatory evaluation of Belinsky in recent Soviet criticism.

> V. G. Belinsky was the initiator of the revolutionary-democractic movement of the last century, the ideological inspirer of the struggle against the landlord-autocratic system in the reactionary reign of Nicholas I. . . . Belinsky's whole conscious life was devoted to the search for a correct revolutionary theory, for the right way to bring about the social transformation of Russian life. . . . Lenin showed that Belinsky and his followers, first and foremost Chernyshevsky, represented the revolutionary-democratic trend in Russia's historical development, which was sharply opposed to the other trend—that of bourgeois and landlord liberalism.[21]

The pivotal ideological conception of Belinsky was the "idea of negation"—nihilism—which involved the critique and destruction of the old forms of society in order that the new, just, social order might come into existence. Without such negation and destruction, he said, human history would become a "stagnant and malodorous swamp." He called Hegel's dialectics the "algebra of revolution." But, like Petrashevsky and other contemporary revolutionists—and most notably like Karl Marx—Belinsky was not so much interested in abstract speculation as he was in concrete praxis. "In Hegel philosophy attained its highest development, but it came to an end with

---

20 Masaryk, *The Spirit of Russia*, I, 367.
21 M. Yovchuk in Belinsky, *Selected Philosophical Works*, viii, ix, li. *Notes From Underground* was a reply to Chernyshevsky's *What Is to Be Done?*—a title later taken over by Lenin.

him as a cognition that is mysterious and alien to life. . . . The beginning of [the] beneficent reconciliation between philosophy and practice was achieved on the left side of present-day Hegelianism." [22]

Fascinating among Belinsky's writings for the student of Dostoevsky is the letter to V. P. Botkin dated March 1, 1841, because of the singular similarity between it and the words of Ivan Karamazov forty years later, as the latter rejects his entrance ticket to the "eternal harmony."

> You will laugh at me, I know . . . but, never mind, I will stick to my view: the fate of a subject, an individual, a personality is more important than the fate of the world. . . . Let me inform you, with all respect for your philosophical philistinism, that if I did succeed in reaching the top of the evolution ladder, I would demand even there an account from you of all the victims of the conditions of life and history, of all the victims of accident, superstition, the Inquisition, Philip II, *etc., etc.*: otherwise I will throw myself headlong from the top rung. I will not have happiness even if you give it to me gratis unless I feel assured about every one of my blood brothers, the bone of my bone and flesh of my flesh. Disharmony is said to be a condition of harmony: that may be very profitable and pleasant for melomaniacs, but certainly not for those whose fates are destined to express the idea of disharmony.[23]

In his impassioned manifesto, of the same year, Belinsky proposed, as the cure for the ills of the world as heretofore organized, the therapy of socialism, and proclaimed his conversion to the new doctrine.

> I am at a new extreme, which is the idea of *socialism* that has become for me the idea of ideas, the being of beings, the question of questions, the alpha and omega of belief and knowledge. It is the be all and end all. It is the question and its solution. It has (for me) engulfed history and

---

[22] Belinsky, *Selected Philosophical Works*, xxxii, 305. Herzen also wrote: "The philosophy of Hegel is the algebra of revolution, it emancipates a man in an extraordinary way and leaves not a stone standing of the Christian world, of the world of outlived tradition." Herzen, *My Past and Thoughts*, II, 121. On the nihilism of Hegel and its Cartesian philosophical roots, see Stanley Rosen, *Nihilism: A Philosophical Essay* (New Haven: Yale University Press, 1969), 88–93.

[23] Vissarion G. Belinsky to V. P. Botkin, March 1, 1841, in Belinsky, *Selected Philosophical Works*, 160. The striking parallel between Belinsky's and Ivan's views, as expressed here has frequently been observed. Cf Robert Payne, *Dostoevsky: A Human Portrait* (New York: Alfred A. Knopf, Inc., 1961), 358ff.

religion and philosophy. And hence I now use it to explain my life, yours
and everybody's whom I have met on the path of life. . . . My God is
negation! In history my heroes are the destroyers of the old—Luther,
Voltaire, the Encyclopaedists, the Terrorists, Byron (*Cain*), and so on.
. . . I prefer the blasphemies of Voltaire to acknowledging the authority
of religion, society, or anything or anybody! I know that the Middle
Ages were a great epoch. . . . But I prefer the eighteenth century—the epoch
of religion's decline: in the Middle Ages heretics, freethinkers and witches
were burnt at the stake; in the eighteenth century the guillotine chopped
off the heads of aristocrats, priests and other enemies of God, Reason,
and Humanity. And there will come a time—I fervently believe it—when
no one will be burnt, no one will be decapitated . . . when there will be
no senseless forms and rites, no contracts and stipulations on feeling, no
duty and obligation, and we shall not yield to will but to love alone; when
there will be no husbands and wives, but lovers and mistresses. . . . There
will be neither rich nor poor, neither kings nor subjects, there will be
brethren, there will be men, and, at the word of the apostle Paul, Christ
will pass his power to the Father, and Father-Reason will hold sway once
more, but this time in a new heaven and above a new world. . . . I want
the golden age, not the former unreasoning golden age of the beast, but
the one that has been prepared by society, laws, marriage, in a word by
everything that was in its time essential but is now stupid and vulgar.
. . . And that will be effected through *sociality*. And hence there is no
object more noble and lofty than to contribute towards its progress and
development. But it is absurd to imagine that this could happen by itself,
with the aid of time, without violent changes, without bloodshed. Men
are so insensate that they must forcibly be led to happiness. And of what
significance is the blood of thousands compared to the degradation and
sufferings of the millions. Indeed: *fiat justitia, pereat mundus!*[24]

The fine exaltation and religious enthusiasm expressed by Belinsky
in 1841 have remained characteristic of the gnostic-ideologue to this
day.

Just four months prior to Dostoevsky's triumphant first meeting
with Belinsky, in January, 1845, the latter had read two early works
of Karl Marx in the first and only issue of the publication *Deutsch-*

---

24 Belinsky to Botkin, September 8, 1841, in Belinsky, *Selected Philosophical
Works*, 170, 175–77. Belinsky's words echo Rousseau's doctrine in *The Social Con-
tract* (bk. 1, chap. 7) that "it may be necessary to compel a man to be free"—the
starting point of modern totalitarianism. See J. L. Talmon, *The Origins of Totalitarian Democracy* (New York: Frederick A. Praeger, Inc., 1952), 42–43.

Französische Jahrbücher, namely, the essay, "On the Jewish Question," and the important "Critique of Hegel's Philosophy of Law." In reacting to them, he had written to Herzen: "I have accepted the truth—and in the words *God* and *religion* I see darkness, gloom, shackles and the knout; and now I love these two words as much as I love the four that follow them." [25] These early works of Marx, together with the influence of Feuerbach, served to complete in Belinsky the education that Marx expressed in the formula, "The critique of religion is the presupposition of all critique." It was precisely on this strategic ground that Dostoevsky encountered Belinsky as a young man and then, in his mature work, returned to do battle with his followers and successors. [26]

2. WESTERN REVOLUTIONISM AND IDEOLOGY

The contour of Dostoevsky's avowed enemy is thus discerned. It came to be identified as the intelligentsia. The tangled etiology of the rise of this element of Russian society cannot here concern us. Suffice it to say that the sprouting intelligentsia of the period from the Dekabrist revolt of 1825 to the death of Belinsky in 1848 reached full flower in the more tolerant atmosphere of the Russia of Alexander II (1855 to 1881). Split into two wings, the Slavophiles and Westernizers, the radical revolutionary intelligentsia emerged in the third quarter of the nineteenth century in that branch of the Westernizers called the *raznochintsy*. The *raznochintsy* were the conveyer belt of Western revolutionism, the ideological heirs of Bakunin and Belinsky in the Russia of the mature Dostoevsky. Their spokesmen were Chernyshevsky and Dobroliubov. In the pages of *The Brothers Karamazov,* it is Ivan who is the chief (if tortured) protagonist of their viewpoint. Exponents of the most radical doctrines of French positivism, German materialism, and socialism, this segment of the intelligentsia represented the end form of atheist humanism as it gathered into the tidal wave that eventually was to overwhelm tsarist and Orthodox

---

25 Quoted by M. Yovchuk in Belinsky, *Selected Philosophical Works,* xxxvii.
26 On the importance of Feuerbach to Dostoevsky, see Reinhard Lauth, *Die Philosophie Dostojewskis in systematischer Darstellung* (Munich: Piper, 1950), 311; cf. Konstantin Mochulsky, *Dostoevsky: His Life and Work,* trans. and with an intro. by Michael A. Minihan (Princeton: Princeton University Press, 1967), 117–20.

Russia. The psychological and metaphysical roots of the *raznochintsy* are laid bare by Dostoevsky both in *The Possessed* and in *The Brothers Karamazov*. Their social and political principles can be summarized in three statements: (1) the injustice and misery suffered by the peasantry were national sins for which the privileged minority was morally and politically responsible; (2) the tsarist theocratic autocracy was the root evil of Russia, the cause of both economic backwardness and social inequality and ought to be destroyed; (3) the application of the radical ideologies of the West to Russia after destruction of the tsarist regime would lead to immediate improvement in all spheres of life and to ultimate perfection of man and society. Atheism and materialism were the marks of a progressive outlook, and Europe was regarded as the light for the East because of its rationalism and irreligion. The whole movement was enthusiastic, permeated by the glow of fanatical conviction and wholehearted dedication characteristic of adherents of a messianic and eschatological doctrine.[27]

Dostoevsky remained a lifelong student of the problem of revolutionary socialism. In the 1860s and 1870s he was keenly alive to the rumble of revolutionism and to the activities of Herzen (whom he visited in 1862) and Bakunin (whom he had heard address the second session of the International Peace Congress of the League for

---

[27] The three-point summary of the radical intelligentsia's doctrine relies on Nicolas Zernov, *Eastern Christendom: A Study of the Origin and Development of the Eastern Orthodox Church* (New York: G. P. Putnam's Sons, 1961), 197. The principal literature upon which the general assessment of the movement is based is the following: Richard Pipes (ed.), *The Russian Intelligentsia* (New York: Columbia University Press, 1961); Marc Raëff, *Origins of the Russian Intelligentsia: The Eighteenth Century Nobility* (New York: Harcourt, Brace & World, Inc., 1966); Michael Prawdin, *The Unmentionable Nechaev: A Key to Bolshevism* (New York: Roy Publishers, Inc., 1961); E. H. Carr, *Studies in Revolution* (New York: Grosset & Dunlap, Inc., 1964); Antole G. Mazour, *The First Russian Revolution 1825: The Decembrist Movement; Its Origins, Development, and Significance* (Stanford: Stanford University Press, 1937); Avrahm Yarmolinsky, *Road to Revolution: A Century of Russian Radicalism* (New York: Macmillan Co., 1959); Franco Venturi, *Roots of Revolution: A History of the Populist and Socialist Movements in Nineteenth Century Russia*, trans. Francis Haskell, and with an intro. by Isaiah Berlin (New York: Grosset & Dunlap, Inc., Universal Library, 1966); John H. Hallowell, *Main Currents in Modern Political Thought* (New York: Holt, Rinehart & Winston, Inc., 1950).

Peace and Freedom, in Geneva in September, 1867). Dostoevsky spoke of his impressions of the session as follows:

> When I arrived here, the Peace Conference was just beginning, to which Garibaldi himself came. He went away immediately afterwards. It was really incredible how these socialist and revolutionary gentlemen, whom hitherto I had known only from books, sat and flung down lies from the platform to their audience of five thousand! It's quite indescribable. One can hardly realize, even for oneself, the absurdity, feebleness, futility, disunion, and the depth of essential contradictoriness. And it is this rabble which is stirring up the whole unfortunate working-class! It's too deplorable. That they may attain peace on earth, they want to root out the Christian faith, annihilate the Great Powers and cut them up into a lot of small ones, abolish capital, declare that all property is common to all, and so forth. And all this is affirmed with no logical demonstration whatever; what they learned twenty years ago, they are still babbling today. Only when fire and sword have exterminated everything, can, in their belief, eternal peace ensue.[28]

Dostoevsky manifests an informed and persistent interest in all varieties of socialism throughout the last two decades of his life. *The Possessed* used the notorious Nechaev affair as its point of inspiration. Leonid Grossman has argued that the character "Stavrogin" in the novel is a literary reincarnation of Bakunin; but the *Notebooks* for the novel do not support the view and the claims for Nicolas Speshnev (a fellow Petrashevist) are perhaps more persuasive, although there is no reason not to allow for a composite, just as Verkhovensky seems to be a composite of Nechaev and Chernyshevsky.[29] In any event, it is erroneous to suppose that Dostoevsky's sole direct knowledge of and interest in the activities of the nihilists, Socialists, and Communists antedates his imprisonment. It is likewise a mistake to contend (as has been done) that the old idea of the forties merely remained "imbedded in his mind like a fossil"—thereby to conclude

---

28 Dostoevsky to his niece, Sofia Alexandrovna, September 29/October 11, 1867, in Mayne (trans.), *Letters of Dostoevsky*, 130.

29 Lampert, *Studies in Rebellion*, 275n27. Cf. Fyodor M. Dostoevsky, *The Notebooks for "The Possessed,"* ed. and with an intro. by Edward Wasiolek, trans. Victor Terras (Chicago: University of Chicago Press, 1968), 153n, 185, 272, 341, 349, 360, 387.

that "Dostoevsky was a typical case of arrested development." [30] The cited slogan announcing atheism as the central tenet of revolutionary socialism (quoted above) came, in fact, from Bakunin's "Programme" for the Alliance of Socialist Democracy of 1868. Dostoevsky was an avid newspaper reader. He remained abroad for most of the period between 1862 and 1871 (including the four years, April 14, 1867, to July 9, 1871), much of which was spent in Switzerland during the height of the activities of the First International and the various other revolutionary groups. His visit to Alexander Herzen occurred in 1862, the same year that Bakunin's Russian translation of the *Communist Manifesto* appeared in Herzen's journal *Kolokol* (*"The Bell"*). Although there appears to be no conclusive evidence that Dostoevsky ever read Marx, he mentioned him in *Grazhdanin*[31] and referred to the International and to the Paris Commune on a number of occasions. Shigalov (in *The Possessed*) may have been modelled on Pëtr Tkachov: a defendant in the Nechaev trial and one of the earliest Russian followers of Marx, he is considered (along with Nechaev himself and his [Bakunin's?] *Revolutionary Catechism*) to have influenced Lenin.[32] Dostoevsky primarily aimed at the nihilists, to be sure, but he was quite prepared for the face of the enemy to change. And which modern reader of Marx's *Theses on Feuerbach* or *Critique of the Hegelian Philosophy of Law* will affirm that Dostoevsky's analyses are inapposite? That Dostoevsky understood Bakunin is incontestable;[33] and Marx and Bakunin start from the same philosophical position—however extensive their later differences—namely from Hegel-Feuerbach and the Hegelian Left. Both learned from Proudhon and the French Socialists and both were positivists and materialists. And while Marx the theorist and Bakunin the practitioner can be distinguished in certain aspects, the distinction must not be driven too far. For at first, as well as even later, Marx's outlook did not es-

---

[30] Avrahm Yarmolinsky, "Dostoevsky: A Study in His Ideology" (Ph.D. dissertation, Columbia University, 1921), 37.

[31] No. 41, 1873. This number is not included in the English translation of the *Diary* by Boris Brasol.

[32] Yarmolinsky, *Dostoevsky: His Life and Art*, 287–88. The authorship of the *Catechism* is disputed. Cf. Venturi, *Roots of Revolution*, 364–68.

[33] See Lampert, *Studies in Rebellion*, 125ff.

sentially differ from that of Bakunin. Marx was himself a revolutionary activist. He took personal part in the revolution of 1848, although somewhat more cautiously than did Bakunin. Marx taught permanent revolution, and by this he intended (among much else) the destruction of the state. And he believed in the speedy attainment of an ideal society as the certain aftermath of revolution.[34]

From the viewpoint of the Marxists of the Soviet Union, there seems little doubt that Dostoevsky strikes home—most obviously, of course, in *The Possessed*. There is great diversity of opinion, both scholarly and political, but the words of V. F. Pereverzev in his *Dostoevsky and Revolution* (1921) are of interest.

> To speak of Dostoevsky for us still means to speak of the most burning and profound questions of our current life. . . . Revolution is cruel and immoral; it treads over corpses and bathes in blood; it prefers torture, scoffing. . . . The real revolutionary is not the noble defender of the weak and the oppressed who is inspired by pity, but the grim man who seizes power, inspired by self-will. . . . The horror of revolution does not lie in the fact that it is immoral, spattered with blood, drunk with cruelty, but in the fact that it offers gold from the devil's treasures which turns into broken shards after all manner of cruelties have been committed for the sake of this gold. . . . Everything has come true as Dostoevsky predicted.[35]

Just as Verkhovensky can say in the novel *The Possessed*: "They shout 'a hundred million heads'; that may be only a metaphor, but why be afraid of it? . . . We believe that our program is correct; that is the reason we have decided on blood," so Lenin can say in the first months after the Bolshevik *coup d'état*: "Why should we be squeamish about the sacrifices to our righteous cause? . . . It does not matter if three-fourths of mankind is destroyed; all that counts is that

---

34 See Masaryk, *The Spirit of Russia*, I, 462–63. The central importance of the early writings of Marx (from the doctoral dissertation of 1841 through the *Address to the Communist League* of 1850) now is well recognized by Western scholars. For a discussion of the point see, for example, Robert C. Tucker, *Philosophy and Myth in Karl Marx* (New York: Cambridge University Press, 1961), 11ff; also Eric Voegelin, "The Formation of the Marxian Revolutionary Idea," *Review of Politics*, XII (1950), 275–302; repr. in M. A. Fitzsimons, *et al.* (eds.), *The Image of Man* (Notre Dame: University of Notre Dame Press, 1959), 265–81.
35 Quoted in Seduro, *Dostoevsky in Russian Literary Criticism*, 128ff.

ultimately the last quarter should become Communist. . . . Later centuries will justify the cruelties to which circumstances have forced us. Then everything will be understood, everything." [36]

Dostoevsky's vision of all this was most clear. He is often called a prophet. However this may be, what is sometimes overlooked is, having been himself a revolutionary, he well understood the mentality of the movement and did not neglect it as of no consequence. He perceived that the Feuerbachian reduction of theology to anthropology undercut the foundations of the social order and prepared the way for the man-god megalomaniac. In a letter to Strakhov in May, 1871, Dostoevsky reflects on the recent activities of the Paris Commune:

> At the bottom, the entire movement is but a repetition of the Russian delusion that man can reconstruct the world by reason and experience (Positivism). . . . Why do they cut off heads? Simply because it is the easiest of all things to do. . . . The burning of Paris is something monstrous: "Since we have failed, let the whole world perish!"—for the Commune is more important than the world's weal, and France's! Yet they (and many others) see in that madness not monstrosity, but only *beauty*.[37]

Or again: "The Paris Commune and Western Socialism do not desire *better men* (*i.e.*, aristocracy of talent) but equality. They would cut off the heads of Shakespeare and of Raphael." [38] One is reminded of Dostoevsky's chilling summation of incipient totalitarianism formulated in 1862 after his first trip abroad: "driven to the final stage of desperation, the Socialist ends by proclaiming '*liberté, egalité, fraternité, ou la mort.*' Well, there is nothing left to say." [39]

---

[36] Quoted in René Fueloep-Miller, *Fyodor Dostoevsky: Insight, Faith, and Prophecy*, trans. Richard and Clara Winston (New York: Charles Scribner's Sons, 1950), 105.

[37] Dostoevsky to N. N. Strakhov, May 18, 1871, in Mayne (trans.), *Letters of Dostoevsky*, 218–19.

[38] Quoted in Yarmolinsky, "Ideology," 38. Cf. Dostoevsky, *The Notebooks for "The Possessed,"* 387.

[39] Fyodor M. Dostoevsky, *Winter Notes on Summer Impressions*, trans. R. L. Renfield (New York: Criterion Books, Inc., 1955), 116. On the French Revolution and the rise of totalitarianism see Talmon, *Origins of Totalitarian Democracy.*

3. SPIRITUAL CURRENTS: ORTHODOXY, SECTARIANISM, AND RUSSIAN MYTH

There is, finally, the question of Dostoevsky's spiritual life and of his elaborate relationship to Russian sectarianism. To be sure, there is no parallel, in this respect, between Dostoevsky and Leo Tolstoy: Tolstoy became a sectarian and forsook both art and Orthodoxy. This did not happen with Dostoevsky; and precisely what was his relation to sectarianism is both complex and obscure because, always a secretive man, he has left no more than hints. It has been suggested that Dostoevsky was, at heart, a Schismatic—covertly, of course, and in a rather special sense: overtly he expressed himself so as to be regarded as the pillar of Orthodoxy and was looked upon in that way by the court and by such high officials as his friend and Saturday evening confidant (and, after 1880, the *Ober-Prokurator* of the Holy Synod) K. P. Pobedonostsev himself. No more than the barest outline of the matter can be attempted here.

Russian sectarianism is both an old and significant phenomenon whose character can be understood only if it is seen in conjunction with the ancient cosmic religiousness of the Slavs, on the one hand, and in relation to Orthodoxy, on the other hand. Because Dostoevsky represents this entire range of experience in his work, it is necessary that at least the fundamental points be discussed. The ostensible Christianization of Russia dates from 988 when St. Vladimir made Orthodoxy the religion of the state. Slav polytheism was not so easily displaced, however. It continued to live side by side with official Christianity, perhaps right into the present day, so that Russia has been called the country of the "twin faith" (*dvoeverie*).[40] The consequences of this fact are difficult to ascertain with precision. But it seems to be certain that the cosmic religiousness and mythology of the ancient Slavs remained vital influences in the Russia of Dostoevsky. They conditioned orthodox Christianity in Russia and persisted in a wide variety of transmutations in the bosom of the official church itself. In symbiosis with Christianity, along with Bulgarian and Persian religious influences, they gained new life in the multiplicity of sectarian movements emerging into particular promi-

---

40 Masaryk, *The Spirit of Russia*, I, 38.

nence in the seventeenth century and later. They maintained un-interrupted continuity of existence in the consciousness, cults, and games of the peasantry.[41] Lastly, they supplied an indispensable matrix for articulation under cover of Christian imagery of the dominant political symbolisms of tsarist Russia: the myth of the saintly prince as this emerged into the figure of the pious tsar, em-bedded from the sixteenth century on in the eschatology of Moscow the Third Rome; and the myth of Holy Russia (coined by Prince Kurbsky out of the tension with the ruler myth in the 1570s), which differentiated as the widely ramified myth of the Land and the People (*Sviataia Rus'*).[42]

Because of the dearth of evidence, authorities are divided with re-gard to the precise configuration of the ancient Russian mythology.[43] Vernadsky emphasizes sun worship as the core of the old Slavic reli-gion, finding philological confirmation for this view in the fact that names of various Slavic tribes (including the *Rus'*) reflect the notion of Sun. Fedotov, while acknowledging a cult of solar deities, finds the worship of the sun to be secondary and sees the core of Russian religion to be the worship of Mother Earth. Stender-Petersen, fol-lowing the lead of Lubor Niederle, attempts to resolve the problem by distinguishing a Russian theology from a demonology, identify-ing the former with the celestial gods of the aristocracy generated under stimulus of Varangian and Iranian influences, and seeing in the latter the cultic contrivance of peasantry preoccupied with the fruitfulness of the earth. All writers agree that the old religiousness is of remarkable vitality and that it persisted until the twentieth cen-

41 Adolf Stender-Petersen, *Russian Studies*, Acta Jutlandica, Humanistisk Serie, XLIII (Copenhagen: Universitetsforlaget I Aarhus, 1956), 57–58.

42 See J. L. I. Fennell (ed. and trans.), *Prince A. M. Kurbsky's History of Ivan IV* (Cambridge: Cambridge University Press, 1965), 168–69; also, Michael Cher-niavsky, *Tsar and People: Studies in Russian Myths* (New Haven: Yale University Press, 1961), 119, 102ff, 51ff, and *passim*.

43 The following discussion of ancient Russian religiousness relies principally upon the following sources: Stender-Petersen, *Russian Studies*; Cherniavsky, *Tsar and People*; George P. Fedotov, *The Russian Religious Mind: Kievan Christianity, the Tenth to the Thirteenth Centuries* (New York: Harper & Row, Publ., Torch-books, 1960); George Vernadsky, *The Origins of Russia* (Oxford: Clarendon Press, 1959); and A. Gieysztor, "Slav Countries: Folk-Lore of the Forests," in Pierre Grimal (ed.) and Patricia Beardsworth (trans.), *Larousse World Mythology* (New York: G. P. Putnam's Sons, 1965), 401–16.

tury. While Stender-Petersen stands at the extreme in doubting "whether Christianity as a religion ever became the spiritual property of the Russian people," Fedotov admits that "heathen survivals were abundant even in the nineteenth century." It is unnecessary here to mediate this dispute, because it resolves itself into being more one of accent than of content.[44]

King (St.) Vladimir established his pantheon of cosmic divinities in 980 in Kiev and Novgorod, and he vigorously fostered revival of their worship by setting up temples and idols and reinstituting the offering of regular human sacrifices. Only eight years later (988) he accepted Christianity, demolished every idol, and had the people more or less forcibly Christianized. The decision in favor of Greek Orthodoxy (rather than Judaism, Mohammedanism, and Roman Catholicism, all of which were considered) is traditionally said to have turned on the impact of the beauty of liturgy and ritual in the service witnessed by the Russian envoys in Sancta Sophia in Constantinople, rather than on any consideration of relative theological merit. They reported to Vladimir, the city elders of Kiev, and the Council of Boyars: "We knew not whether we were in heaven or on earth." The divinity of the cosmos found expression in the old Russian mythology primarily through symbolisms venerating Sun and Fire, Clan, and Mother Earth. An affinity with Mithraism and with the Hellenic cult of Helios is suggested by the sun symbolisms. Various names were used to designate the Sun in his several aspects and functions.[45]

Perun was the God of the Thunderbolt and the oak tree and perhaps the oldest of the gods.[46] *Khors* denoted the luminous celestial body, the Light and absolute Good as opposed to the Dark and Evil. *Dazhbog* is variously understood as the Giver of Wealth and as the

---

[44] Vernadsky, *The Origins of Russia*, 108; Fedotov, *The Russian Religious Mind*, 10–12, 346; L. Niederle, *La civilisation*, Vol. I of Niederle, *Manuel de l'antiquité slave* (2 vols.; Paris: E. Champion, 1923–26), 46–55; Stender-Petersen, *Russian Studies*, 46–55; Cf. Roman Jakobson, "Studies in Comparative Slavic Metrics," *Oxford Slavonic Papers*, III (1952), 21–66.

[45] Stender-Petersen, *Russian Studies*, 54; Vernadsky, *The Origins of Russia*, 288–96.

[46] Gieysztor, "Slav Countries: Folk-Lore of the Forests." The following summary of Russian mythology relies principally upon Varnadsky, "Religious Foundations of the Old Russian Culture," chap. 4 of Vernadsky, *The Origins of Russia*.

Burning or Ardent God, and in the latter sense was also designated *Iarilo (iaryi*=ardent). *Veles* and *Volos* were twin designations which suggest a kinship to the Greek Apollo but combine an allusion to hair (beard: a symbol of power) which protectorship over flocks and with holy breath or wind—hence with music, poetry, and ultimately Holy Spirit. Thus, Bayan, the inspired poet of *Igor's Tale* (twelfth century), is Veles's grandson. *Svarog* seems to have been the highest god in the Slavic patheon and was the divinity of White Light. Fire was associated with both light and sun and was worshipped long after conversion to Christianity as *Svarozhich* ("Son of Svarog"). In a popular poem of the late Middle Ages, the *Glubinnaia Kniga* (*Book of Deep Wisdom*), Prince Vladimir and King David are in dialogue. The latter explains the genesis of the divine Light: "The White Light originated from God's Heart; the Sun, from God's face." Vladimir took as his epithet *Krasnoe Solntse*, which meant "Ardent Sun."

In Slavic folklore the Tsar-Sun rules from a radiant throne, flanked by two maidens (dawn and evening glow). In some versions there are seven judges (planets) and seven messengers (comets); in other accounts Tsar-Sun rules twelve kingdoms, each under a sign of the Zodiac, and his sons abide in the stars, all assisted by the Sun's maidens. In its annual course through the four seasons, the Sun enacted the divine cosmic drama of death and rebirth. He was regarded as the source of life on the earth, and solar festivals were celebrated at the appropriate times. His birth came with the winter solstice, and in Christian times this festival was fused with the Nativity. The Russian Christmas carols (*koliady*, from L. *Calendae*; Sl. *kolo* = wheel, round dance: symbol of the sun) take as their principal subject prayer for a bountiful harvest in the coming year and also contain elements of ancient magical incantations. In some of the older songs, mention is made in particular of the sacrifice of a young goat. The vernal equinox symbolized the awakening of the ardent forces of procreation as represented in *Iarilo*, the Ardent God who reigned supreme until the summer solstice. In Kievan Russia the new year began in this season (March 1). Because of the conflict with Lent after Christianization, the ancient rites of spring were moved to the period of the Carnival and called *maslenitsa* (butter week). At this time the expected abundance of crops in the year to come was anticipated and assured by ritual orgies of eating and drinking, the special dish of the week being the *bliny* ("pancakes") whose round form symbolized the sundisk. The ancient festivals of *Semik* and *Ivan Kupala* were celebrated just before and just after the summer solstice: the former on the seventh Thursday after Easter (hence, before Pentecost), the latter on the day of the birth of St. John the Baptist (June 24). Both of these festivals are Dionysian in character and are celebrations of the fertility cult of Iarilo, whose effigy displayed an enormous phallus. *Semik* brought the symbolisms of water, trees, and water nymphs (*rusalki*) into prominence and was celebrated in the forests and along the shores of lakes and streams as a festival of youth and premarital love, dedicated to the souls of the dead. At *Kupala* bonfires were built, men, women, and maidens danced around and jumped through them in ritual purification, and fire wheels were kindled and rolled down hillsides. The male effigy of Iarilo and the female effigy of Kupala (perhaps denoting the vulva) were burned together. The festivals took place between villages where the people gathered for dancing, games, and "other devilish amusements," in the words of the old *Russian Chronography*: "the men on these occasions carried off wives for themselves, and each took any woman with whom he had arrived at an understanding. In fact, they even had two or three wives apiece." The turning of the sun after the solstice was thus symbolized by the rolling wheel, and the funeral of Iarilo was celebrated, along with rites appropriate to the god of procreation and fecundity. Orgiastic tendencies seem recognizable behind the *kupalskie pesni* or "Kupala songs" sung on St. John's Day. The Baptist himself, as portrayed in these songs, "had practically lost his Christian stamp completely and had become wholly paganized. In the general fraternization which was customary on this day are found traces of a bacchantic hetairism." The cosmic calendar drew to a close in the harvest festivals of autumn.[47]

---

[47] Stender-Petersen, *Russian Studies*, 68–69; Vernadsky, *The Origins of Russia*, 112–14, 118, 154; S. H. Cross and O. P. Sherbowizt-Wetzor (trans.), *The Russian Primary Chronicle* (Cambridge, Mass.: Mediaeval Academy of America, 1953), 56. *The Brothers Karamazov* ends with a juxtaposition of Christian and cosmological symbolisms of immortality: " 'Karamazov,' cried Kolya, 'can it be true what's

From Iarilo the connection is made with the clan cult. Clan in Russian is *rod*, which in Old Russian connoted genitor or procreator. Sacrifices still were made in the Christian period to *Rod* and *Rozhanitsy* (plural), the female counterparts of Rod. "In concrete terms, *rod* might have denoted the phallus and *rozhanitsa* the vulva." The *Radunitsa* is a spring feast of the dead or funeral banquet in which the veneration of ancestors occurs (at the time of Easter Week), symbolically in the churches, and more passionately in church yards and on the graves where wine plays a great part. It sometimes ends "in real orgies." The impact of the *rod* or clan cult was such that it shaped all social life in Russia, extending to it the form of family life so that all moral relations among men were symbolized at the level of blood kinship. The patriarchal character of life found expression in a wide variety of ways. The entire Russian nation could be regarded as an immense clan of whom the tsar was the earthly father—an idea well developed in the nineteenth century by the Slavophiles. The collective consciousness of the *mir*, or Russian village community, was but one aspect of the veneration of parents characteristic of the *rod* cult. The experience of personality emerged only gradually in Russia: the immortality, freedom, rights, and separate life of the individual were overwhelmed by the experience of consubstantiality with the generations of ancestors. Even in Christian Russia the dead were honored on no fewer than ten different "Parents' Saturdays," days consecrated and set aside for prayer for ancestors: from parents one comes and to parents one returns. And at this juncture the clan cult can be seen to be linked with the veneration of Mother Earth as the parent from whom all come and to whom all return. This connection is present in the mention of the *Rusalki* at the festival of Semik, for these female spirits were identified as the souls of dead maidens and children who had committed suicide or

---

taught us in religion, that we shall all rise again from the dead and shall live and see each other again, all, Ilusha [who has just died] too?'

"'Certainly we shall all rise again, certainly we shall see each other!' Alyosha answered. . . .

"'Well, now we will finish talking and go to his funeral dinner. Don't be put out at our eating pancakes [*bliny*]—it's a very old custom and there's something nice in that!' laughed Alyosha. 'Well, let us go! And now we go hand in hand.'"
See Masaryk's comment, *The Spirit of Russia*, III, 55.

otherwise met violent death. They were believed to be released from the netherworld for the period from Easter to Pentecost and permitted to appear on earth and share communion with the living and receive their gifts. The old Russian image of *Mati Syra Zemlia* ("Mother Moist Earth") can be identified with the only female deity of Vladimir's pantheon, *Mokosh* ("moisture" in Old Russian), as the successor of *Api-Anahita*, the Great Goddess of the Scythians.

> Mother Earth becomes clearer to us against the background of the *gens* [clan] religion. The sacred motherhood of the earth is intimately akin to the worship of the parents. The double mystery of birth and death is experienced as well in the life of the *rod* as in the yearly cycle of the earth. From the sperm of the parents man is brought forth into the everlasting *rod* for his short existence, just as the seed, buried in the earth's womb, gives a new life to the ear of corn which is procreated through the death of the seed itself. Was not this symbolical association of the life of man and corn the fundamental mystery of Eleusis?

The Russians venerated no virgin goddess, and womanly purity and beauty formed but a negligible part in their representation of Sacred Womanhood. Mother Earth has neither shape nor face. Her beauty is that of the embracing and enveloping sensuous nature with which man feels himself involved and permeated. From the *Rozhanitsy* to *Mokosh* and their absorption into Mariology in the Mother of God (*Theotokos*) image of the Greeks, the accent of Russian veneration is on fecund motherhood. In the *Bogoroditsa* of the Christian centuries (which is a literal translation of the Greek *Theotokos*), no abstract and spiritual experience is fundamental. Rather there is palpable, emotional power: the accent lies on *tokos*, on "the Parent, the Birthgiver, the Mother." The Russian Mary is not only the Mother of God or Christ but the universal Mother, the Mother of all mankind. "In the first place she is of course Mother in the moral sense, a merciful protector, an intercessor for men before the heavenly Justice, the Russian version of redemption. But in another ontological sense she was really believed by the folk to be the Giver of life to all creatures, and in that dignity she rightly succeeded to the modest and nameless, somewhat shadowy Rozhanitsy."

As great as were the heights of spirituality achieved by Russian Christianity in the centuries after Vladimir, the fascination and immediacy of the old nature religion never lost either its power or pertinence in the land of the twin faith. The characters of Dostoevsky's novels are themselves embedded in a reality experienced predominantly as sacred matter on the pattern of the ancient consciousness. The Mother Moist Earth, made fruitful in the generations of men by the beneficent life-giving celestial Light, describes a center of gravity in the Russian soul still alive in the pages of our author. To be sure there is much more than this. But the old cosmic religiousness of the *Rus'* is one of the essential keys to the manifold mysteries of the *rod* Karamazov. The immanence of God in material reality, the experience of the divinity of the cosmos, and the consubstantiality of man with all universally divine being are experiences decisive for the Russian mind. Fedotov remarks that the greatest temptation for the Russian is sensual patheism (hylozoism). The object of veneration is too easily sacred matter rather than spirit. Sensual mysticism supports in an essential way the social discipline of the clan. "The spirit of Dionysus is perpetually attempting to infringe upon the laws of Mother Earth." [48]

The residue of pagan religiosity was but one of the circumstances enhancing proliferation of sects outside of the established church. The long and tangled history of Russian sectarianism cannot be told here.[49] Suffice it to say that during the two decades from 1860 to 1880 there occurred a mass influx into the more radical sects. By 1880 the best sources estimate that, in a total Russian population

---

[48] Vernadsky, *The Origins of Russia*, 117–23; Fedotov, *The Russian Religious Mind*, 16–20, 351, 361–62. The symbolism of Dostoevsky's epigraph for *The Brothers Karamazov* may be recalled: "Verily, verily, I say unto you, Except a grain of wheat fall into the ground and die, it abideth alone: but if it die, it bringeth forth much fruit" (John 12:24).

[49] See Paul Miliukov, *Outlines of Russian Culture*, ed. Michael Karpovich, trans. Valentine Ughet and Eleanor David (3 vols.; Philadelphia: University of Pennsylvania Press, 1943) I, 116. See also Frederick C. Conybeare, *Russian Dissenters*, Harvard Theological Studies, X (New York: Russell and Russell, Publ., 1962). Karl Grass, *Die russischen Sekten* (1907–14; 2 vols.; repr. ed.; Leipzig: Zentral-Antiquariat, 1966) remains the best account; cf. Serge Bolshakoff, *Russian Nonconformity: The Story of "Unofficial" Religion in Russia* (Philadelphia: Westminster Press, 1950), 92.

of eighty million, there were about fourteen million sectarians and Schismatics. The *Khlysty* and their more radical offshoot, the *Skoptsy*, made particular headway during the reign of Alexander I (1802–25). His predecessor on the throne, Paul I (1796–1801), had been fascinated by the Skoptsy, perhaps especially because their leader, Konrad Selivanov (or "Christ" as he was proclaimed), insisted that he was the assassinated father of Paul, Tsar Peter III. He was worshipped as Christ Peter III.

In *The Diary of a Writer* Dostoevsky alluded rather often to the various sects and unorthodox spiritual phenomena. Moreover, in *The Brothers Karamazov* much that is said and done is not fully comprehensible unless seen against the background of sectarianism, a conclusion supported by the evidence of the *Notebooks*. Religious enthusiasm and mysticism in Russia first appeared in the writings of St. Nilus in the fifteenth century and reached a climax in the time of Dostoevsky in the work of Theophan the Recluse (1815–94). A direct impetus to the nineteenth century developments came from the monk Paissey Velichkovsky (1722–94), whose work included translating the *Philokalia* (in part) into Slavonic and publishing it in 1793. The tradition Velichkovsky established was carried on by many of his pupils who gathered together in the monastery of Optino-Pustyn near Kozelsk in the province of Kaluga. Dostoevsky and Solovyov visited this monastery together in June, 1878. Theophan belonged to the same movement. He became Bishop of Tambov in 1859 and, shortly afterwards, of Vladimir. Together with the monks at Optino-Pustyn, he translated the *Philokalia* into Russian. It appeared in five volumes beginning in 1876.[50]

These developments are of pertinence here for several reasons. First, there is a direct relationship between monasticism and sectarianism: both arise out of a thirst for spiritual perfection. Dos-

---

[50] Bolshakoff, *Russian Nonconformity*, 83; H. A. Hodges, "Introduction," in Lorenzo Scupoli, *Unseen Warfare*, trans. E. Kadloubovsky and G. E. H. Palmer (London: Faber & Faber, Ltd., 1952), 58–60. Cf. Fyodor M. Dostoevsky, *The Notebooks for "The Brothers Karamazov,"* ed. and trans. Edward Wasiolek (Chicago: University of Chicago Press, 1971), 110–59; Dostoevsky, *The Notebooks for "A Raw Youth,"* ed. and with an intro. by Edward Wasiolek, trans. Victor Terras (Chicago: University of Chicago Press, 1969), 27, 32, 58, 172, 235, 272, 295, 308, 379–80, 401, 445, 454, 465–67, 480, 493, 518, 523, 528, 544–52.

toevsky was well aware of this and remarks with respect to Stundism,
"for instance . . . observe its popularity among the masses. What
does that signify?—Quest for truth and anxiety for it." He then
makes the political connection:

> The people, in our day, are morally "disturbed." I am convinced that if,
> thus far, nihilistic propaganda has failed to find its way to the people,
> this has been exclusively due to the incompetence, stupidity and un-
> preparedness of the propagandists, who did not even know how to ap-
> proach the people. However, with the slightest skill they would have
> penetrated the people just as Stundism has. Oh, one must guard the
> people: "The time will come to pass when ye shall be told: Here is
> Christ, or yonder. Do not believe it." [51]

The ardent desire of the monk, of the sectarian, and also—as Dostoevsky perceived—of the revolutionary is perfection in truth. The
truth may vary but the eschatological drive remains. In sectarianism,
as an expression of the religion of the heart, Dostoevsky saw the
spiritual aspiration of the people. He recognized that it could be
used by those who came bearing stones for bread. The goal toward
which Dostoevsky sought to direct men, on the contrary, is expressed
on the first page of one of the principal books of spiritual exercises
of the time, the *Unseen Warfare*. After quoting Matthew 5:48, "Be
ye therefore perfect, even as your Father which is in heaven is perfect," the writer says: "I will tell you plainly: the greatest and most

---

[51] Dostoevsky, *Diary*, II, 1026–27; cf. *ibid.*, I, 62ff; II, 560ff, Cf. the assessment
by Venturi, *Roots of Revolution*, xivn, 114–17, 200–201, 577–80. The interest of the Populists in the revolutionary potential of the sectarians is
fervidly expressed in the reaction of V. I. Kelsiev to *Raskol'* documents given
him by Herzen in London in 1859: "I didn't sleep all night and carried on
reading. . . . Suddenly, in one night, there was revealed to me the emasculates with
their mystic rites, their choruses and their harvest songs, full of poetry; the
flagellants with their strange beliefs; the dark figures of the 'priestless' sects; the
intrigues of the leaders of the Old Believers. . . . they thought, thought of the
most important problems that can concern the human soul—truth and untruth,
Christ and anti-Christ, eternity, man, salvation. . . . The *Raskol'* reflects honor
on the Russian people, showing that it does not sleep, that every peasant wants
to keep a lively independent eye on dogmas, wants to think for himself about
truth, that the Russian people *searches for truth*, and then follows what it has
found, and does not allow itself to be frightened by floggings or by caves with
their entrances blocked up, or by emasculation, or by human sacrifice and cannibalism." Quoted in Venturi, *Roots of Revolution*, 115, from Kelsiev's *Confession*.

perfect thing a man may desire to attain is to come near to God and dwell in union with Him." [52] The mysticism of the cloister is shadowed and often grotesquely caricatured by popular enthusiasm. A second reason why a discussion of sectarianism is germane here is that Dostoevsky specifically tells us it is his intention to portray the manifestations of sectarianism in *The Brothers Karamazov*. This directly expressed intention is confirmed by both the content of the novel as well as the geographic setting which it is given. A third reason has been mentioned in passing. The sectarians and Schismatics have a twofold significance: on the one hand, they genuinely and freely express from the heart of the *narod*, from the very soul and soil of Russia, the distinctive religious consciousness of the people; on the other hand, they are essentially revolutionary and anarchistic, living examples of the refractory thirst for freedom and the adamant defiance of all authority except the free conscience. Bakunin and Dostoevsky alike shared an admiration for the sects and the Schismatics for this reason. In the fourth place, there is the question of the content of the sectarian doctrine and consciousness as contributing factors to the broadly gnostic element in Dostoevsky's thought.

The chief point to secure is Dostoevsky's interest in and acquaintance with these sects, particularly with the Khlysty. One of the references in the *Diary* speaks of the "sects . . . awaiting the millennium, and . . . the Khlysty (a universal and very ancient sect)" and continues: "in the philosophical essence of these very sects—these tremblers and Khlysty—sometimes there lie concealed very profound and vigorous ideas."

It is said that around the Twenties, at the home of Tatarinova, in the Mikhailovsky Castle, alongside with herself and her guests—among them, for example, a Minister of those days—her serf domestics also used to whirl and prophesy. This means that there must have been an impetus of thought and emotion if such an "unnatural" communion of believers could have arisen: and it would seem that Tatarinova's sect belonged to the Khlysti or to one of their innumerable ramifications. [53]

---

[52] Scupoli, *Unseen Warfare*, 77. Dostoevsky knew this volume and had Zosima in *The Brothers Karamazov* quote and paraphrase from it, *e.g.*, in bk. 2, chap. 4 See Lauth, *Die Philosophie Dostojewskis*, 48n.

[53] Dostoevsky, *Diary* I, 268.

The direct connection of the sects with Dostoevsky's art is made in a letter to Maikov from Florence in December, 1868. Speaking of the vicissitudes of the "Atheist," Dostoevsky charts this course for him: "He tries to attach himself to the younger generation—the atheists, Slavs, Occidentalists, the Russian Sectarians, and Anchorites, the mystics: amongst others he comes across a Polish Jesuit; thence he descends to the abysses of the Khlysty-sect; and finds at last salvation in Russian soil, the Russian Saviour, and the Russian God." [54] The juxtaposition of the Khlysty and the Russian soil and salvation is noteworthy. It is not necessary to inquire in detail just how far the other elements of the plot of the projected great work ever were realized. It is enough here to affirm that the sectarian element was, in fact, retained and constitutes an important dimension of the later art of Dostoevsky. In the same letter Dostoevsky equates the "New Man" of the socialists with the Russian sectarian. He writes: "Do you know what the new Russians are like? Well, for example, look at the muzhik, the 'sectarian' of the time of Paul the Prussian. . . . If he's not precisely typical of the coming Russian, he is undoubtedly one of the Russians of the future." [55] In a later letter to the same correspondent Dostoevsky states his intention to include Tsar Paul I as one of the characters in the "Great Sinner." The reference is almost certainly to Konrad Selivanov, the Skoptsy "God the Son."

Another current of spiritual influence to be mentioned is the Schismatics, or "Old Believers." The origin of the *Raskol'* [56] was the

---

54 Dostoevsky to Apollon N. Maikov, December 11, 1868, in Mayne (trans.), *Letters of Dostoevsky*, 158; see, also, the letter to Maikov, March 25, 1870, *ibid.*, 190. For references to the Khlysty in the Notes to the *Life of a Great Sinner*, see Fyodor M. Dostoevsky, *Stavrogin's Confession and the Plan of the Life of a Great Sinner*, trans. S. S. Koteliansky and Virginia Woolf (Richmond: Hogarth Press, 1922), 119, and the commentary by N. Brodsky (ed.), *ibid.*, 151–52, 154n, 168. Cf Fyodor M. Dostoevsky, *The Notebooks for "The Possessed,"* 66–68; see also n. 50 above.
55 Cf. Dostoevsky to Maikov, March 25, 1870, in Mayne (trans.), *Letters of Dostoevsky*, 191.
56 In light of Dostoevsky's relationship to the Schismatics and sectarians, one must look behind the psychological condition of the hero of *Crime and Punishment* fully to comprehend the significance of Raskolnikov. On the Russian sect devoted to the worship of Napoleon as Christ, see Grass, *Die russischen Sekten*, I, 562–63.

liturgical reforms instituted by Patriarch Nikon, who was appointed in 1652 and personally condemned in 1666 by the Holy Synod. Despite his personal fate, Nikon's reforms were retained. In the view of the Old Ritualists the age of the Antichrist began with Nikon (1666), and both church and state were organs of Antichrist and Satan.[57] The Schismatics split into a number of sects and subsects and blended the sectarian movements in existence long before Nikon. Among these there was great heterogeneity of belief. The name "Khlysty" is probably a corruption of Christŭ (their sect's oldest traceable title), meaning those who have Christ in their midst. While they outwardly conform to the Orthodox church and attend Confession and Holy Communion, they despise the state church and spit out the wine after communion. The Orthodox church, in their eyes, is the "world" and the kingdom of Satan, the clergy "popes," Jewish priests, and Pharisees. In contrast, they regard themselves as the only true Church, the Kingdom of God on earth, because they alone possess the Spirit of God. They are neither mystics nor flagellants but dancers and ecstatics: dancing (radenie) is the proper ritual means for bringing the Spirit from heaven. Those capable of achieving this are known as "Christ" or "God Sabaoth" (Christ of the highest rank) or "Mother of God." They are highly ascetic, characterized by fasting and complete sexual abstinence. The earliest report of the sect was in 1691. Khlysty traditions reach back at least to the fourteenth century, however. In this context it is of interest to note that one of the "Christs" of the mid-eighteenth century, Andreyan Petrov, was known as the "Happy Idiot" and had entrée to the houses of the Moscow aristocracy, where he propagated his views with some success.[58] The source of the beliefs of the sect is disputed; quite possibly it is a derivation from the Bogomils (Paulicians), although Grass finds the Khlysty entirely devoid of the Bogomilian

---

57 A. von Stromberg, "Russian Sects," in James Hastings (ed.), *Hastings' Encyclopedia of Religion and Ethics* (12 vols.; New York: Charles Scribner's Sons, 1928), XI, 337, hereinafter cited as *Hastings' Encyclopedia.*

58 Karl Grass, "Men of God," in *ibid.*, VIII, 545–46. On the holy fool or idiot (*urodivi*) see Mochulsky, *Dostoevsky*, 339n; also, Dostoevsky, *The Notebooks for "The Idiot,"* ed. and with an intro. by Edward Wasiolek, trans. Katharine Strelsky (Chicago: University of Chicago Press, 1967), 69, 97, 105, 129, 143. Cf. chap. 3, n. 20, *below.*

cosmology, suggesting their affinity instead with the Messalians or Euchites.

Whatever the relationship of the Khlysty to the Bogomils, common to both is the Manichaean dualism of good and evil, God and Satan, heaven and world, soul and body. The Bogomils originated in Bulgaria and are considered to be the connecting link between the "heretical" sects of the East and West. Serge Bolshakoff suggests not only Manichaean and Bogomil sources for the sect but also the possible influence of Hindu teaching, particularly that of certain Vishnuite sects. The Manichaean writings were known in Russia for many centuries. Some Russian scholars believe the Khlysty to be purely Russian in origin, an outgrowth of the dualism of the old pagan religion as well as of a misunderstood Christianity. A few scholars believe that they reflect some of the Western mystical sects, such as the Adamites and Quakers, as well as the influence of such mystics as Jakob Boehme, Quirinus Kuhlmann, Madame Guion, and Jung-Stilling. Although the later Russian sectarians were familiar with these writers and movements, the earlier leaders of the *Liudi bozhie* (the God-Fearing or People of God, as the Khlysty were sometimes called) could not have known them.[59]

According to an old tradition, the Khlysty was founded by a peasant named Daniel Filippov who, in 1631, proclaimed himself "God Sabaoth" on Gorodno Hill near Murom in the province of Vladimir. A Vladimir peasant named Ivan Suslov was selected to become his chief prophet and so became "Christ" and began to preach the new doctrine. Avvakum Kopylov appeared in Tambov as a new "Christ" at the beginning of the nineteenth century. The Skoptsy arose in the neighboring province of Orel through Selivanov, who was considered the seventh "Christ" of the Khlysty. The great convert to this sect was the Tula peasant Alexander Shilov, and the Khlysty prophetess

---

[59] Cf. Dmitri Obolensky, *The Bogomils: A Study in Balkan Neo-Manichaeism* (Cambridge: Cambridge University Press, 1948), especially app. 4, "Bogomilism in Russia, Serbia, Bosnia and Hum," 276ff, who finds (p. 283) that it "is probable that Bogomilism, as a sectarian movement, never struck deep roots in medieval Russia." Cf. Fedotov, *The Russian Religious Mind*, 43. 168, 353–56, 411; F. J. Powicke, "Bogomils," in *Hastings' Encyclopedia*, II, 784; Bolshakoff, *Russian Nonconformity*, 88.

from Orel, Aquilina Ivanova, also was an important early convert. As previously mentioned, the Skoptsy were particularly influential during the first quarter of the nineteenth century, and their following included some of the aristocracy. The circle of Madame Tatarinova (Katherine von Buxhoevden, d. 1856) was noteworthy for its inclusion of princes, high officials of state, and for the interest taken in it by the tsar himself. Tatarinova was a Lutheran who became Orthodox and in 1815 founded the "Brotherhood in Christ" in Petersburg. Sectarianism, Western mysticism, and pietism blended in this gathering as they did also in such other active groups as the Freemasons and Rosicrucians. The similarity between the teaching with respect to Sophia by the Dukhobor sect, on one hand, and Russia's greatest philosopher, Vladimir Solovyov, on the other hand, is worthy of mention.[60]

The triangular region Vladimir-Orel-Tambov appears to have been the center of sectarian activity in nineteenth century Russia. Of interest here is that this region of fervid sectarian activity is precisely the setting both of Dostoevsky's childhood and of the novel *The Brothers Karamazov*. The family retreat of Chermashnia was situated near Tula and is mentioned in the novel. The significance of this usually is attributed to the parricide theme, of course; Dostoevsky visited the old estate in the summer of 1877 as he was meditating his novel. He chatted with the peasants and walked the road

[60] Cf. Bolshakoff, *Russian Nonconformity*, 194 and 149. Daniel Filippov is mentioned by Dostoevsky as a prototype of his projected "Great Sinner" in an entry dated January 1, 1870, in Dostoevsky, *The Notebooks for "The Possessed"*, 67. A Joachite movement (derived from the teachings of Joachim of Flora, see chap. 5, sec. 2, *below*) of some significance was founded by Alexander Kapitonovich Malikov in the Orel region and gained in importance because the religion was embraced by Nikolai Vasilevich Chaikovsky, one of the "boldest revolutionaries of *Narodnaya Volya*" (Venturi, *Roots of Revolution*, 473) and was broadcast in his revolutionary movement. This was a sect of "God-men," who were perfected in the Holy Spirit, each of whom achieved "the status of which Christ was forerunner" (Cherniavsky, *Tsar and People*, 196n). The Chaikovskists throve in the early 1870s. As M. F. Frolenko described it: "Chaikovsky saw in this preaching a revelation from above. . . . There was no need for conspiracies, secrecy, revolution and revolts. It was enough to free oneself of shortcomings and vices, to feel oneself a God-man, to believe that one was this. He believed with absolute faith." Venturi, *Roots of Revolution*, 473. See also M. F. Frolenko, "Chaikovsky i Ego Bogochelovechestvo," *Katorga i Ssylka* (1926), no. 5; J. H. Billington, *Mikhailovsky and Russian Populism* (London: Oxford University Press, 1958).

between Darovoye and Chermashnia on which his father was murdered. It was his first visit there in more than forty years, and it was to be his last—as he himself felt it would be.[61] Dostoevsky's first wife Marya Issayeva used to winter in Vladimir, and he is known to have been there in the winter of 1859 and the fall of 1863. In the summer of 1878 Dostoevsky again ventured into the region of his childhood, of the sectarians, and of the setting of the novel when he visited the Optino monastery, traveling from Moscow to Kozelsk with Solovyov. He spent two days in the monastery; his interviews with the Elder Ambrosius profoundly impressed him, and the elder was an important source for his character Zosima. Interestingly enough, the monastery of Saint Tikhon (prototype of Zosima) was located at Zadonsk in Tambov province. And, further, both the Dukhobors and Molokans had their centers in Tambov province.

The sectarian influence on Dostoevsky's last novel has been suggested as partial explanation of the name "Karamazov." The suspected connection is with the medieval Jewish sect of Karaites which were known in Russia as *Karaimi*. A colony of these people lived at Semipalatinsk where Dostoevsky was stationed while in exile during the years 1854 to 1859. This may have been a contributing idea, for Dostoevsky surely was not averse to combining and synthesizing notions into a single symbol. Komarovich has argued, however, that the name is derived from the Turkish root, *Kará*, meaning black and the Russian one, *maz'*, meaning tar. Matlaw has pointed out that the Russian *kára* (meaning punishment or retribution) is studiously avoided and occurs but once in the entire 400,000 words of the novel.[62] The symbolism here is fascinating, suggesting as it does primordial, brooding, evil, chthonic forces, devoid of light and grace, on one hand, and, regeneration, renewal, purification, and redemption on the other hand.

---

[61] Yarmolinsky, *Dostoevsky: His Life and Art,* 338. See the letter by Dostoevsky to his wife Anna Grigorievna, July 15, 1877, in Dostoevsky, *The Letters of F. M. Dostoevsky to His Wife,* 240.

[62] See Payne, *Dostoevsky,* 346n; W. L. Komarovich, *Die Urgestalt der Brüder Karamasoff: Dostojewkis Quellen, Entwürfe und Fragmente* (Munich: Piper, 1928), 93; Ralph E. Matlaw, *The Brothers Karamazov: Novelistic Technique* (The Hague: Mouton, 1957), 31n.

One can but wonder whether Dostoevsky, through his acquaintance with the life and writings of St. Tikhon, did not construct the
Karamazov name at least partly on the basis of an anecdote told
about him in Chebaterev's *Memoirs*: "When visited by temptation,
he (Tikhon) would say: . . . 'Do you not smell an evil odor in this
cell?' I would answer, 'No,' and he would say, 'Go and fetch some tar
and pour it on the floor.' (For he liked the smell of tar.)" [63]

---

[63] "Memoirs by Chebaterev of the Life of Saint Tikhon of Zadonsk," in George
P. Fedotov (ed.), *A Treasury of Russian Spirituality* (New York: Sheed & Ward,
1948), 193.

CHAPTER II

FAITH AND THE NATURE OF MAN

1. MAN AND THE DIVINE

The anthropological question is explored by Dostoevsky with maturity and the drive of purpose and conviction from the appearance of *Notes From Underground* (1864)—"his most metaphysical work"—throughout the pentalogy of great novels published in the last fifteen years of his life, culminating in *The Brothers Karamazov*.[1] Indeed, as is clear from Dostoevsky's correspondence, not only did the years of penal servitude in Siberia deepen his grasp of the nature of man through excruciating experience, but they elicited a more or less clear conception of its artistic embodiment. In January, 1856, Dostoevsky wrote A. N. Maikov from Semipalatinsk as follows:

> I couldn't at all tell you how very much I suffered from not being allowed to write in prison. My mental labour comes only thus to the boil. Some things were all right; I felt it. I planned out in that way a great novel, which I consider will be my definitive work. I was dreadfully afraid that the first passion for my work would have gone cold when the years had passed, and the hour of realization struck at last—that passion without which one cannot write. But I was mistaken: the figure which I had

---

[1] Renato Poggioli, *The Phoenix and the Spider* (Cambridge: Harvard University Press, 1957), 23; Marcel I. Weinrich, "Ideological Antecedents of *The Brothers Karamazov*," *Modern Language Notes*, LXIV (1949), 404. The pentalogy specified is comprised of *Crime and Punishment* (1866), *The Idiot* (1868), *The Possessed* (1871), *A Raw Youth* (1875), and *The Brothers Karamazov* (1880).

conceived, and which is the basis of the whole book, needed some years for its development, and I am convinced that I should have ruined all if I had then, unready as I was, begun the work in the first flush of zeal. But even when I left the prison, I did not set to, though all was quite ready in my mind. I simply could not write. . . . I have not been wholly idle. I have done some work; but the carrying-out of my *chef d'oeuvre* I have postponed. . . . One should . . . await the synthesis, and think more; wait till the many single details which make up an idea have gathered themselves into a nucleus, into a large, imposing picture; then, and not till then, should one write them down. The colossal figures, created by the colossal writers, have often grown out of long, stubborn labor. But the attempts and sketches that go to the picture should not be displayed at all.[2]

Dostoevsky was careful to conceal from public view "the attempts and sketches that go to the picture" from all who would investigate the unfolding of his great idea from its inception to its realization, but the process became apparent with the publication of his private notebooks. It is in a sense true that the pentalogy of late novels realizes Dostoevsky's great conception; but it is in another sense also true that the idea never was fully realized. The author's intention was that *The Brothers Karamazov* should have a sequel. The great work conceived in Siberia first received the name "Atheism" in Dostoevsky's correspondence and notes; subsequently, it was called "The Life Story of a Great Sinner"; and, finally, it became (in part) *The Brothers Karamazov.* Within this novel, it is the Legend of the Grand Inquisitor which most perfectly articulates the great "idea-feeling" of Dostoevsky.

But bits and pieces of the masterwork found their way into all of the late novels. For example, in *The Idiot* Dostoevsky realized something of his idea through the person of Myshkin. A glimpse of his literary intention is given in a letter of January, 1868, to his beloved niece Sonia:

The idea of the book is the old one which I always have so greatly liked; but it is so difficult that hitherto I never have had the courage to carry it

---

[2] Dostoevsky to Apollon N. Maikov, January 18, 1865, in Mayne (trans.), *Letters of Dostoevsky to his Family and Friends* (New York: Horizon Press, 1961), 87, 89.

out; and if I'm setting to work at it now, it's only because I'm in a desperate plight. The basic idea is the representation of a truly perfect and noble man. And this is more difficult than anything else in the world, particularly nowadays. All writers, not ours alone but foreigners also, who have sought to represent Absolute Beauty, were unequal to the task, for it is an infinitely difficult one. The beautiful is the ideal; but ideals, with us as in civilized Europe, have long been wavering. There is in the world only one figure of absolute beauty: Christ. That infinitely lovely figure is, as a matter of course, an infinite marvel (the whole Gospel of Saint John is full of this thought: John sees the wonder of the Incarnation, the visible apparition of the Beautiful). I have gone too far in my explanation. [N. B.] I will only say that of all the noble figures in Christian literature, I reckon Don Quixote as the most perfect. But Don Quixote is noble only by being at the same time comic. . . . The reader feels sympathy and compassion with the Beautiful, derided and unconscious of its own worth.[3]

In this same letter Dickens' Pickwickians and Hugo's Jean Valjean are mentioned as noteworthy, but lesser, examples of the "truly perfect and noble man."

From the time of the letter to Maikov of December 11, 1868, Dostoevsky is almost wholly preoccupied with his great novel. Its subject would be God and man, the problem of faith; it would probe the *conditio humana* through the whole range of human types and the gamut of experience: from the mystical exaltation of the saintly recluse to the slobbering sensuality of the spiritually obtuse satyr. On March 24, 1870, he wrote to N. N. Strakhov from Dresden: "I have been meditating the idea of this novel for three years. . . . I have set myself this idea as the goal of my literary future, for I can't at all hope to live and work more than six or seven years longer." [4] The next day, in a letter to Maikov, Dostoevsky expresses a continuing concern with the central problem of the truly good man.

This will be my last novel; it will be as long as "War and Peace". . . . The novel will consist of five longish tales. . . . The tales are complete in themselves, so that one could even sell them separately. . . . The funda-

---

3 Dostoevsky to Sofia Alexandrovna, January 1, 1868, in *ibid.*, 142–43.
4 Dostoevsky to N. N. Strakhov, March 24, 1870, in *ibid.*, 187–88.

mental idea, which will run through each of the parts, is one that has tormented me, consciously and unconsciously, all my life long: it is the question of the existence of God. The hero is now an atheist, now a believer, now a fanatic and sectarian, and then again an atheist. The second story will have for its setting a monastery. On this second story I base all my hopes. Perhaps people will admit at last that I can write something but pure nonsense. (I will confide to you alone, Apollon Nikolayevitch, that in this second story the principal character is to be taken from Tikhon Zadonsky; of course under another name. . . .) Don't talk to anybody about Tikhon. . . . Perhaps I shall succeed in creating a majestic, authentic saint. . . .[5] I shall probably not *create* at all, but present the real Tikhon, who has long been enshrined in my heart. But even a close, faithful delineation I should regard it as a great achievement to succeed in. Don't talk to anyone about it.[6]

A postscript to this letter adds: "How do we know—perhaps it is in fact Tikhon who represents our *positive* Russian type, which is so eagerly sought after in our literature." [7] Tikhon appears by name in *The Possessed,* and the portrayal of the holy man is attempted in the person of the godly *Makar* in *A Raw Youth* (1875). The first drafts of *The Brothers Karamazov* contain the name "Tikhon," subsequently replaced by "The Hermit" and "Elder Zosima." Vasily Rozanov has pointed out that Tikhon, while the prototype of Elder Zosima in *The Brothers Karamazov,* is also "in" Alyosha.

In a covering letter dated August 7, 1879, to the associate editor of *Russky Vestnik,* N. A. Liubimov, Dostoevsky calls particular attention to a passage of the Karamazov manuscript (bk. 6, "The Russian Monk"), *Of Holy Writ in the Life of Father Zosima*: "This chapter is enthusiastic and poetic; the model is certain sermons of Tikhon Zadonsky's and the naïve exposition is in the spirit of the book *The Pilgrimages of the Monk Parfeni*." [8]

---

5 In Nadeida Gorodetsky, *Saint Tikhon Zadonsky: Inspirer of Dostoevsky* (London: S.P.C.K., 1951), 183, this sentence is translated: "If only I could depict a *positive* holy figure."

6 Dostoevsky to Apollon N. Maikov, March 25/April 6, 1870, in Mayne (trans.), *Letters of Dostoevsky,* 190–92.

7 Quoted from Gorodetzsky, *Saint Tikhon Zadonsky,* 183.

8 Dostoevsky to N. A. Liubimov, August 7, 1879, in S. S. Koteliansky (trans.), *New Dostoevsky Letters* (London: Mandrake Press, 1927), 94.

2. The Experiential Ground of Faith

Dostoevsky's chief concern, it may be said, was for goodness and for the redemptive in man and human experience. The configuration which this concern took has come clearly into view. His answer to the question, What is man? is comprehensible only in light of his experience of the good. When a youth of seventeen he had written to Michael, his brother, of the gnosis gained through faith in language akin to that of Pascal in the *Pensées*. "We know truth," Pascal wrote, "not only by the reason, but also by the heart, and it is in this last way that we know first principles; and reason, which has no part in it, tries in vain to impugn them." It is the heart which "naturally loves the Universal Being," and "which experiences God, and not the reason. This, then is faith: God felt by the heart, not by the reason. Faith is a gift of God." Further, "Reason must trust these intuitions of the heart, and must base on them every argument. . . . Principles are intuited, propositions are inferred." [9] Dostoevsky, for his part, expressed the matter in this way:

> What do you mean precisely by the word *know?* Nature, the soul, love, and God, one recognizes through the heart, and not through the reason. Were we spirits, we could dwell in that region of ideas over which our souls hover, seeking the solution. But we are earthborn beings, and can only guess at the Idea—not grasp it by all sides at once. The guide for our intelligences through the temporary illusion into the innermost center of the soul is called *Reason*. Now, Reason is a material capacity, while the soul or spirit lives on the thoughts whispered by the heart. Thought is born in the soul. Reason is a tool, a machine, which is driven by the spiritual fire. When human reason . . . penetrates into the domain of knowledge, it works independently of the *feeling*, and consequently of the *heart*. But when our aim is the understanding of love or of nature, we march towards the very citadel of the heart. . . . Philosophy cannot be regarded as a mere equation where nature is the unknown quantity. Remark that the poet, in the moment of inspiration, comprehends God, and consequently does the philosopher's work. Consequently poetic inspiration is nothing less than philosophical inspiration. Consequently philosophy is nothing but poetry, a higher degree of poetry! It is odd

---

[9] Blaise Pascal, *Pensées and Provincial Letters*, trans. W. F. Trotter and Thomas M'Crie (New York: Random House, Inc., Modern Library, 1941), Nos. 277, 278, 282; cf. No. 1 *et seq.*

that you reason quite in the sense of our contemporary philosophy. What a lot of crazy systems have been born of late in the cleverest and most ardent brains! To get a right result from this motley troop one would have to subject them all to a mathematical formula. And yet they are the "laws" of our contemporary philosophy! [10]

Already prefigured here is Dostoevsky's dedication to realism in the higher sense that became his emblem as a philosophical poet.[11] The opposition between the knowledge of the heart and the instrumental quality of reason later (especially in *Notes From Underground*) resulted in the deprecation of "Euclidian reasoning" in a way reminiscent of Paul's words in II Corinthians 10:5: "We refute arguments and reasonings (*logismous*) and every proud and lofty thing that sets itself up against the (true) knowledge (*gnosis*) of God." [12] For Dostoevsky, Vyacheslav Ivanov notes, " 'Euclidian' reasoning is concerned only with form: the comprehension of essence is a property of love alone. Only love can say 'Thou art,' and thus affirm the existence of the beloved." [13] In Pauline usage the Christian gnosis gained through revelation in faith expands to signify "supernatural mystical knowledge." It is of particular relevance to note that as a technical term "gnosis" has this amplitude of meaning in Eastern Orthodox theology where it is a concept of pivotal importance.[14]

---

10 Dostoevsky to his brother, Michael, October 31, 1838, in Mayne (trans.), *Letters of Dostoevsky*, 6–7.

11 Cf. Ernest J. Simmons, "Dostoevsky—'A Realist in the Higher Sense,' " chap. 3 of Simmons, *Introduction to Russian Realism* (Bloomington: Indiana University Press, 1965).

12 Slightly condensed from the translation in *The Amplified New Testament* (11th ed.; Grand Rapids: Zondervan, 1958); cf. W. R. Nicoll (ed.), *The Expositor's Greek Testament* (5 vols.; Grand Rapids: Eerdmans, n.d.), III, 95–96. For elucidation of the Pauline usage, see also I Cor. 2:4; II Cor. 9:13; 13:8. On Christian and heretical *gnosis*, see the inventory of passages and bibliography in H. A. Wolfson, *Faith, Trinity, Incarnation*, Vol I of, *The Philosophy of the Church Fathers* (1 vol. to date; 2nd ed., rev.; Cambridge: Harvard University Press, 1964), 498ff.

13 Vyacheslav Ivanov, *Freedom and the Tragic Life: A Study in Dostoevsky*, ed. S. Konovalov, trans. Norman Cameron (New York: Noonday Press, 1957), 113.

14 Cf. Walter Bauer, *Greek-English Lexicon of the New Testament and Other Early Christian Literature*, ed. and trans. W. F. Arndt and F. Wilbur Gingrich (Chicago: University of Chicago Press, 1957), 163. See Vladimir Lossky, *The Mystical Theology of the Eastern Church* (London: James Clarke & Co., 1957), 215, 229, 246, and *passim*. Lossky's book was originally published as *Essai sur la Théologie Mystique de l'Eglise d'Orient* (Paris, 1944). The tragic opposition be-

Dostoevsky wrote his own confession of faith from Omsk in 1854 shortly after release from prison. The same tragic tension between the knowledge of the intellect and that of the heart can be seen in its language.

> I want to say to you, about myself, that I am a child of this age, a child of unfaith and scepticism, and probably (indeed I know it) shall remain so to the end of my life. How dreadfully has it tormented me (and torments me even now)—this longing for faith, which is all the stronger for the proofs I have against it. And yet God gives me sometimes moments of perfect peace: in such moments I love and believe that I am loved; in such moments I have formulated my creed, wherein all is clear and holy to me. This creed is extremely simple; here it is: I believe that there is nothing lovelier, deeper, more sympathetic, more rational, more manly, and more perfect than the Savior; I say to myself with jealous love that not only is there no one else like Him, but that there could be no one. I would even say more: If anyone could prove to me that Christ is outside the truth, and if the truth really did exclude Christ, I should prefer to stay with Christ and not with truth.[15]

The issue of the relationship of the truth of the intellect to the truth of the soul is the theoretical pivot of Dostoevsky's life and work, as it is also a leading question of modern philosophy. It is a major theme in *A Raw Youth* and in *The Brothers Karamazov* and recurs in an interesting way twenty-six years after the letter from Omsk in one of the last things Dostoevsky wrote: his reply (written while he was working on the twelfth and last book of *The Brothers Karamazov*) to the criticisms levelled by Professor A. D. Gradovsky against the Pushkin Speech. He writes:

> you uttered an important word: "enlightenment." I wish to ask what you

---

tween heart and intellect expressed by Pascal and reflected in Dostoevsky's exploration of human existence as its very core is repeatedly formulated in the notes; see, for example, Dostoevsky, *The Notebooks for "A Raw Youth,"* ed. and with an intro. by Edward Wasiolek, trans. Victor Terras (Chicago: University of Chicago Press, 1969), 368, 379, 380, 443, 512, 518, 551; Dostoevsky, *The Notebooks for "The Brothers Karamazov,"* ed. and trans. Edward Wasiolek (Chicago: University of Chicago Press, 1971), 27, 40, 49, 72, 77, 81, 99–102, 111, 151, 175, 178–79, 186, 189–95, 219–21, 224, 235, 270.

[15] Dostoevsky to Mme. N. D. Fonvisin, beginning of March, 1854, in Mayne (trans.), *Letters of Dostoevsky*, 70–71.

mean by it? Western science, useful knowledge, handicrafts, or spiritual enlightenment? The former, *i.e.*, science and trades, in truth should not evade us, and there actually is no reason for us to seek to evade them. I am also in full accord with you that these can be acquired only from Western European sources, for which Europe deserves praise and our eternal gratitude. But my conception of enlightenment ... coincides with what this word literally implies, *i.e.*, spiritual light illuminating the soul, enlightening the heart, guiding the mind and indicating to it the road of life. If this be so, I wish to state to you that there is no reason for us to borrow such enlightenment from Western European sources because Russian sources are fully available—and not absent. You are surprised? ...

I assert that our people have long been enlightened, having embraced in their hearts Christ and His teachings. ... I shall express my thought only in its essential thesis: If our people have long been enlightened by the fact of their acceptance of the quintessence of Christ and His teachings, together with Him, they have embraced *genuine* enlightenment. With this fundamental supply of enlightenment, Western sciences will become a real blessing to the people. They will not dim the image of Christ as in the West, where, however, it was dimmed not by science, as liberals maintain, but by the Western Church itself.[16]

This statement is of importance for several reasons. It illustrates a consistency of viewpoint from age seventeen until the very end of life forty-two years later: Dostoevsky died less than six months after publication of the reply to Gradovsky.[17] It is, moreover, a viewpoint which—so far from being that of an obscurantist political crackpot who happens also to be one of the undeniably great artists of history, as is argued by some critics—is comparable with that of such eminent figures in modern philosophy as Pascal and Bergson, to name but two.[18]

---

[16] Fyodor M. Dostoevsky, *The Diary of a Writer,* trans. Boris Brasol (2 vols.: New York: Charles Scribner's Sons, 1949), II, 982–83, hereinafter cited as Dostoevsky, *Diary.* Serial publication of *The Brothers Karamazov* was completed in the October, 1880, issue of the *Russian Messenger.*

[17] He died January 28, 1881.

[18] A comparison between Dostoevsky and Pascal, in view of the latter's relation to the new philosophy of Bacon and Descartes, on the one hand, and to the Jesuits, on the other hand, might prove particularly rewarding. The similarity of Dostoevsky's thought with that of the late Bergson in its metaphysical and epistemological aspects is striking. Cf. Ellis Sandoz "Myth and Society in the Philosophy of Bergson," *Social Research,* XXX (1964), 171–202; also, Alois Dempf, *Die drei Laster: Dostojewkis Tiefenpsychologie* (Munich: Karl Alber, 1946), 17–18, 77.

Dostoevsky once said of himself: "I am weak in philosophy (but not in my love for it); in my love for it I am strong." [19] Berdyaev, on the other hand, calls him "a dialectician of genius and Russia's greatest metaphysician." [20] However this may be, one can scarcely either contend that Dostoevsky has written philosophy or deny that his insights into the nature of man and the structure of being are surpassed by any other modern thinker. Moreover, his strict sense of causality in the Gradovsky reply is to be admired as philosophically perspicacious. There is no inherent conflict between science and religion, provided the two operate in their proper spheres and do not commit "boundary transgressions." [21] Spiritual effects follow from spiritual causes. Dostoevsky believed (as Miliukov has since confirmed) that the breach between the intellectuals and the people in Russia actually occurred a half century before Peter the Great and derived primarily from a religious cause rather than from economic and political causes.[22] Similarly, a danger inherent to Western science and Enlightenment in the French sense was its tendency toward perversion into scientism of the Comtean and Marxian kinds, thereby becoming a religious movement.[23] Dostoevsky was among the first to understand that the modern political

---

[19] Dostoevsky to N. N. Strakhov, June 6, 1870, as quoted in David Magarshack (ed.), *The Best Short Stories of Dostoevsky* (New York: Random House, Inc., Modern Library, n.d.), xixn.
[20] Nicholas Berdyaev, *Dostoevsky*, trans. Donald Attwater (New York: World Publ. Co., Meridian Books, 1957), 11.
[21] Cf. W. H. Werkmeister, "Scientism and the Problem of Man," in Charles A. Moore (ed.), *Philosophy and Culture: East and West* (Honolulu: University of Hawaii Press, 1962), 135–55.
[22] Cf. Paul Miliukov, *Outlines of Russian Culture*, ed. Michael Karpovich, trans. Valentine Ughet and Eleanor Davis (3 vols.; Philadelphia: University of Pennsylvania Press, 1943), I, 38–39.
[23] Cf. Matthew Spinka, *Christian Thought from Erasmus to Berdyaev* (Englewood Cliffs: Prentice-Hall, Inc., 1962), especially chaps. 8 and 9; Eric Voegelin, "The Origins of Scientism," *Social Research*, XV (1948), 462–94; John Wellmuth, *The Nature and Origins of Scientism* (Milwaukee: Marquette University Press, 1944); R. G. Owen, *Scientism, Man, and Religion* (Philadelphia: Westminster Press, 1952). Fundamental for understanding the eschatological and messianic ("religious") components of the Enlightenment and its nineteenth century political and ideological sequels are J. L. Talmon's books: *The Origins of Totalitarian Democracy* (New York: Frederick A. Praeger, Inc., 1952) and *Political Messianism: The Romantic Phase* (New York: Frederick A. Praeger, Inc., 1960.)

mass movements are secular religions ("irreligions"),[24] aping science, dedicated to the destruction of God and the humanity of man, and at bottom are spiritually and intellectually bankrupt. Even without having seen the text, he knew that the "scientific" socialist's answer to the fundamental metaphysical questions about the origin of man and the world, the ground of being, and the source of order, could only be something like that given by Marx.

> Your question is itself a product of abstraction. Ask yourself how you arrived at that question. Ask yourself whether your question is not posed from a standpoint to which I cannot reply, because it is wrongly put. Ask yourself whether [that problem] exists for a reasonable mind. When you ask about the creation of nature and man, you are abstracting . . . from man and nature. You postulate them as non-existent, and yet you want me to prove them to you as *existing*. Now I say to you: Give up your abstraction and you will also give up your question. . . . Don't think, don't ask me, for as soon as you think and ask, your abstraction from the existence of nature and man has no meaning. . . .
>
>   . . . . for the socialist man the *entire so-called history of the world* is nothing but the creation of man through human labor, nothing but the emergence of nature for man, so he has the visible, irrefutable proof of his *birth* through himself, of the *process of his creation*. Since the *real existence* of man and nature—since man has become for man as the being of nature, and nature for man as the being of man has become practical, sensuous, perceptible—the question about an *alien* being, about a being above nature and man—a question which implies the admission of the unreality of nature and of man—has become impossible in practice.[25]

Critical issues of this kind must not be raised. Metaphysical questions are forbidden. The socialist man is a "reasonable" man in just the sense ridiculed by Dostoevsky from the time of *Notes From*

24 Cf. Eduard Thurneysen, *Dostoevsky: A Theological Study*, trans. K. R. Crim (London: Epworth, 1964).

25 Karl Marx, *Economic and Philosophic Manuscripts of 1844*, ed. Dirk J. Struik, trans. Martin Milligan (New York: International Publishers Co., 1964), 145; Marx, *Die Frühschriften*, ed. Siegfried Landshut (Stuttgart: Kroener, 1953), 247–48. Cf. the analysis and the parallel passage in Comte, *Cours de Philosophie Positive*, Vol. I in Eric Voegelin, *Wissenschaft, Politik und Gnosis* (Munich: Koesel, 1959), 33ff; Voegelin, *Science, Politics and Gnosticism: Two Essays*, trans. William J. Fitzpatrick (Chicago: Regnery, 1968), 22–28. Italics as in original.

Underground onward; and by Marx's definition, *he* does not ask these questions. The entire enterprise rests upon a conscious intellectual swindle enforced by moral sanction. Dostoevsky understood even this.[26]

The existential centrality of Christ was not a conception of only the post-Siberian Dostoevsky. Christianity was regarded from his youth as "the foundation" of the spiritual order of the world. In one letter, written at age eighteen, a comparison is drawn between Homer and Christ as divine *nomothetai* of ancient and modern mankind. "Homer (a legendary figure, who was perhaps sent to us by God, as Christ was) can only be placed with Christ. . . . Homer, in the *Iliad*, gave to the ancient world the same organization in spiritual and earthly matters as the modern world owes to Christ." [27]

There is no need to enter here into the vexed question of a religious conversion of Dostoevsky in the prison years, or to explore in any detail the ambiguity of his life or the technique of ambiguity in his art, or even to do more than mention the highly dialectical character of his thought. It is, however, essential to notice that for Dostoevsky the mystery of man finds its highest resolution and ultimate synthesis in the mystery of the Incarnation of the divine Word.[28] That the supersession of the mystery of man by the mystery of Christ is the (or even *a*) "solution" to the problem of man is a point lost on the majority of Dostoevsky's readers—as he feared it would be. Failure to apprehend this is responsible for the most fantastic of the "critical" literature dealing with the author. In this respect, above all others, Dostoevsky speaks neither to his age nor ours but to all the ages of man. The work in which this "word" is most successfully expressed is *The Brothers Karamazov,*

---

26 See *The Brothers Karamazov*, bk. 11, chap. 9; cf. Voegelin's analysis of "the swindle" in Marx in *Science, Politics and Gnosticism*, 25. For "the swindle" of the Grand Inquisitor, see Dostoevsky, *The Notebooks for "The Brothers Karamazov,"* 72, 82, 86.

27 Dostoevsky to his brother, Michael, January 1, 1840, in Mayne (trans.), *Letters of Dostoevsky*, 13. Similar thoughts are expressed in *The Notebooks for "The Brothers Karamazov,"* 186–91, 255.

28 See *The Notebooks for "The Brothers Karamazov,"* 96, 100: "The mystery of God surrounds man, the mystery of great order and harmony. . . . *Keep* the image of Christ and if possible picture him in yourself."

particularly in the fifth and sixth books ("Pro and Contra" and "The Russian Monk"). Yet writers of the penetration and scholarship of E. H. Carr can say that: *"The Brothers Karamazov* is a mighty *tour de force* by one whose zenith already is passed, and lacks the eager, stumbling spontaneity of its predecessors"; and Ralph Matlaw can report the consensus of the critics that book 6 is "generally . . . thought to be the weakest in the novel." [29] Despite Dostoevsky's own reservations and his agonies over this portion of the manuscript, the shortcomings here appear to lie not so much with the author as with the readers. Whether Dostoevsky was a decadent or a mystic has been a fashionable question for a century. Among his Russian readers the range of comment can be bracketed by statements by another great writer, Turgenev, and by a leading contemporary scholar, Nicolas Zernov. The former wrote, shortly after Dostoevsky's death, that the recently deceased was the Russian "Marquis de Sade. . . . And when one thinks that all the Russian Bishops said masses for the soul of *this* Marquis de Sade, and even preached sermons about his great love for all mankind! Truly, we live in a remarkable age." [30] Zernov writes: "With Dostoevsky, Russian culture of the nineteenth century reaches its climax. He is one of the greatest novelists the world has known, and one of the most original psychologists of all times. But he is more than a gifted writer; he is also a mystic whose utterances about God and man equal in significance any ever made by a Christian thinker." [31]

One must be attentive, in any event, to Dostoevsky's meaning when, he explains with respect to "The Russian Monk": "I have written this book for the few and consider it the culminating point of my work." [32] And what, indeed, does Dostoevsky mean by this

---

[29] Edward H. Carr, *Dostoevsky (1821–1881): A New Biography* (London: Allen & Unwin, 1931), 231; Ralph E. Matlaw, *The Brothers Karamazov: Novelistic Technique* (The Hague: Mouton, 1957), 42. Edward Wasiolek concurs in Matlaw's (if not in Carr's) judgment; see his remarks in *The Notebooks for "The Brothers Karamazov,"* 89–90.

[30] Ivan Turgenev to M. E. Saltykov, September 24, 1882, as quoted in Mayne (trans.), *Letters of Dostoevsky,* 336.

[31] Nicholas Zernov, *Three Russian Prophets: Khomyakov, Dostoevsky, Solovyov* (2nd ed.; London: S. C. M. Press, 1944), 82.

[32] Dostoevsky to K. P. Pobedonostsev, August 9/21, 1879, in S S. Koteliansky and J. Middleton Murry (trans.), *Dostoevsky: Letters and Reminiscences* (New

sentence? He has written for the few (and not for fools), firstly, because the subject matter can in any case only be penetrated by the few: the mountain peaks of human experience can be gained only rarely. The view from there can achieve the lucidity of reflective apprehension and articulation only in those charismatic persons who, as prophets, artists, sages, saints, and philosophers, link man through the ages with the eternal, illuminate the opacity of existence with the truth of being, and subtly help to shape the course of human destiny. The work in which Dostoevsky was consciously participating is the perennial enterprise of the aristocrats of the spirit—even of those who think of themselves as proletarians of literature.[33] He has written for the few, secondly, because he knew society was disintegrating around him as a result of Westernization in its ideological dimension. He knew that the destruction of faith was a primary characteristic of the times and that it was precisely and solely on the foundation of the living faith experience that what he had written could be comprehended with anything like its real power and authority. The reader capable of identifying at all levels of the work would, in any event, be the rare exception. Berdyaev suggests there never has been even one. The two points enumerated are, of course, merely different aspects of the same problem: the mountain peaks of human experience cannot be scaled without faith. In a discussion of Eros in Plato's *Symposium* F. M. Cornford points out that, when man encounters "ultimate reality" through an experience of transcendent being, "the distinction between the metaphysical and the religious may become meaningless." [34] And it is well to recall that Plato coined the term "theology" (*Republic,*

York: Alfred A. Knopf, Inc., 1923), 247. The point is bluntly stated elsewhere by Dostoevsky: "I am not writing for fools." Dostoevsky, *The Notebooks for "A Raw Youth"*, 426. The opposition between the many fools and the few *spoudaioi* is as old as philosophy itself. Stanley Rosen aptly remarks that "the many have always disliked philosophy; the new historical phenomenon after Hegel is the acceptance of the tastes of the many by the few, in however esoteric a manner this acceptance might be phrased." Stanley Rosen, *Nihilism: A Philosophical Essay* (New Haven: Yale University Press, 1969), 92.

33 Cf. Dostoevsky to N. N. Strakhov, September 18, 1863, in Mayne (trans.), *Letters of Dostoevsky*, 108ff.

34 F. M. Cornford, *The Unwritten Philosophy and Other Essays* (Cambridge: Cambridge University Press, 1950), 78.

379a)—precisely to establish the new concept as the center of philosophical thought.[35]

Faith as presented by Dostoevsky is existential rather than doctrinal. This is in no way to suggest that he was not well read in
theological literature: indeed, nothing would be further from the
truth. But like all the other experiences of men which fell within
his purview to find dramatic expression in his work, Dostoevsky
portrayed faith from within—turned inside out, as it were, after the
necessities of his art. The perspective is suggested by the often-quoted
statement reported by Strakhov: "They call me a psychologist: it is
not true. I am merely a realist in the higher sense of the word, that
is, I depict all the depth of the human soul." [36] In a letter to Maikov,
in which the problem of faith is of direct concern, Dostoevsky wrote:

> I have a totally different conception of truth and realism from that of
> our "realists" and critics. My God! If one could but tell categorically all
> that we Russians have gone through during the last ten years in the way
> of spiritual development, all the realists would shriek that it was pure
> fantasy! And yet it would be pure realism! It *is* the one true, deep realism;
> theirs is altogether too superficial. . . . With such realism, one couldn't
> show so much as the hundredth part of the true facts. But our idealists
> have actually *predicted* many of the actual facts—really, that has been
> done.[37]

The perspective of the psychologist is external and analytical. That
of Dostoevsky is of the man conscious of the mystery of being and
conscious of his participation in it. He illumined the mystery by
embodying the endless variety of its configurations in the concrete
depictions and imagery of art. The articulation is, on each occasion,
the mythopoeic utterance of the mystery. His art is, therefore, all
together a topography of the inner dimension of human experience
—a voyager's chart of the soul. The tension of existence supplies the

---

[35] Cf. Werner Jaeger, *Humanism and Theology* (Milwaukee: Marquette University Press, 1943), 46.

[36] Quoted in Poggioli, *The Phoenix and the Spider*, 25. Psychology is consistently
deprecated as a deficient mode of understanding. See, for example, Dostoevsky,
The Notebooks for "The Brothers Karamazov," 179, 180, 247, 251, 259, 264.

[37] Dostoevsky to Maikov, December 11, 1868, in Mayne (trans.), *Letters of
Dostoevsky*, 158–59.

matrix of reality which Dostoevsky illuminates from within as a self-conscious participant and existent. The immersion of existence itself in a larger reality (being) does not dispel the mystery of man. It only particularizes mystery into types and varieties so that mystery yields further mystery and knowledge descends and ascends to increasing degrees of awareness of a reality which is essentially unfathomable but *is* and comprises both the substance of man and his condition.

In the life of individuals and the history of societies, faith illumines and structures existence. Dostoevsky's perception of this was expressed early in life, as has been seen. It constitutes the centerpiece of his conception of human existence and history. Insofar as faith is viewed by Dostoevsky as spiritual action, as a reciprocal experience in the continual unfolding of the drama of being, his perspective approximates the view of revelation taken by H. Richard Niebuhr, for he says that

> revelation . . . shines by its own light and is intelligible in itself . . . it illuminates other events and enables us to understand them. Whatever else revelation means it does mean an event in our history which brings rationality and wholeness into the confused joys and sorrows of personal existence and allows us to discern order in the brawl of communal histories. Such revelation is no substitute for reason; the illumination it supplies does not excuse the mind from labor; but it does give to that mind the impulsion and the first principles it requires if it is to be able to do its proper work. In this sense we may say that the revelatory moment is revelatory because it is rational, because it makes the understanding of order and meaning in personal history possible.[38]

3. Suffering and Faith

An understanding of faith is ineluctable if the full stature of Dostoevsky's art is to be glimpsed. The core of his effort dramatically to portray, or externalize, the faith experience as the sovereign solution to the riddle of existence is especially to be found in those places where the undeserved suffering of the innocent becomes thematic. Surely one of the most tormenting of these passages is the chapter en-

---

[38] H. Richard Niebuhr, *The Meaning of Revelation* (New York: Macmillan Co., 1941), 199–200.

titled "Rebellion" in *The Brothers Karamazov* (bk. 5, chap. 4), the prologue to the "Legend of the Grand Inquisitor." The question of theodicy is presented in the most searing terms. The chapter supplies the key to Ivan's rebellion in that, on the one hand, Euclidian rationality can provide no satisfactory answer to the problem with which he is agonized; and, on the other hand, the answer of faith is incomprehensible and, therefore, existentially unpersuasive because the experience of divine grace is absent. With relentless acumen Dostoevsky strips away layer after layer of husk until the kernel problem in all its horror and brutality is confronted. The alternative solutions to the encounter are *rebellion* and *faith*. The novel shows the irrationality of the "rational" solution as the consequences of rebellion are unfolded to culminate in the murder of Fyodor Pavlovitch and the psychic destruction of Ivan. The rationality of the "irrational" solution is, in fact, the high motif of the novel, the climax of which is reached in the portrayal of Christ in the Legend. Here the ineffability of transcendent being becomes, in Dostoevsky's hands, as much of a real encounter with the sublime as modern literature affords: "Christ keeps a silence so eloquent that The Legend is one of the few pieces of world literature, outside the New Testament, that gives a living picture of Jesus Christ." [39]

Yet what can be the possible meaning of such a tribute? Wherein is this at all rational or even intelligible? Even if the barbarity, futility, and tragedy of Ivan's rebellion can, with the empirical evidence of the consequences of contemporary worldwide rebellion, be understood, what—beyond a sort of nauseous milk and water nostrum of humane good will and pity derided by Dostoevsky—that is "intersubjectively transmissible" [40] can be said of Dostoevsky's high,

---

[39] Nicolas Zernov, *Eastern Christendom: A Study of the Origin and Development of the Eastern Orthodox Church* (New York: G. P. Putnam's Sons, 1961), 199.

[40] Cf. Arnold Brecht, *Foundations of Twentieth Century Political Theory* (Princeton: Princeton University Press, 1959), chap. 13, especially from 469 on. Dostoevsky's ridicule of sugary, sentimental Christianity is especially evident in the *ad populam* arguments of the defense attorney, Fetiukovich, at Dmitri's trial, as sketched in the notes; see Dostovesky, *The Notebooks for "The Brothers Karamazov,"* 237–39, 248–49, 253–54, 263. The prosecutor is the foil for unmasking this perversion, along with the audience; but he is himself a dogmatist and fundamentalist. Both versions of Christianity are radically defective, in Dostoevsky's view, and the defense attorney and the prosecutor alike are consciously cor-

true solution of the problem? One must be reminded of Ivan: nothing could be communicated to Ivan that was existentially cogent.
Indeed, this fact is emphasized to the point of grotesqueness by Dostoevsky: the superb portrayal of Christ is one ostensibly done by
this very Ivan! The forms, paraphernalia, and intimate knowledge
of all the biographical, doctrinal, and historical data and accoutre-
ments are to no avail. Was not Feuerbach a biblical scholar and
theologian? Is not the intellectual brilliance and erudition of Ivan
clear from the characterization? Probably the basic model for Ivan
was P. J. Chaadaev (1794–1856), although he is, of course, only
drawn in caricature as part of a composite derived from many other
sources; and it is impossible to deny Belinsky a prominent part in
the character of Dostoevsky's hero.[41] That Ivan is an encyclopedist
and *polymathes* is clear even to the casual reader. A dissection of
Ivan's lines shows him to be quoting (to give but a partial list) John
the Merciful, Voltaire, Polonius, Richard of Geneva, John Damascene, Nekrasov, the newspapers, Schiller, Gogol, sixteenth century
mystery plays, Dante, Victor Hugo, Hamlet, the Bible, Tiuchev,
Pushkin, Tolstoy, Goethe, Belinsky, Descartes, and Heine.[42] Endowed so richly, in what is Ivan lacking? Not in feeling, not in
sympathy of at least a grandiose and all-embracing kind, not in

---

rupt sophists, as the prosecutor says in the notes: "But what difference does the
Bible make, we glance at it on the eve of our speech so as to shine with our eloquence." *Ibid.*, 249. It is suggested that Mitia's and Fetiukovich's kinds of Christianity are immature and roughly equivalent: infected by the sentimental,
Schilleresque, romantic idealism of the St. Petersburg intellectuals.

[41] See Thomas G. Masaryk, *The Spirit of Russia: Studies in History, Literature,
Philosophy*, Vols. I and II, trans. Eden and Cedar Paul (2nd ed.; London: Allen &
Unwin; New York: Macmillan Co., 1955); Vol. III, ed. George Gibian, trans.
Robert Bass (New York: Barnes & Noble, Inc., 1967), I, 229. Dostoevsky had expressed the intention of characterizing Chaadaev in this novel: "Of course it is
not to be the actual Chaadaev; I only want to display the type." (Dostoevsky to
Maikov, March 25, 1870, in Mayne (trans.), *Letters of Dostoevsky*, 191. The
actual role of Ivan in the novel is considerably different from the one sketched
in this letter, but the central importance of the figure is retained. Matthew Spinka
makes a point-blank identification of Ivan with Belinsky and the "Westernists"
(Spinka, *Christian Thought*, 202–203). Valuable for an understanding of the
conflict basic to the political and religious tensions in *The Brothers Karamazov* is
Raymond T. McNally, "Chaadaev versus Khomyakov in the late 1830s and the
1840s," *Journal of the History of Ideas*, XXVII (1966), 73–91.

[42] Cf. Matlaw, *The Brothers Karamazov*, 17.

idealism and nobility of soul. He lacks only faith. And the gigantic *superbia cognoscendi* of his philosophical gnosticism not only cannot substitute for faith but even bars approach to it.

But Dostoevsky is yet subtler than this. He displays the trace of Ivan's faith which reflects the ambiguity that "It's not God" (*The Brothers Karamazov*, I, 250)[43] he rejects but the order of His creation and His revelation in Christ. It does not do merely to suppose that Ivan lacks faith. The problem is not so simple as that. To borrow Karl Barth's characterization of Feuerbach, Ivan's "feeling is positive. He, too, is singing his *Magnificat*." [44] Ivan's faithlessness is concentrated in the rejection of Christ as the climax of revelation and the means of salvation. Like the Inquisitor, he is moved by the divine encounter but "adheres to his idea" (*The Brothers Karamazov* I, 269). Dostoevsky's message is that without faith in Christ there can be no redemption.

The contours of this peculiarly and precisely *Christian* conception of faith must be sketched because Dostoevsky makes it the heart of his greatest novel: if one is to enter into a discussion of *The Brothers Karamazov*, then one must be prepared to consider faith, because this is what the book is about. The reader is confronted by an effort to transmit through depiction a mystical experience of transcendent being in the Christian tradition. The content of such an experience has aptly been summarized in principle as follows:

> No religion has brought the mystery of the need for atonement or expiation to so complete, so profound, or so powerful expression as Christianity. . . . the distrust and suspicion which so widely obtains with regard to this mystery is only to be explained from the general custom . . . of taking into account only the rational side of religion. Yet this atonement mystery is a "moment" which no Christian teaching that pur-

---

[43] References to *The Brothers Karamazov* are to the "Everyman Edition" (2 vols.; London: J. M. Dent & Sons, Ltd., 1927), trans. Constance Garnett, unless otherwise indicated. As is generally the case, the presentation of the novel is more refined than in the notes; there Ivan boldly states: "I would like to destroy completely the idea of God" (Dostoevsky, *The Notebooks for "The Brothers Karamazov*," 72).

[44] Karl Barth, *Protestant Thought: From Rousseau to Ritschl; Being the Translation of Eleven Chapters of "Die Protestantische Theologie Im 19. Jahrhundert,"* trans. B. Cozens (New York: Harper & Row, Publ., 1959), 356.

ports to represent the religious experience of the Christian and biblical tradition can afford to surrender. The teacher will have to make explicit, by an analysis of the Christian religious experience, how the "very numen," by imparting itself to the worshipper, becomes itself the means of "atonement." . . . For the God of the New Testament is not less holy than the God of the Old Testament, but more holy. The interval between the creature and Him is not diminished but made absolute; the unworthiness of the profane in contrast to Him is not extenuated but enhanced. That God none the less admits access to Himself and intimacy with Himself is not a mere matter of course; it is a grace beyond our power to apprehend, a prodigious paradox. To take this paradox out of Christianity is to make it shallow and superficial beyond recognition. But if this is so, the intuitions concerning, and the need felt for, "covering" and "atonement" result immediately. And the divinely appointed means of God's self-revelation, where experienced and appraised as such—"the Word," "the Spirit," "the person of Christ,"—become that to which the man "flees," in which he finds refuge, and in which he "hides" himself, in order that, consecrated and cleansed of his "profaneness" thereby, he may come into the presence of Holiness itself.

. . . Whoever . . . penetrates to the unique center of the religious experience, so that it starts awake in his own consciousness, finds that the truth of these intuitions is experienced directly, as soon as he penetrates their depths.[45]

In Dostoevsky's work the efficacy of faith as the answer to suffering in the world occupies the place of primacy. No merely intellectual or ethical solutions will suffice, and in the desperate thirst for justice, Ivan is driven into his tragic rebellion. The emphasis upon suffering is no chance one. Nor is it an index to "Dostoevsky's very strong destructive instinct, which might easily have made him a criminal, [but which] was in his actual life directed mainly against his own person [inward instead of outward] and thus found expression as masochism and a sense of guilt"—even if "masochistic characters" are imputed to "all the great men to whom mankind is indebted for progress and increased joy of life." [46] The emphasis on suffering has

45 Rudolf Otto, *Idea of the Holy: An Inquiry into the Non-Rational Factor in the Idea of the Divine and Its Relation to the Rational*, trans. J. W. Harvey (2nd ed.; London: Oxford University Press, 1950), 56–57.

46 Sigmund Freud, *Collected Papers*, ed. J. Strachey (5 vols.; New York: Basic Books, Inc., 1959), V, 224; Theodore Reik, *Masochism in Modern Man*, trans. M. H. Beigel and G. M. Kurth (New York: Farrar, Straus, Inc., 1941), 393.

its explanation, rather, in the dynamics of the Christian consciousness and its solution also is to be found there, as the quotation from
Otto suggests. The merit of the discoveries of modern psychoanalysis should not be permitted to obscure the truth of the drama
of the soul here unfolded and resolved. Even Freud himself (amid
the lamentations of his more sanguine latter-day enthusiasts, it is
true) has conceded that "before the problem of the creative artist
analysis must, alas, lay down its arms." [47]

Zernov has observed that Dostoevsky "never used theological terms,
and he never spoke about Christ's redemptive work. But his whole
life was based on the experience of redemption." [48] This experience
both suffused his art at its highest levels and comprises the centerpiece of Christianity. Concisely stated: "redemption is throughout
the purport of the Gospel even in its first and simplest form, a
redemption which is both to be fulfilled by God hereafter and yet at
the same time already experienced here and now." [49] The fact of
suffering in existence and the uncommon capacity of the *narod* to
bear suffering without fear and lapse of faith is the clue to the religious depth and identity of the Russian people as a Christ-bearing
nation. This subject is raised in an early number of *The Diary of a
Writer* as follows:

> I believe that the main and most fundamental spiritual quest of the
> Russian people is their craving for suffering—perpetual and unquenchable
> suffering—everywhere and in everything. It seems that they have been
> affected by this thirst for martyrdom from time immemorial. The suffer-
> ing stream flows through their whole history—not merely because of ex-
> ternal calamities and misfortunes: it gushes from the people's very heart.

---

[47] Freud, *Collected Papers*, V, 222. For a psychoanalytical approach to Dostoevsky, see Lawrence Kohlberg, "Psychological Analysis and Literary Form: A Study
of the Doubles in Dostoevsky," *Daedalus*, XCII (1963), 345–62, who finds the key
to the "double" in the novelist to lie in the "autoscopic syndrome" (353ff). See
especially Table I, p. 356. Essays by Claire Rosenfield and Simon O. Lesser in the
same number of this journal take the psychoanalytical approach to the author;
see also Harry Slochower, "Incest in *The Brothers Karamazov*," in Hendrik M.
Ruitenbeek (ed.), *Psychoanalysis and Literature* (New York: E. P. Dutton & Co.,
1964), 303–20.
[48] Zernov, *Three Prophets*, 107.
[49] Otto, *Idea of the Holy*, 167.

Even in happiness there is in the Russian people an element of suffering; otherwise, felicity to them is incomplete. . . . the Russian people know the Gospel poorly . . . but they do know Christ, and they have been carrying Him in their hearts from time immemorial . . . the heart-knowledge of Christ, a true conception of Him, does fully exist . . . it has merged with the heart of the people. Perhaps, Christ is the only love of the Russian people, and they love His image in their own way, to the limit of sufferance.[50]

The paradigm of this image is the Passion of Christ. To the earthbound, Euclidian logic of Ivan this very dysteleology is the most repulsive (and dubious) element of Christian reality. The biblical context and solution supply the setting.

It is . . . clear that it is in the Passion and death of Christ that the objects of the strongest religious intuition must be sought. If His Incarnation, His mission, and the manner of His life come to be considered as a piece of self-revelation, in which an eternal Will of Love is mirrored, before all else is this Love and Faith seen accomplished in the Passion. The Cross becomes in an absolute sense the "mirror of the eternal Father" *(speculum aeterni Patris);* and not of the "Father" alone—the highest rational interpretation of the holy—but of Holiness as such. For what makes Christ in a special sense the summary and the climax of the course of antecedent religious evolution is pre-eminently this—that in His life, suffering, and death is repeated in classic and absolute form that most mystical of all the problems of the Old Covenant, the problem of the guiltless suffering of the righteous, which reechoes again and again so mysteriously from Jeremiah and deutero-Isaiah on through Job and the Psalms. The thirty-eighth chapter of Job is a prophecy of Golgotha. And on Golgotha the solution of the problem, already adumbrated in Job, is repeated and surpassed. It lay . . . entirely in the non-rational aspect of deity, and yet was none the less a solution. In Job the suffering of the righteous found its significance as the classic and crucial case of the revelation, more immediately actual and in more palpable proximity than any other, of the transcendent mysteriousness and "beyondness" of God. The Cross of Christ, the monogram of the eternal mystery, is its completion. Here rational are enfolded with non-rational elements, the revealed commingled with the unrevealed, the most exalted love with the "wrath" of the numen, and therefore, in applying to the Cross of Christ the category

---

50 Dostoevsky, *Diary* (*The Citizen*, No. 4, 1873), I, 36, 38–39.

"holy," Christian religious feeling has given birth to a religious intuition profounder and more vital than any to be found in the whole history of religion.[51]

The encounter through faith with the numen is a mingling of the soul through grace with the fascinating, august, *mysterium* of Divine Being. It assuages sorrow and appeases anguish. It reconciles man to God in the tribulation of existence. It implants the consciousness of the supreme goodness of the incomprehensible embracing reality which cannot be assimilated to rational human thought but must remain a fact and an irreducible mystery.[52]

A mystical faith experience is thus foundational to Dostoevsky. It outruns conceptualization and discursive statement to find symbolization in the mythopoeic representations of the saintly persons of his novels. It also finds expression in the glimpses of sublimity and evanescent tendencies toward the holy accorded even the most depraved and discordant characters in his formidable rogues' gallery.

The face and figure of Christ as the Incarnation of divinity in history emerges from the dark night of the misery of existence. He illuminates life with ineffable splendor, and it is this that is so powerfully evoked in the symbolization of the Legend. In the wake of this transcendental encounter, Dostoevsky utters through the words of Zosima those things which *can* be said of the essentially unspeakable *Realissimum*. It is, therefore, in terms of the philosophical impossibility of expressing transcendental experiences through necessarily immanent propositions that Dostoevsky's apparently contradictory and paradoxical assertions are to be reconciled that the Legend, on the one hand, and the words of the dying Zosima, on the other hand, each constitute the "culminating point" of the novel: one in the way of apophatic mysticism, the other in the way of cataphatic theology.[53] Berdyaev's assertion is similarly to be understood, that the Legend is the climax of Dostoevsky's Christian metaphysics. The encounter with the transcendental numen shapes the soul and transforms existence through the individual experience called "conversion" in the

---

51 Otto, *Idea of the Holy*, 172–73.
52 *Ibid.*, 77–80.
53 See this chapter, sec. 4, *below.*

Christian tradition. This movement of reorientation in the ground of the soul and subsequent repetitions of the divine encounter do not dispel the quality of mystery or overcome the problem of ineffability. On the contrary. The mystery deepens, the gulf is made more absolute. Its unutterability becomes the absolute silence of the mystic. The phenomenon is commonplace to Christian mysticism, well known to the discipline of Russian contemplatives. Hellenic philosophy affords an instructive parallel in Plato's handling of the problem in the Vision of the Agathon in the *Republic*: although the Myth of the Cave is the keystone of the dialogue, nothing at all is said about the content of the Good. It lies strictly beyond discursive statement, which can bring to grasp only the immanent in being.[54]

The mystical faith experience finds its highest expression by Dostoevsky in the Legend. Therefore, it is proper to proceed directly to this passage in his writing, the more so that the Legend (not all of Dostoevsky) is the subject of this essay. Nonetheless, in raising the problem of Dostoevsky's conception and experience of faith for consideration, it is necessary also to acknowledge certain other problems ancillary to it. Dostoevsky wrote that the subject which had tormented him all his life and which was to be the topic of his definitive work was the question of the existence of God. This appears to be not quite accurate, or at least to be fragmentary and misleading. The position ascribed to Ivan is, at least in this respect, more nearly that of Dostoevsky. The problem with which Dostoevsky is agonized is not the existence of God, but the relation of God and His truth (known through revelation and faith) to the creation, to nature, and to human society. What are the consequences of faith and the truth of faith for man's life in society as this unfolds historically? This is the preeminently political question. The problem is one of the relationship between the divine and the social orders, between the order of transcendent being and the order of immanent being. The problem is complex. This is especially true because Dostoevsky's work and thought are completely existential in thrust. He was acutely aware

---

[54] Cf. Eric Voegelin, *Plato and Aristotle* (Baton Rouge: Louisiana State University Press, 1957), Vol. III in Voegelin, *Order and History* (3 vols. to date.; Baton Rouge: Louisiana State University Press, 1956—), 112.

of the immersion in existence, in the life throes of what he called the *élan vital* (*zhivaia zhizn'*) of "our Russia, which is eternally in a state of creation." [55] With the social order jeopardized on all sides, and particularly by nihilism and incipient revolutionism from within, the question became one of how to meet the all-too-justified criticisms of the Belinskys and Chernyshevskys without, at the same time, succumbing to the radical defectiveness of their solutions.

The question is related to faith because Dostoevsky's opposition to Belinsky and his epigoni was founded on the insight that any solution to the social problem which excluded Christ was destructive of man and the essentially human. The consequences of this view will be of concern in the Conclusion.

4. MYTHOPOESIS AND MYSTICAL THEOLOGY

The argument here is that Dostoevsky has in the Legend given mythopoetic expression to an experience of transcendence in the Christian mystical tradition. He has set down an apocalypse. In the interest of cogency and plausibility some further evidence of Dostoevsky's mastery of the Bible and the mystical theology of Eastern Orthodoxy will be offered and a brief analysis be given of a mystical tradition but little known in the West.

"I come from a Russian and religious family," the author once wrote. "We in our family knew the New Testament almost from early childhood." [56] According to Madame A. G. Dostoevsky, her husband had learned to read from the volume entitled *A Hundred and Four Sacred Stories from the Old and New Testament*. At the age of eight he was greatly impressed by an account of Job which he heard in a

---

55 Dostoevsky, *Diary*, I, 342.

56 Quoted in Fyodor M. Dostoevsky, *Stavrogin's Confession and the Plan of the Life of a Great Sinner*, ed. N. Brodsky, trans. S. S. Koteliansky and Virginia Woolf (Richmond: Hogarth Press, 1922), 160. The biblical implications of the Legend are considered in Antanas Maceina, *Der Grossinquisitor: Geschichtsphilosophische Deutung der Legende Dostojewskijs* (Heidelberg: Kerle, 1952), especially pt. 3, pp. 157–236; Cyrille Wilczkowski, "Regards sur l'évolution réligieuse de Dostoievski," in Dostoevsky, *La Légende du Grand Inquisiteur* (Bruges: Desclée de Brouwer, 1958), 207–51; Roger L. Cox, *Between Earth and Heaven: Shakespeare, Dostoevsky, and the Meaning of Christian Tragedy* (New York: Holt, Rinehart & Winston, Inc., 1969), especially chap. 9.

sermon.[57] The only book permitted him during the five years of imprisonment in Siberia was the New Testament which he "constantly read," probably the first Russian translation, published in St. Petersburg in 1822.[58] These five years brought Dostoevsky from age twenty-nine to thirty-four and must be considered decisive to his spiritual development. They were five years of excruciating psychic and physical suffering, spent in thought, meditation, and prayer; spent in communion with God and self, and with a variety of human types ranging from the criminally insane and perverse peasant to political revolutionaries of aristocratic descent. It is not difficult to suppose that in this period Dostoevsky pondered every sentence and thought of the New Testament or that he applied the biblical truths to his plight, to the suffering of the innocent, to the riddles of the human condition as he lived it. A lesser man might have done as much. That a great intellect and spirit failed to do so is inconceivable.

More than a decade prior to the creation of his great work, *The Brothers Karamazov*, he wrote that "before I attack it, I shall have to read a whole library of atheistic works by Catholic and Orthodox-Greek writers. Even in the most favourable circumstances, it can't be ready for two years. . . . when I have written this last novel, I shall be ready to die, for I shall have uttered therein my whole heart's burden." [59]

It can be established from external evidence that Dostoevsky was an omnivorous reader. But it is mainly the internal evidence of his artistic production which confirms that he did, in fact, make the

---

[57] Cited in Dostoevsky, *Stavrogin's Confession*, 160. He wrote of this to his wife in 1875: "I am reading Job and it brings me to a state of painful ecstasy; I leave off reading and I walk about my room, almost crying, for an hour. This book, dear Anna, it's strange, it was one of the first to impress me in my life. I was then practically an infant" (cited from Dostoevsky, *The Notebooks for "The Brothers Karamazov*, 95n). Zosima recounts the story of Job in the novel, bk. 6, chap. 3.

[58] Simmons, "Dostoevsky—'A Realist in the Higher Sense'," 107. A page from Dostoevsky's New Testament is reproduced by Komarovich, *Die Urgestalt der Brüder Karamasoff*, opposite 384. Cf. A. Yarmolinsky, *Dostoevsky: His Life and Art*, 397n. The 1822 Russian translation was apparently the one used by Dostoevsky: *Gospoda nashego Iisusa Khrista Novyi Zaviet na slavjanskom i russkom iazyke* 3. Tisneniem (St. Petersburg: V Tip. Rossiiskago bibleiskago obva, 1822) vi and 818.

[59] Dostoevsky to Apollon P. Maikov, December 11, 1868, in Mayne (trans.), *Letters of Dostovesky*, 157–58.

study outlined in the letter of 1868. The survey of formative intellectual influences in Dostoevsky's life and work in the preceding
chapter has covered much that is pertinent here. The concern with
theology and politics, in addition to the general literature of Russia
and Europe and contemporary philosophical currents, is confirmed
not only by the substance of the five great novels but also by the
variegated fare of *The Diary of a Writer*. His personal library "contained many serious works; for instance, it was rich in the literature of the Old Believers." [60] Dostoevsky's continuing concern
with religious questions in all of their ramifications and, particularly, his interest in the significance of sectarianism, the Schism
in the Russian church, and the messianic destiny of Holy Russia
have been documented.

Because the themes of religion and politics are the warp and woof
of the Legend, it will be instructive to quote further from his correspondence with A. N. Maikov. A letter in the spring of 1868, for
example, proposed a *"whole poem . . . about the Raskolniki . . . or a
verse novel."* [61] Theological and political conceptions are intertwined
a few weeks later when Dostoevsky wrote that the "constitution" of
Russia "is the mutual love of the Monarch for the people and of the
people for the Monarch. This principle of the Russian State, the principle of love not of strife . . . is the greatest of all ideas." [62] In the
spring of 1869 Dostoevsky again proposed a religious-political theme,
this time for a cycle of ballads which would deal with the ecumenical
and "pan-Orthodox significance of Russia," its future hegemony in
the wake of "the disintegration of the West, a disintegration which
will occur when the pope distorts Christ finally and thereby begets
atheism in the defiled humanity of the West." [63] He explained the
meaning of *The Possessed* in the following: "he who loses his people
and nationality, loses also the belief of his fathers, and God. Well, if
you want to know,—this is precisely the theme of my novel." [64]

---

60 A. G. Dostoevsky, "Reminiscences of 1871", in Fyodor M. Dostoevsky, *Dostoevsky: Letters and Reminiscences*, trans. S. S. Koteliansky and J. M. Murry (New
York: Alfred A. Knopf, Inc., 1923), 116.
61 Dostoevsky to Apollon P. Maikov, February 18/March 1, 1868, *ibid.*, 38.
62 Dostoevsky to Maikov, March 20/April 2, 1868, *ibid.*, 63–64.
63 Dostoevsky to Maikov, May 15/27, 1869, *ibid.*, 74.
64 Dostoevsky to Maikov, October 9/21, 1870, *ibid.*, 92.

Dostoevsky's religious education, then, was built around a lifelong familiarity with the Bible and with the doctrines, liturgy, iconography, and hagiography of the Russian Orthodox church. He systematically interested himself in Greek and Russian theology, and to a lesser extent he doubtless read Roman Catholic and Protestant writers, maintained a lively interest in the varieties of sectarianism in Russia, and was broadly acquainted with radical revolutionary literature with its religious implications.

Gleanings from this material were evidently available to the author in an uncommonly full way. His mind so functioned that "files" were accumulated about "the vagaries of the psyche" and knowledge could be called up from all levels of awareness. "One has the feeling that in Dostoevsky the barriers between unconscious, pre-conscious and conscious were exceptionally permeable." [65] As a result, information and experience lay at his disposal in extraordinary completeness. He deployed his theological knowledge and spiritual experience with facility, and his gift for adapting borrowed material into new creations served here as elsewhere.[66] The inference to which one is led is that in Dostoevsky's novels there is concealed and concentrated a great deal of theology indeed, far more than the reader is at first apt to suspect. For the purpose of interpretation the hidden theology of Dostoevsky must be made somewhat more apparent.[67]

Mysticism does not stand apart either from theology or from liturgical worship in Eastern Orthodoxy. Both theology and liturgy are suffused by the experience of persons and the common experience of the church. There is no notion of a cleavage between individual experience and the common faith as in Western mysticism. Dogmas are defined in light of experience and serve, in turn, to guide persons toward the attainment of an increasingly profound life in the Spirit. Neither faith nor theology is conceivable without mysticism. Empha-

---

[65] Simon O. Lesser, "Flaubert and Dostoevsky," *Daedalus,* XCII (1963), 374–75.

[66] Cf. Charles E. Passage, *Dostoevsky the Adapter: A Study in Dostoevsky's Use of the Tales of Hoffmann* (Chapel Hill: University of North Carolina Press, 1954), 175ff.

[67] The following account relies upon Vladimir Lossky, *The Mystical Theology of the Eastern Church* (London: James Clarke & Co., 1957).

sis upon existential faith in Dostoevsky is, thus, eminently correct.[68]

The goal of faith is union with God. This is the end of the Christian life and is termed "deification" (*theosis*): "God became man in order that man might become god, to use the words of Ireneus and Athanasius, echoed by the Fathers and theologians of every age." Hence, the substance of revelation is the covenant that men might become "partakers of the divine nature" (*theias koinonoi physeos*, II Pet. 1:4). While looked forward to as a perfection to be consummated only in eternity, this is a process really begun in the here and now, one made possible by man's participation in the divine energies which manifest in creation what is knowable of the essentially unknowable Triune God. The nature (*ousia*) of God is strictly unknowable. He can be known only through His energies (*dynameis*). *Concerning Mystical Theology*, by Pseudo-Dionysius Areopagita, supplies the cornerstone of the Eastern mystical tradition.[69] A crucial distinction is there drawn between: (1) the superessential Nature of God (the "unions" = *henoseis*) which is absolutely ineffable, unknowable, divine Darkness that can be apprehended only as the Incomprehensible; and (2) the divine Energies (the "distinctions" = *diakriseis*) in which everything that exists participates and by means of which God is revealed. The Nature of God can be approached only through the apophatic or negative way which is theology in the strict sense of the term; the Energies are the subject of the cataphatic or speculative theology of the Names of God. The latter realm is properly the divine economy (*oikonomia*: the administration or construction of a house, a regimen, a dispensation) and embraces the exterior manifestations of God, the Holy Trinity known in its relation to created being. As this doctrine is summarized by St. Gregory Palamas, who gave it precise formulation: "The divine and deifying illumination and grace is not the essence but the energy of God," a "divine power and energy common to the nature in three" hypostases; hence, "to say that the divine nature is communicable not in itself but through its energy, is to remain within the bounds of right devo-

---

68 *Ibid.*, 20ff; 9, 14, 236.
69 *Ibid.*, 196; 9, 10, 23, 67, 134, 237.

tion (*eusebeia*)." [70] St. John Damascene (following St. Gregory Nazianzen) states that what can be said "positively (*kataphatikos*) of God manifests not His nature but the things about His nature." The divine energies are otherwise called "rays of divinity" penetrating the created universe, "uncreated light," or simply "grace." Cataphatic theology, then, discloses the divine names and forms images and conceptual representations that conceal God even as they make Him more intelligible. It can serve only to form steps in a ladder whereby knowledge yields to contemplation in the controlling apophatic attitude: intellection's gains defer to the reach of experiences which outrun any symbolization. It is in this sense that gnosis ("knowledge") is understood to be inferior to the agnosia ("unknowing") of mystical contemplation (*mystika theamata*): "It is necessary to renounce both sense and all the workings of reason, everything which may be known by the senses or the understanding, both that which is and all that is not, in order to be able to attain in perfect ignorance to union with Him who transcends all being and all knowledge." In the Eastern tradition, "all true theology is fundamentally apophatic." [71]

From this vantage point the meaning of faith (*pistis*), defined by Paul as "the assurance of what we hope for, the proving of what we cannot see" (Heb. 11:1), becomes magnificently meaningful. The mysterious numen of Rudolf Otto is the equivalent of the nameless Unknown of the Eastern mystics, of Him Who is accessible only through grace in the silence of contemplation. "This awareness of the incomprehensibility of the divine nature thus corresponds to an experience: to a meeting with the personal God of revelation." Man is not divine by nature but is destined for divinity. Salvation is worked out in existence by the free will of man who responds to grace and chooses to harmonize himself with the will of God to create the synergy which is the cooperation of the two wills—the human and the divine. The end of man is the acquisition of the Holy Spirit. [72]

Essential to this existential ascent is the understanding that it is not a question of knowledge of the objective *God*; rather, it is a

---

70 *Ibid.*, 70–72. Cf. *ibid.*, 23ff, 27, 38ff, 42ff.

71 *Ibid.*, 73; *ibid.*, 27, 39, 238ff.

72 *Ibid.*, 34, 117, 196ff.

question of experiential union with the incomprehensible uncreated Light Who lies beyond (transcends) the relation of subject-object, Who escapes all conceptualization and resists analysis to leave only an irrational residue. One is thrown fully onto revelation. It alone is the source of the distinction between created being and the uncreated Incomprehensible, ever to be encountered only in wonder—Him whose highest name is the irreducible antinomy Holy Trinity—the God who is neither one nor many. The way of faith is the going forth from being toward that Who transcends the reality susceptible of conceptualization, Who not only is *not* earth, *not* fire, *not* the sun, but also Who is *not* being, *not* good, *not* love, *not* light. "The divine nature is like a sea of essence, indeterminate and without bounds, which spreads far and wide beyond all notion of time or of nature. If the mind tries to form a faint image of God, considering Him not in Himself but in that which compasses Him, this image eludes it even before it can attempt to seize it, illuminating the superior faculties as a flash of lightning which dazzles the eyes." [73] The superessential nature of God—Who is a subject neither for speech nor for thought nor, ultimately, even for contemplation in His otherness and ineffability—is indicated in a formulation of St. Gregory Nazianzen: "For if God be nature, then all else is not nature. If that which is not God be nature, God is not nature, and likewise He is not being if that which is not God is being." [74]

In the apophatic attitude—to repeat—God no longer presents himself as object nor does man know himself as subject in a cognitive relationship. Rather it is a question of union with the Unknowable Who Is. The quest for union is experienced as a *katharsis*, or inward purification, which differs however from the catharsis of both Plato and Plotinus in that it is essentially a "refusal to accept being as such, in so far as it conceals the divine non-being." This renunciation of the realm of created things so as to gain the realm of the uncreated is an existential liberation which heightens participation into mystical union and effects a real change in the person who undergoes it. The new condition entails a progress, an acquisition of something

---

[73] *Ibid.*, 36.
[74] *Ibid.*, 37.

not possessed of man by nature. It effects a transition or translation from the created into the Light of the uncreated. The mystical journey of perfections toward the divine Darkness is a struggle of ascent through the divine Light in which the Godhead manifests itself.[75]

Mystical experience cannot be separated from the way of union, and it can "only be gained in prayer and by prayer." The stages in the way are threefold: penitence and conversion (*metanoia, epistrophe*), purification, and perfection: "that is to say, conversion of the will, liberation from the passions, and the acquisition of that perfect love which is the fullness of grace." The discipline whereby mystical experience is achieved is typically the technique of interior prayer called "hesychasm": in accordance with strict regimen to attain spiritual concentration, the Publican's prayer ("O Lord Jesus Christ, Son of God, have mercy on me a sinner!") is uttered rhythmically with every aspiration. The term "gnosis" is used to signify the highest stage of spiritual awareness: the "experience of light, the experience itself being light." [76]

It is generally a distinction of Eastern mysticism that, while it is sometimes ecstatic, lapses from Light into the "Dark Night of the Soul" (regarded as typical in Western mysticism) are not characteristic.[77] Rather, in the experience of Greek and Russian contemplatives, the passing mystical ecstasy is supplanted at spiritual maturity by a sustained conscious life in Light, in an endless communion with God. This is known as the beginning of the transfiguration of the created nature and its entry before death and resurrection into the new heaven and earth of eternal life.[78] At this pinnacle the goal of union—*theosis*—is reached in an earthly prefiguration of deification,

---

[75] *Ibid.,* 38, 218ff, 244. Cf. Acts 2:3; Eph. 5:8, 14.

[76] Cf. Luke 18:13. Lossky, *The Mystical Theology,* 204, 210, 218. Hesychasm is from St. Hesychius of Sinai (eighth century).

[77] Lossky, *The Mystical Theology,* 208, 225, 237. Cf. Evelyn Underhill, *Mysticism: A Study in the Nature and Development of Man's Spiritual Consciousness* (12th ed.; New York: World Publ. Co., Meridian Books, 1955), especially 380ff. Lossky notes that St. Tikhon Zadonsky (Dostoevsky's model for Zosima) experienced the dark night (*The Mystical Theology,* 227n). He acknowledges, also, that no hard and fast distinction in this respect can be drawn because, for example, St. Bernard's mysticism was not characterized by the dark night.

[78] Lossky, *The Mystical Theology,* 229–30. Cf. Underhill, *Mysticism,* 413ff, on the transition from illumination to union or unity.

the perfection of the person into a created god by grace of the Un-created Lord. Yet, although this is the supreme mystical state, the perfections of divinity do not diminish or grow stale with the at-tainment of the contemplative heights. Indeed, just the opposite occurs. For the soul of man—unlike the body which becomes sated when appetites are met and overflowed, only to recur in cyclic fashion to the old hungers again—dilates as participation matures into union. It experiences a steady movement from perfection to perfection in growing awareness and increasing fulfillment without limit.

Here a final symbolism of the faith gained through Christ is shown. The quest of the contemplative is a suffering, an *agon* or "unseen warfare" of the soul. One runs and is not wearied, eats and is not filled, drinks and yet is not quenched. Like the Shulamite of the *Song of Songs* in search of the Bridegroom whom she cannot find—and who is indeed inaccessible and unattainable—the contemplative learns that "to progress and rise without cease" is the true enjoyment of the Beloved, because desire fulfilled engenders at every moment a new desire. "She sees the heartbreaking, unencompassable Beauty of the Beloved revealed perpetually more perfect throughout the eter-nity of the aeons, and is consumed by a more burning desire." [79]

The ultimate symbol of the Christian is "Abraham, who sets out for an unknown country that God will show him." [80] For in the celestial heights of union the journey of the soul becomes a fearless quest of faith into the uncircumscribed infinitude of the Unknown God. Hope is made substantial and the Unseen apprehended. Every step in the way is a new creation. It is a movement of perpetual crea-tion (*epektasis*),[81] of new modalities in the metamorphosis of the cosmos toward ultimate redemption at the culmination of sacred history. In this dynamic, man simultaneously participates as a will-ing partner to the transformation wrought by the Spirit, yet ever

---

[79] Jean Daniélou, "The Dove and the Darkness in Ancient Byzantine Mysticism," in Joseph Campbell (ed.), *Man and Transformation: Papers from the Eranos Yearbooks,* Bollingen Series, XXX (5 vols.; New York: Random House, Pantheon Books, 1964), V, 290ff.
[80] *Ibid.*, 290.
[81] Cf. Philipp. 3:13.

strives after the always transcendent God in an ascent from glory to glory.[82]

Life in faith is an adventure of the soul, to conclude with St. Gregory Nyssa, in which "every perfection (*telos*) is the beginning (*arche*) of a greater good:"

> We see the soul as in the mounting of a ladder, guided by the Word, ascending toward holiness. Called to approach the light, it has become beautiful, taking in the light the form of the dove. Then, having participated in the good as much as it could, it is drawn once more by the Word to participate in supernatural beauty, as though it were still at the beginning and had had no part in it. Thus in proportion to its progress its desire increases for what is always manifested to it more—and because of the superabundance of goods that it never ceases to discover in the transcendent, it believes that it is only at the beginning of its ascension. That is why the Word says again: Arise, to the soul that is already arisen and: Come, to the soul that has already come. He, indeed, who really arises, must forever arise, and he who runs toward the Lord will never lack wide space. For one must always arise and never cease to run toward Him who says: Rise and come, and always gives one the strength to rise toward the better.[83]

---

82 Cf. Daniélou, "The Dove and the Darkness," 289.
83 *Ibid.*, 293–94.

PART TWO

THE LEGEND
OF THE
GRAND INQUISITOR

CHAPTER III

THE LEGEND AS POLITICAL APOCALYPSE

Nowhere has Dostoevsky more profoundly probed the mystery of the *conditio humana*—the experiential confluence of man, history, and being—than in the "Legend of the Grand Inquisitor." The dramatic power and trenchancy of the episode, which holds a unique place in world literature, stagger the reader. It will be the task of this portion of the study to seek the explanation of the extraordinary effectiveness of the Legend as literature and to give as exhaustive an account as resources permit of its meaning. The present chapter seeks to identify the principal sources of the Legend, to discern Dostoevsky's intentions in writing it, and to establish its literary form as political apocalypse. It also sets forth this author's presuppositions and outlines the method of meditative reconstruction by which the inquiry proceeds. Chapter 4 identifies and analyzes the major threads of meaning which run through the Legend and shows their interrelationship. Chapter 5 considers the significance of the temptation whose employment is such as to transform the Inquisitor's monologue into a dialogue of great profundity with the formally silent Christ. Chapters 6 and 7 are devoted to the specific problems of rebellion and human nature, respectively, in light of the Legend and of the novel as a whole; they complete this part of the study.

1. DOSTOEVSKY'S INTENTIONS: SURVEY OF MATERIALS

Dostoevsky's insight into contemporary political movements was not that of a detached visionary but of an informed student of politics. In 1870 he wrote: "I have been assiduously reading for the last three years all the political papers [of Europe], that is, the most important of them." A theme of importance to the Legend is then given sharp formulation: "The whole destiny of Russia lies in Orthodoxy, in *the light from the East*," which will suddenly shine forth to Western humanity which has become "blinded and has lost Christ. The course of the whole misfortune of Europe, everything, everything without exception, has been that she gained the Church of Rome and lost Christ, and then they decided that they could do without Christ." It is out of this conviction that Russia's "exclusive Orthodox mission to mankind" has been formulated.[1]

Nine years later, in covering letters written to his editor, N. A. Liubimov, Dostoevsky supplied brief exegetical comments to book 5 of *The Brothers Karamazov* and to the Legend, included there as a chapter. The book, entitled "Pro and Contra," was divided into two installments for its initial appearance in the *Russkii Vestnik*, the division lying between chapter 4, "Rebellion," and chapter 5, the "Legend." With reference to the first installment Dostoevsky wrote: "Its idea . . . is the presentation of extreme blasphemy and of the seeds of the idea of destruction at present in Russia among the young generation that has torn itself away from reality." In this book, Ivan expresses

> his basic convictions. These convictions form what I consider as the synthesis of contemporary Russian anarchism. The denial not of God, but of the meaning of his creation. The whole of socialism sprang up and started with the denial of the meaning of historical actuality, it arrived at the program of destruction and anarchism. The principal anarchists were, in many cases, sincerely convinced men. My hero takes a theme,

---

[1] Dostoevsky to Apollon P. Maikov, October 9/21, 1870, in Fyodor M. Dostoevsky, *Letters and Reminiscences*, trans. S. S. Koteliansky and J. Middleton Murry (New York: Alfred A. Knopf, Inc., 1923), 94, 95. Cf. the comments of Edward Wasiolek in Fyodor M. Dostoevsky, *The Notebooks for "The Brothers Karamazov"*, ed. and trans. Edward Wasiolek (Chicago: University of Chicago Press, 1971), 62–63, 89–92.

in my view, an unassailable one: the senselessness of the suffering of children, and from it deduces the absurdity of the whole historical actuality. . . . And my hero's blasphemy will be triumphantly refuted in the next [June] number on which I am working now with fear, trembling and awe, as I consider my task (the refutation of anarchism) a civic exploit.[2]

A few days later (on May 19) Dostoevsky wrote to K. P. Pobedonostsev saying,

this book of the novel is the culminating one. It is entitled "Pro and Contra," and the theme of the book is: denial of God and the refutation of this denial. The denial now is finished and sent off, but the refutation will only come in the June number. The denial I described just as I felt it myself and realized it strongest, that is, just as it is now taking place in our Russia in nearly the *whole* upper stratum of society, and above all with the young generation. I mean, the scientific and philosophical refutation of the existence of God has been given up, it no longer occupies at all *socialists* of today (as it occupied them throughout the whole of the last century and the first half of the present one); instead men are denying with all their might and main the divine creation, the world of God and *its meaning*. These are the only things which modern civilization finds utter nonsense. I flatter myself that even in such an abstract theme I have not betrayed realism. The refutation of this (not a direct, not a face to face refutation) will appear in the last word of the dying old monk.

In a further passage of this same letter Dostoevsky, speaking of the current case of one Dubrovin, makes the following illuminating remarks:

. . . mad men have their logic, their doctrine, their *esse,* their God even, and they are planted in them as firm as firm can be. This is left out of consideration. Nonsense, people say. It is not like anything they know, therefore it is nonsense. It is *culture* we have not got, dear Konstantine Petrovich (the culture which exists everywhere else), and it is not there because of the nihilist, Peter the Great.[3] It was torn out by the root. And

---

2 Dostoevsky to N. A. Liubimov (associate editor of *Russkii Vestnik*), May 10, 1879, in Fyodor M. Dostoevsky, "Dostoevsky on *The Brothers Karamazov*," trans. S. S. Koteliansky, *New Criterion*, IV (1926), 552–53.

3 Dostoevsky seems to have derived this conception of "culture" from Solovyov. See chap. 5, sec. 7, *below*.

since man does not live by bread alone, our poor, uncultured man involuntarily invents something most fantastical, most absurd, and most unlike anything. (For although he has taken absolutely everything from European socialism, yet even this he has remade so that it is unlike anything.)[4]

The following month, speaking specifically of the Legend, Dostoevsky again wrote to Liubimov.

The day before yesterday I sent to the editorial office of the *Russkii Vestnik* the continuation of *The Brothers Karamazov* for the June number (the end of the chapter "Pro and Contra"). In it is finished what *the lips speak proudly and blasphemously*. The modern *denier*, the most vehement one, straightway supports the advice of the devil and asserts that that is a surer way of bringing happiness to mankind than Christ is. For our Russian socialism, stupid, but terrible (for the young are with it)—there is a *warning*, and I think a forcible one. Greed, the Tower of Babel (*i.e.* the future kingdom of socialism), and the completest overthrow of conscience—that is what the desperate denier and atheist arrives at. The difference only being that our socialists (and they are not only the underground nihilists—you are aware of that) are conscious Jesuits and liars, who will not confess that their idea is the idea of the violation of man's conscience and of the reduction of . . . mankind to the level of a herd of cattle. But my socialist (Ivan Karamazov) is a sincere man who frankly confesses that he agrees with the "Grand Inquisitor's" view of mankind, and that Christ's religion (as it were) has raised man much higher than man actually stands. The question is forced home: "Do you despise or respect mankind, you, its coming saviors?"

And they do all this in the name of the love of mankind, as if to say: "Christ's law is difficult and abstract, and for weak people intolerable"; and instead of the law of liberty and enlightenment they bring the law of chains and subjection by means of bread.[5]

In late August, Dostoevsky again wrote his friend Pobedonostsev

---

[4] Dostoevsky to K. P. Pobedonostsev, May 19, 1879, in Dostoevsky, *Letters and Reminiscences*, 241–42, 243–44. The susceptibility of men to fantastic doctrines which, however, provide meaning to existence already had been noted by Aristotle: "conscious of their ignorance, they admire those who proclaim some great ideal that is above their comprehension." *Nicomachean Ethics* 1095a25–27.

[5] Dostoevsky to N. A. Liubimov, June 11, 1879, in Dostoevsky, *Letters and Reminiscences*, 554–55. Both this letter and that of May 10 have been published in S. S. Koteliansky (trans.), *New Dostoevsky Letters* (London: Mandrake Press, 1927), 80–92. Italics Dostoevsky's.

and outlined the character of his response in book 6 (mailed to the *Russian Messenger* earlier in the month) to the arguments of the nihilist and rebel expressed in book 5. "In my reply is represented something directly opposite to the world-conception expressed in the earlier book, but again [N. B.] it is represented not point by point, but, so to say, in an artistic picture. And that's just what worries me, that is, shall I be understood and shall I achieve even a particle of my aim." [6] Not only by means of the words of the dying Zosima did Dostoevsky seek to refute the Inquisitor, but he attempted this in the Legend itself through his portrayal of Christ. The technique explicitly outlined in this letter is also that of the Legend and this is clearly stated in the letter to Liubimov of May 11. The anxiety that a refutation of this kind might be lost on a majority of readers proved to be well founded. Dostoevsky's expressed apprehensions have become partly the basis in some quarters both for condemning as weak literature book 6 (not to speak of the positive, "triumphant" aspect of the Legend) and for suspecting Dostoevsky of spiritual bankruptcy and wholehearted alliance with Ivan's atheistic rebellion.

Four months later, in December, 1879, Dostoevsky prepared a brief introduction to the Legend, which he then included in a public reading for some students. The introduction, too, contains valuable hints for interpretation of the Legend.

An atheist, sick with disbelief, composes in a moment of torment a wild-fantastic poem. . . . The suffering from which the poet is ill has its immediate source in the fact that he, in the fantasy-form of the Grand Inquisitor and his Catholics, has fallen so far away from the old apostolic orthodoxy and view of the world that he knew as a youth and servant of Christ. His Grand Inquisitor is, however, himself really an atheist. The fundamental thought is: Yon spirit, he that caricatures Christianity, the moment he brings it into harmony with the goals of the world, annuls the entire purpose of Christendom and must without any question drive toward absolute disbelief. A second Tower of Babel stands in the place of the high ideals created by Christ. The sublime Christian view of human nature sinks down to the view of an animal herd and, under the

---

[6] Dostoevsky to K. P. Pobedonostsev, August 24, 1879, in Dostoevsky, *Letters and Reminiscences*, 251.

banner of Social Love, shows entirely unconcealed its contempt for mankind.[7]

The thematic substance of the Legend, of high interest to political philosophy, clearly emerges from these quoted materials: the onto-logical character of revelation and the fundamental opposition of the two conceptions of the nature of man; the historical tension which lies between immanent being and the revealed order of transcendent being; and the political consequences of the naturalistic reduction of man to a mere species of animal.

2. PERSPECTIVE AND METHOD OF ANALYSIS

The "Legend of the Grand Inquisitor" is generally agreed to be Dos-toevsky's masterpiece. Nicholas Berdyaev warns of its "fathomless depth" and speaks of the author as "the climax of Russian literature" and of the Legend as "the high point of Dostoevsky's work and the crown of his dialectic." [8] The art of Dostoevsky has aptly been de-scribed as "a Whitmanesque song of himself," [9] and in the Legend one confronts both the grotesque and the magnificent, a last agonized hymn of dirgeful prophecy and hopeful hosanna. A word must, then, be said about the method employed in this study and about the particular problems the subject poses.

Dostoevsky, of course, was a consummate artist, but his art seems never to be merely art for art's sake. First and last he was passionately engaged in a no-holds-barred combat for existence in truth and freedom—insofar as man, being what he is, the world and society, being what they are, and God, being what He is, make this possible. The arena of the struggle is human existence. The novels are an-thropocentric, preoccupied with the *conditio humana*, not from the perspective of the curious onlooker, but as a totally committed actor

---

[7] Translated from W. Komarovich, *Die Urgestalt der Brüder Karamasoff: Dos-tojewskis Quellen, Entwürfe und Fragmente* (Munich: Piper, 1928), 540–41.

[8] Nicholas Berdyaev, *Dostoevsky*, trans. Donald Attwater, (New York: World Publ. Co., Meridian Books, 1957), 210, 30, and 188. Dostoevsky himself is said to have regarded the Legend as the culminating point of his artistic life. See Komarovich, *Die Urgestalt der Brüder Karamasoff*, ix.

[9] Avrahm Yarmolinsky, "Dostoevsky: A Study in his Ideology" (Ph.D. disserta-tion, Columbia University, 1921), 7.

in the drama of existence. Ultimately, Dostoevsky's work is theocentric for, as has already been said, at the center of his anthropology lies man's mysterious participation in the divine. Romano Guardini remarked that whoever attempts to deal with the religious in Dostoevsky's work quickly sees that he has taken for his subject the entire world of the writer. The work of the novelist finds its highest resolution in the realm of the spirit. Dostoevsky is not only a single actor in the drama of human existence under God but he is all of his characters as well; or, all together, they are Dostoevsky. The Karamazov family is a symbolism evoking the universal-historical drama of existence: mankind itself with its light and its dark, its sordidness, pettiness, and sensuality, its exaltation, nobility and grandeur.[10]

The vastness of the canvas and complexity of the subject account for the fact that, despite a substantial critical literature and a number of able and resourceful commentators among the Dostoevsky scholars, the import of the Legend has never been adequately expounded. The attempt to gain access to its meaning will be made here through a series of associative aggressions, each of which reconstructs a facet of the author's meaning. This is an essentially meditative method of analysis which commends itself as the one best suited to the exploration of a deeply stratified composition such as the Legend. It partly avoids fragmenting the work and permits the emergence of a metaphysically integrated image of the author's vision. But, the technique necessarily entails some reiteration and, moreover, does not simplify the meaning but achieves exactly the opposite effect by bringing to explicit statement the substance of the work in all its range and subtlety. In short, the attempt is made to expound discursively through a theoretical analysis what Dostoevsky has expressed in dramatic imagery and allegorical discourse through mythopoesis.

Such a translation, one must quickly add, can provide only the approximate content of the original for reasons partly stated above (in

---

[10] Romano Guardini, *Religiöse Gestalten in Dostojewskijs Werk* (Munich: Kösel, 1951), 7, 235–36. Cf. Fyodor M. Dostoevsky, *The Notebooks for "The Brothers Karamazov,"* ed. and trans. Edward Wasiolek (Chicago: University of Chicago Press, 1971), 234, 243–47.

chap. 2, sec. 2). Not only is any translation likely to be inferior to the original in shading and nuance, but whole dimensions of human experience which profoundly engaged Dostoevsky's attention cannot be rendered through discursive statement and can only be articulated mythically and dramatically. The analysis cannot supplant the work of art itself any more than the critic can substitute for the artist. But one gains indices to the meaning which can be of assistance in grasping the meaning itself as artistically embodied. The meditative reconstruction of the meaning of the Legend is especially appropriate. Dostoevsky was himself a contemplative; and there is persuasive evidence that the creative process in him ran from experience to idea to particular embodiment in the highly detailed, four-dimensional reality of his prose-poetry, the direction being from abstraction to dramatization.[11] A meditative analysis seeks to recover both the predramatic abstraction and the theoretical gains registered through dramatization of the idea, translating the whole range of content into the language of philosophy and placing it in the context of this mode of inquiry and understanding. A perceptive student of the Legend cryptically concludes concerning V. V. Rozanov's analysis and of a portion of his own: the work "communicates considerably more than these ideas." [12] This statement has a permanent application not only to the work of Rozanov or to that of Ralph Matlaw or to the present study in advance because the irreducible mythopoesis of the Legend makes ideational communication inherently deficient in some respects. The analysis of the Legend must therefore be prepared to proceed both in terms of ideas and in terms of the opaque imagery of myth if it is to capture the experiential substratum of movement in the subconscious and supraconscious levels of the psyche. While it is indubitably true (as Dostoevsky himself tells us) that much of what he says he expresses as he does because of limits imposed by his art, it must also be noted that some of what he says can be uttered in no way other than the one he has so superbly mastered. The same

---

11 See Dostoevsky, *The Notebooks for "The Brothers Karamazov,"* 22.
12 Fyodor M. Dostoevsky, *Notes from Underground and the Grand Inquisitor,* ed., trans., and with an intro. by Ralph E. Matlaw (New York: E. P. Dutton & Co., 1960), xxii.

conditions—including the same hazards of objectivism—are imposed as ineluctably on the interpreter as on the thinker and artist.

This study directs attention especially toward the vertical dimension of the Legend. It claims to be no more than a crude chart of the domain of the Legend, something of a guide for the perplexed. Not only must the crudeness of the chart be acknowledged, but also its incompleteness in another direction: concern is primarily for the politics of Dostoevsky. While this term is understood in the broad sense of Classical philosophy, literary considerations are largely left aside as better to be examined by more expert commentators.

The meditation begins from the shattering existential impact of the Legend upon the reader of *The Brothers Karamazov*. While he realizes that something extraordinary has been said, like Alyosha he does not quite understand what it is. And involvement and anguish are soon swallowed up as he yields himself to the more tangible concerns of the "feverish" and breathless art of Dostoevsky in the unfolding drama of the novel. As we leave the Legend, we seek here, then, to overcome the feeling that we have not touched bottom, as it were. We find encouragement in our task from the impression in reading the literature that neither has any one else touched bottom; and from the experience that, as we ourselves reach what appears to be "bottom," a new bottom is sensed lying below. Berdyaev's challenge to plumb the depths of the Legend is accepted.

3. STRUCTURE AND SOURCES

The structure of the Legend provides the clue to its nature and meaning. For purposes of analysis it can be divided into nine parts articulated according to the following plan.

FIGURE 1

Parts of the Legend

1. Prologue: a literary preface
2. *Dramatis personae*
   a. Christ and the Inquisitor
   b. Ivan and Alyosha
3. Encounter: "Is it Thou?"—the Inquisitor's monologue

4. First Interlude: "I don't understand." Alyosha's outburst; Ivan's exegesis.
5. The temptation as trial: "What is truth?" Satan and Caesar.
6. Conviction and condemnation: "Thou art to blame!" Golgotha and Armageddon.
7. Second Interlude: the secret
8. *Finis*: the Kiss. The power of the Spirit.
9. Epilogue: the pathos of existence. A brother's kisses.

The understanding of the Legend's structure can best be advanced by first directing attention to the central passage (pt. 5 of fig. 1). This part is built around the temptation of Christ in the wilderness according to the account in Matthew 4. This is the "chief part" of the Legend as Ivan says, and the Inquisitor begins it with an encomium to Satan and the three questions of the temptation as a "miracle" and "the whole future history of the world and humanity. . . . For in those three questions the whole subsequent history of mankind is, as it were, brought together in one whole and foretold, and in them are united all the unsolved historical contradictions of human nature." But the tenor of the temptation in the Legend is not that of the Gospel account. Rather, it is that of the trial of Christ before Pilate. And this lengthy passage is in fact succeeded by part 6 in which culpability for the unhappiness and suffering of man is charged against the Prisoner and, in the name of just retribution and because He has returned to "hinder" their work, He is sentenced to be burnt at the stake. The central motif of Christ as the divine Hinderer (*katechon*) is thereby sounded. The Inquisitor sentences Him to a second Golgotha on the morrow: "I shall burn Thee for coming to hinder us. For if anyone has ever deserved our fires, it is Thou. Tomorrow I shall burn Thee. *Dixi*." This imagery is overlaid and encompassed, however, by the imagery of Armageddon and the specific citation of the coming of the Antichrist with his legions in the form of the Great Beast who is Rome. The Apocalypse is quoted here (Rev. 17:3ff) just as it has been quoted in the opening section of the Legend (pt. 1; Rev. 8:10–11). The analysis must concern itself in some detail with these various elements which are now mentioned only in a preliminary way.

These central passages are flanked by what have been called a First and Second Interlude (pts. 4 and 7) in which Alyosha and Ivan converse. The First Interlude opens with Alyosha's timidly incredulous "I don't understand," thrice repeated with increasing alarm. Its third statement closes the interlude with the interrogation: "And what's the meaning of 'no lack of admonitions and warnings'?" Ivan, like his Inquisitor, is preeminently one who *knows*. And the *"I know"* of the rationalist-gnostic's *superbia cognoscendi* rattles through the monologue like a drum beat. Ivan, in his exegesis, makes explicit the thematic substance of the Inquisitor's narrative: freedom, happiness, and rebellion. The Second Interlude is, once again, occasioned by Alyosha's interruption of the narration, this time in anguish and outrage as he protests the Legend as a monstrosity and supplements his earlier observation of Ivan's rebellion with the insight that the Inquisitor's "secret" is his atheism and "simple lust for power." Even before he has heard its conclusion, Alyosha says: "Your poem is in praise of Jesus, not in blame of Him—as you meant it to be." He grudgingly admits the possibility of aspirations like those of the Inquisitor within Roman Catholicism but accuses Ivan of perhaps being a Mason himself, and that is just as evil: " 'You don't believe in God.' "

The close of the chapter now comes quickly. Part 8 stresses the attentive *silence* of the Prisoner who answers only with a kiss: "His silence weighed down upon him. . . . The old man longed for Him to say something. . . . But He suddenly approached the old man in silence and softly kissed him on his bloodless aged lips." The Epilogue (pt. 9) echoes Ivan's motifs. Alyosha speaks of the "hell in your heart and head" and Ivan of the "strength of Karamazov baseness." Alyosha extracts from Ivan a scowling admission of this creed: "Yes, if you like, 'everything is lawful' since the word has been said. I won't deny it. . . . The formula 'all is lawful,' I won't renounce—will you renounce me for that, yes?" And Alyosha answers with a kiss, then with another. The pathos of existence is affirmed in the brother's kisses. This theme, introduced into the Epilogue by Alyosha's appeal to Ivan's loves in the sentence: "But the little sticky leaves, the precious tombs, and the blue sky, and the woman you love! How will you live, how will you love them?" now is echoed by Ivan: "if I am really able to care for the sticky little leaves I shall only love them, remembering you. . . . Good-bye, kiss me once more." This faith in man, even in the good man Alyosha his brother, proves inadequate to sustain Ivan as his destiny works out in the pages of the novel. But this is a matter beyond immediate concern.

The mention of the Masons in part 8 raises explicitly a theme prefigured and enunciated on principle in the Prologue (pt. 1), Ivan's "literary preface" to the Legend. From the viewpoint of the Orthodox, the Masons are sectarians. By a play upon the theme of wandering, through detailed references to a blasphemous sixteenth century poem and a quotation from Tiuchev's "These Humble Villages," Dostoevsky already had inserted the sectarian element into the Legend and the personality of the Grand Inquisitor: he is a Russian new man of the future. The implied reference is to the *Stranniki* (Wanderers) sect.

> "Oppressed with bearing the cross,
> The heavenly King in slave's guise,
> Throughout our native land
> Wandered (*Izkhodil*) , blessing as he went." [13]

The symbol of the Wanderer is persistent in Dostoevsky from the time of *The Possessed,* with its chapter headings "Puteshestennica" and "Stranstvovanie," to the *skitalets* who is the high theme of the Pushkin Speech.[14] This symbolism will be of subsequent concern. It is to be noticed, however, that in addition to the fundamental experiential identification with sectarian Russia of the nihilistic intelligentsia, the symbolism embraces these further elements: (1) the broadly human thirst for happiness and blessedness (so central to the meaning of the

---

13 Fyodor M. Dostoevsky, *Polnoe sobranie sochinenii* (12 vols.; 4th ed.; St. Petersburg: Panteleevkh, 1891–92), XII *(Brat'ia Karamazovy),* 287; modified translation from Dostoevsky, *Notes From Underground,* 121.

14 Dostoevsky, *Polnoe sobranie sochinenii,* VII *(Besy)* , 519, 579 (pt. 3, chaps. 5 and 7): cf. Fyodor M. Dostoevsky, *The Diary of a Writer,* trans. Boris Brasol (2 vols.; New York: Charles Scribner's Sons, 1949), II, 967–80. All levels of the problem of the wanderer are brought together in this short presentation.

Legend); (2) the theme of *déjà vu* and *anamnesis*;[15] (3) the theme of the eternal recurrence which Dostoevsky shares with Nietzsche; and which, (4) together with the motif of the rejected truth, he has, perhaps, inherited from Comenius;[16] and (5) the apocalyptical religiousness of Russian Christianity, with its pronounced chiliasm. Then, in full recognition of the technique of ambiguity so characteristic in Dostoevsky, and the fact that as symbol the Wanderer intrinsically entails ambiguity,[17] the kenotic or humiliated and suffering Christ also is evoked by the image. The words of Cyril of Turov to describe the soteriology of Christ are apposite in this context:

> . . . having abandoned the sceptre of the Kingdom above, I am wandering in the service of those below; for I came, not in order to be served, but to serve. For thy sake, being fleshless, I put on flesh to heal spiritual and bodily sicknesses of all. For thy sake, being invisible to angel hosts, I

15 The experience of *déjà-vu* and of *anamnesis* in Dostoevsky are discussed by Reinhard Lauth, *Die Philosophie Dostojewskis in systematischer Darstellung* (Munich: Piper, 1950), especially 99ff: "Der Traum. Das vorpersönliche und das anamnestische Unbewusste." Nietzsche considered "eternal recurrence," to be the end form of nihilism and wrote: "Denken wir diesen Gedanken in seiner furchtbarsten Form: das Dasein, so wie es ist, ohne Sinn und Ziel, aber unvermeidlich wiederkehrend, ohne ein Finale ins Nichts: 'die ewige Wiederkehr'. Das ist die extremste Form des Nihilismus: das Nichts (das 'Sinnlose') ewig!" *Der Wille zur Macht* (Stuttgart: Kroener, 1930), bk. I, I/4, p. 44. The connection with Dostoevsky is made by Lauth, *Die Philosophie Dostojewskis*, 254–55ff. Lauth says little in his long and excellent study that bears directly on the Legend, although the present point relates directly to *The Brothers Karamazov*. See Antanas Maceina, *Der Grossinquisitor; Geschichtsphilosophische Deutung der Legende Dostojewskijs* (Heidelberg: Kerle, 1952), 20n.

16 John Amos Comenius, *Labyrinth der Welt* (1623). See Dmitri Chizhevski, "Comenius' *Labyrinth of the World*: Its Themes and their Sources," in Horace G. Lunt (ed.), *Harvard Slavic Studies* (3 vols.; Cambridge: Harvard University Press, 1953), I, 83–135, especially 107, 108n67, and 129: "In his speech to the pilgrim, Christ sums up all the sad experiences of the pilgrim in the 'labyrinth of the world.'" See also the same author's "Die vertriebene Wahrheit," in his *Aus zwei Welten* (The Hague: Mouton, 1946), especially 122ff and the cited literature. He suggests (p. 124) the continuity of the theme of the rejected Christ from the first half of the sixteenth century when the diplomat Fedor Karpov wrote a letter to the Metropolitan Daniil and, with allusion to Ovid's *Metamorphoses*, said: "Auch wenn Petrus, das Haupt der Apostel, heute mit seiner Theologie und verschiedenen Wundern käme, würde er verschlossene Türen finden und vertrieben werden, wenn er nichts mitbrächte." See also Ernst Benz, "Der wiederkehrende Christus," *Zeitschrift für Religions- und Geistesgeschichte*, VI (1954), 305ff.

17 Cf. Austin Farrer, *A Rebirth of Images: The Making of Saint John's Apocalypse* (Boston: Beacon Press, Beacon Paperbacks, 1963), 19.

have appeared to all men: for I do not wish to despise my image lying in corruption, but I wish to save him and to lead him to the understanding of truth.[18]

The Wanderer, however encountered, is spiritual man, whether infested by destructive demons or invested with the Holy Spirit. But as a vessel that thirsts and will be filled, he is a seeker after truth. Dostoevsky shares with Pascal the insight that to seek is to find.[19] In an essential aspect, therefore, ambiguity is driven to a frightening polarity in *The Brothers Karamazov*. The Wanderer is the emblem of both the diabolical and the holy. Together with the tormented minions of hell, he is the familiar pilgrim who lives by faith as one of the fools for Christ (*urodivi Khrista radi*) who spurns the glory of the world in feigned imbecility—and perhaps also in pretended profaneness.[20]

An allusion to Christ "in that human shape in which He walked among men for three years fifteen centuries ago" suggests an adoptionist Christology so prominently characteristic of the sectarians (of the Khlysty, for example) and so distinctly non-Orthodox.[21] The work of Luther (later mentioned when Ivan throws his cup at the devil) and the Protestant Reformation as the work of Satan and the rationalist element of sectarianism are made explicit in the sentences: "But the devil did not slumber, and doubts were already arising among men of the truth of these miracles. And just then there appeared in the north of Germany a terrible new heresy. 'A huge star like to a torch' (that is, to a church) 'fell on the sources of the waters and they became bitter.' " This quotation from a favorite passage of Dostoevsky's in the

---

18 George P. Fedotov, *The Russian Religious Mind: Kievan Christianity, the Tenth to the Thirteenth Centuries* (New York: Harper & Row, Torchbooks, 1960), 75.

19 Cf. Pascal, *Pensées*, No. 243.

20 Cf. Fedotov, *The Russian Religious Mind*, 147–48; Nicholas Arseniev, *Russian Piety*, trans. Asheleigh Moorhouse (London: Faith Press; Clayton, Wisc.: American Orthodox Press, 1964), 108–109. See the explicit statements in Dostoevsky, *The Notebooks for "The Brothers Karamazov,"* 44–45, 56.

21 See Vladimir Lossky, *The Mystical Theology of the Eastern Church* (London: James Clarke & Co., 1957), 44ff, 143ff; also Nikos A. Nissiotis, "The Importance of the Doctrine of the Trinity for Church Life and Theology," in A. J. Philippou (ed.), *The Orthodox Ethos: Essays in Honour of the Centenary of the Greek Orthodox Archdiocese of North and South America* (Oxford, Eng.: Holywell, 1964), especially 40ff.

Apocalypse (Rev. 8:10–11) together with the allusion to the coming of the Antichrist from the original account in Daniel (11:40) sound the chord which dominates the Legend.

The veritable deluge of quotations, literary allusions, and symbolisms introduced by Ivan into his "preface" has the avowed purpose of distinguishing the genre of his poem (*poema*; later, disparagingly, *poemka*): "my poem would have been of that kind"—that is, a legend, ballad, mystery play. In short, it is a *myth* of "heavenly powers on earth"; indeed, it is an *apocalypse*: a vision and a prophecy charged with Danielic and Johannine eschatology. It is the kind of thing, Ivan remarks, which might have been dramatized in "Moscow too, up to the times of Peter the Great." This may be taken as thinly veiled reference to Tsar Peter I as the Antichrist. He was widely accorded this distinction by the Schismatics who reckoned the Age of the Antichrist from the time of the ritual and liturgical reforms of Patriarch Nikon which were confirmed by the Holy Synod in 1666 and resulted in the secession of the Old Believers in the following year. After having directly attacked Roman Catholicism and Protestantism as heresies— with enthusiastic Orthodox approval—Dostoevsky, through Ivan and behind the screen of ambiguity, attacks Christianity itself, Russian Orthodoxy, the church, the tsar and tsardom. Dostoevsky's intimate friendship with Pobedonostsev from 1871 (and especially after 1873) until the end of his life and their revealing correspondence about the Grand Inquisitor are by no means conclusive proof that Masaryk erred in suggesting Pobedonostsev himself as the model for the Grand Inquisitor. The Legend is the "expression of extreme blasphemy." It is the ostensible creation of the nihilist Ivan, an acknowledged foe of Orthodoxy and the tsardom. But his attack, though expected, is blunted in the novel in comparison with the notes and could, in my case, only come allegorically in the Russia of Alexander II.[22]

---

22 The overt attack on Christianity, Orthodoxy, and the church, as well as Ivan's blasphemy, is considerably stronger in the notes than in the published novel. See Dostoevsky, *The Notebooks for "The Brothers Karamazov,"* 72, 76, 78, 79, 82; also 105; and 62–63 for Wasiolek's comment. It is, of course, chronologically impossible for Pobedonostsev *as* chief procurator of the Holy Synod to have been Dostoevsky's model for the Grand Inquisitor: he came to that office only in 1880, after the chapter was written. Masaryk's point is that the Inquisitor's doctrines became Pobedonostsev's own in the years following assassination of Alexander II.

Part 2 of the Legend is the dramatic entrance of the principals: Christ, who is never named, comes unobserved but triumphant; the Grand Inquisitor, attired in "his coarse, old, monk's cassock" stands upstage and from a distance "sees everything." Whatever the lesser sources for the character, the Inquisitor certainly has been drawn in many respects after John the Baptist and may well convey a half-earnest interpretation of the biblical significance of John (in Russian, Ivan).

The identification is justifiable if only because of the obvious superficial parallels between the early life of the Inquisitor and that of John the Baptist as, for example, the stalwart faith, confidence of the Coming of the Christ, the life in the wilderness where he "too . . . lived on roots and locusts" (cf. Matt. 3:4; Mark 1:6; Luke 3:2; John 1:23). But the connections also are profound and subtle: the proximity of John the Baptist to Christ as He assumed His Messiahship, the fulfillment of John's prophecy in the appearance of Jesus, the declaring of the Messiah by John (John 1:29), the baptism of Christ which is followed immediately by his being driven into the wilderness and temptation, and the report of John's imprisonment at the hands of Herod, so that John became the prototype of the holy prisoner of Rome (Luke 3:20). And John was, indeed, mistaken for the Messiah Himself (John 1:19–27), executed and believed by Herod to have been resurrected from the dead in the person of Christ (Mark 6:14). There is the further, if indirect, evidence of familiarity by the Inquisitor with the Prisoner which—if expected in any man—might have been expected in John the Baptist. John was lauded above all other men by Jesus (Matt. 11:11). A satanic incarnation, the Inquisitor speaks as a veritable eyewitness to the temptation. But, while the Gospel account gives no indication of this, it is not difficult to suppose that had there been a mortal witness of the temptation it would have been John (Matt. 3:16–4:2). The impression of impudent familiarity is borne out in the language of the Inquisitor. He speaks in colloquial Russian so that Christ

---

Cf. Thomas G. Masaryk, *The Spirit of Russia: Studies in History, Literature and Philosophy*, Vols. I and II, trans. Eden and Cedar Paul (2nd ed.; New York: Macmillan Co., 1955); Vol. III, ed. George Gibian, trans. Robert Bass (New York: Barnes & Noble, Inc., 1967), II, 199; III, 25, 86, 135–54.

is, in effect, addressed as "You," rather than reverentially as "Thou" as the Garnett translation has it. Indeed, who could have been more disappointed, dismayed, embittered, angered, and capable of titanic rebellion because of the paltry achievement of the Messiah he as prophet had proclaimed and served through all worldly misery than the faithful first believer grown old with the world and devoid of faith, hope, and love. The place of John the Baptist in gnostic theology also is of interest. In the doctrine of the Mandaeans, John the Baptist is exalted at the expense of Christ, Who is alleged to have stolen and falsified the teaching of His master, John.

The subtleties of the New Testament account of John the Baptist pass beyond the elements just mentioned and exceed present interests. But the degree to which the Legend is saturated with biblical content makes it proper to recall the popular imputation of a devil or demon to John (Matt. 11:18) and the striking juxtaposition in the Gospel narrative of the departure of the devil after the temptation and the information that John had been arrested and imprisoned (Matt. 4:11–12). John was the last of the prophets and yet "superior to a prophet" (Matt. 11:13, 9).

The riddle of John, however, is how he regarded Jesus at the end of his life. This aporia in the Gospel account is precisely the uncertainty upon which Dostoevsky plays in his evocation of the biblical John in the Inquisitor. The proclamation of the Messiah by John was the heralding of the Divine Ruler Whose Coming would end history and inaugurate the Kingdom of God. He did not proclaim an earthly man such as Jesus, but One Who would baptize with "the Holy Spirit and with fire," and "Whose sandals I am not worthy *or* fit to take off *or* carry (Matt. 3:11)." The question that John in prison sent his disciples to ask of Jesus (Matt. 11:3) is the question of the Inquisitor: "Are You He Who was to come?"—"Is it You? You?" And the refrain, infinitely impoverished, is heard again before Golgotha: "Are you the King of the Jews?" (Matt. 27:11). Indeed, this is the eternal question. The answer of Jesus is one sufficient only to the faithful. In it one senses the perceived disappointment of John in the meekness and lowliness of the Son of Man. Jesus answers by indirection. He tells of His works and ministry and concludes: "And blessed is he who takes no offense at Me, *and* finds no cause for stumbling in or through me, *and* is not hindered from seeing the Truth" (Matt. 11:6) . Whether John believed is not recorded.

To suppose John the Baptist to have been the prototype of Dostoevsky's Grand Inquisitor is no less than shocking if considered from the perspective of an author who is regarded as a great Christian. Christ's regard for John has secured his place throughout Christendom as one who was more than a prophet. It is even more astonishing if one further considers the high place held by St. John in the Orthodox mind, for certainly he is one of the most popular and widely venerated of the saints of the Eastern church. Indeed, when the Orthodox worshipper stands before the iconostasis or picture wall which conceals the altar in his church, he beholds four icons: Christ, the Virgin, the saint of the particular church—and St. John the Baptist. Yet the plausibility of this connection with the Grand Inquisitor is unmistakably suggested by the words used to characterize the figure of the novel. And there is additional support for the identification. From the side of ancient Russian religious cultism there is the fact, previously mentioned, that the day of the birth of St. John (Ivan Kupala) is the occasion for orgiastic celebration of bacchanalian proportions among even the modern peasantry, a time when the Kupala songs characterize John in such a way as to make him appear "wholly paganized." [23] This constitutes the substantial identification of the Baptist in the mind of the *narod* with the fertility rites of the primordial cosmic religiousness. This assimilation of John to the cult of

---

[23] Adolf Stender-Petersen, *Russian Studies,* Acta Jutlandica, Humanistisk Serie, XLIII Copenhagen: Universitetsforlaget I Aarhus, 1956), 69. Cf. chap. 1, sec. 3, *above.* The celebration of Kupala in the same fashion was characteristic also in Bulgaria. Cf. Dmitri Obolensky, *The Bogomils: A Study in Balkan Neo-Manichaeism* (Cambridge: Cambridge University Press, 1948), 67, 247. The attitude of the Bogomils is of high interest for the present analysis of John the Baptist. In this key sect of the Slav world John was characterized *both* as the forerunner of the Antichrist and as the emissary of Satan sent in response to the appearance of Christ to oppose Him. John's baptism by water kills the baptism of the Spirit by fire. *Ibid.,* 129, 228. See also similar observations in Steven Runciman, *The Medieval Manichee: A Study in the Christian Dualist Heresy* (Cambridge: Cambridge University Press, 1960), 78, 84, 151; also Ign. v. Doellinger, *Geschichte der gnostischmanichäeischen Sekten im früheren Mittelalter; Beiträge zur Sektengeschichte des Mittelalters, Erster Theil,* (2 vols.; repr. ed.; New York: Burt Franklin, Research and Source Works Series No. 8, n.d.), I, 154, 169, 190; II, 34, 65, 90, 283, 375.

Mother Moist Earth is, in turn, intertwined with the sectarian religiousness which is represented in *The Brothers Karamazov*. The Khlysty, for example, whose "violent motions, or frenzied dances" suggested the "Dionysian orgy," was a sect that "sanctioned an exaggerated and wild asceticism which, following the ecstasies, passed into savage sexual orgies, not unlike certain gnostic sects. This was the old leaven of an ecstatic naturalism going hand in hand with a false and fundamentally anti-Christian spiritualism." [24]

Is this not just the spirit of "Karamazov baseness" which provides the dual idealism of mingled opposites, of Sodom and the Madonna, in the quest for beauty and holiness by the characters of the novel before us? What distance separates Zosima's mystical teaching, "Love sins! In truth life is paradise. Once in a myriad of centuries it is given," from Ivan's rebellious affirmation, "Everything is permitted"? [25]

---

[24] Arseniev, *Russian Piety*, 70. Dancing and whipping have striking prominence in Dostoevsky's notes to books 7 and 8. The controlling symbolism is *"GRUSHA. THE LITTLE ONION,"* i.e., the divine cosmos to whom Alyosha flees in revolt after decomposition of Zosima's corpse sets in and which Dmitri orgiastically celebrates at Mokroe with Grushenka; see *The Notebooks for "The Brothers Karamazov,"* 110; 108–60, especially 118, 124, 132, 136, 152, 155, 158–59. Solar symbolism is included, as on a page written in Polish (transliterated into Cyrillic characters): "Pan father and Pani mother—Holy, Priest, Sun." *Ibid.,* 143; cf. 114. A connection with Catholicism is a plausible connotation.

[25] Dostoevsky, *The Notebooks for "The Brothers Karamazov,"* 96, 40; cf. 72, 104, 137, 201–203, 209, 212, 216, 225. Cf. also Temira Pachmuss, *Dostoevsky: Dualism and Synthesis of the Human Soul* (Carbondale: Southern Illinois University Press, 1963), 46, 60ff, and *passim.* This common theme in Dostoevsky is expressed by Valkovsky, the underground man, Versilov, and others. Its fullest statement is by Dmitri Karamazov: "Beauty is a terrible and awful thing! It is terrible because it is indefinable, and it cannot be defined because God has given us nothing but riddles. Here the shores come together; here all contradictions live side by side. I'm very uneducated . . . but I have thought a great deal about this. There are a terrible lot of mysteries! . . . Beauty! I can't endure the thought that a man of lofty mind and heart begins with the ideal of the Madonna and ends with the ideal of Sodom. Even more terrible: a man with the ideal of Sodom in his soul does not renounce the ideal of the Madonna, and his heart truly burns, truly burns—just as in his youthful, innocent days. No, man is broad, even too broad: I'd have him narrower. The devil only knows what it's all about! What the mind regards as shame is sheer beauty to the heart. Is there beauty in Sodom? Believe me, it is exactly in Sodom that it resides for the great majority of people—did you know that secret? It's awful that beauty should be mysterious as well as terrible. God and the devil are fighting there and the battlefield is the hearts of men." Donald Fanger, *Dostoevsky and Romantic Realism: A Study in Relation to Balzac, Dickens, and Gogol* (Cambridge: Harvard University Press, 1965), 227. See Dostoevsky, *The Brothers Karamazov*, I, 106 (pt. 1, bk. 3, chap. 3, *ad fin.*)

How far removed from the core of ancient naturalism is the Grand Inquisitor's perversion of Christianity? At last, the Bread of Life becomes the earthly bread and Sodom and the Madonna can be embraced simultaneously with the blessing of Christ through his Vicar the Inquisitor! Here is the dream come true, just as it came true each year on Ivan Kupala! The saying of St. Isaac the Syrian succinctly designates the foe of Russian Christianity: "The world is . . . the extension of a common name to distinct passions." [26] The beast in man, which once ritually served to propitiate the gods and secure attunement with them, became the captor of the soul imprisoned in the flesh with the rise of Christian consciousness. The whole of Christian asceticism is a monument to this fact. The John represented in Dostoevsky's Inquisitor is the Baptist vanquished by Herod, not simply in body but in spirit as well. The evils of Herod and Pilate are here blended in a symbol of pride, ferocity, and lust triumphant over the spirit traditionally represented by the image of the great Forerunner and first believer.[27] There is a last intimation in this. The Legend is the supposed creation of Ivan Fedorovich Karamazov: the scabrous and the sacred,[28] together with a connecting link to John

---

[26] Quoted from Lossky, *The Mystical Theology*, 199.

[27] The characterization is reminiscent of Kurbsky's account of a sermon by Saint John Chrysostom on Herod, quoted in rebuke of Ivan the Terrible. " 'Today, when the virtues of John and the ferocity of Herod were announced to us, our innermost parts were disturbed, our hearts trembled, our vision was dimmed, our mind was blunted. Oh what is firm in the feelings of man when the multitude of evils destroys the majesty of virtues? . . . . Rightly were our innermost parts disturbed and our heart trembled, for Herod defiled the Church, removed the priesthood'— just as you destroyed, if not John the Baptist, then Archbishop Philipp and other holy men—'befouled the priestly order, shattered the kingdom; what there was of piety, or rules, of life, of customs, of faith, of instruction—he ruined all this and put to confusion. Herod—the torturer of citizens and warriors, the robber, the destroyer of his friends'; but your majesty's wickedness is still greater, for with your children of darkness [the *oprichnina*] you not only destroy your friends, but also you lay waste the whole holy Russian land. . . . I return to what Chrysostom wrote about Herod: 'The murderer of those around him, he soaked the earth in blood and persisted in blood-thirstiness' " Quoted from J. L. I. Fennell (ed. and trans.), *Prince A. M. Kurbsky's History of Ivan IV*, (Cambridge: Cambridge University Press, 1965), 167–71; cf. 8–9.

[28] See Mario Praz, *The Romantic Agony*, trans. Angus Davidson (2nd ed.; London: Oxford University Press, 1951). On the grotesque in Dostoevsky, see Fanger, *Dostoevsky and Romantic Realism*, 228ff. On the link of name symbolism with the old cosmic religiousness of the *rod*, see Fedotov, *The Russian Religious Mind*,

the Baptist, are brought together in the symbolism of the name of the Inquisitor's author.

Part 3 of the Legend opens with a play on darkness and light which moves the symbolism of light, burning, fire, and knowing into the center of the Legend to dominate it throughout. Again, the ambiguity of symbolism is recalled. The "light that shines on in the darkness" (John 1:5) of the dungeon of Seville is both that of the Christ and that of the gnostic Paraclete (John 14:12–18; Matt. 23:34; I Cor. 13:8–10) whose gnosis illumines the darkness of the cell of the Holy Prisoner with his coming, just as he has lighted the darkness of the world and the lives of men. "In the pitch darkness the iron door of the dungeon is suddenly opened and the Grand Inquisitor himself slowly comes in with a light in his hand." [29] At the end of the poem, the Prisoner is released and disappears into the darkness. One is reminded of the God whose nature is Darkness, whose manifestation, Light. The Inquisitor's entrance is followed by the interrogation: "It is You? You?" Then follows the threat which combines the symbolism of baptism and Golgotha: baptism by the fire of the Holy Spirit at the hands of the Paraclete, and sacrificial death through burning at the stake: "tomorrow I shall condemn you and burn you at the stake as the worst of heretics." From the perspective of gnostic sectarianism, Jesus is a devil.[30] But, just at this point, it is well to be reminded that the gnostic and sectarian elements of the Legend are only two of the components of the "synthesis" of "anarchism" which Dostoevsky has included—albeit a preponderantly important two. The core elements of the Legend are representations of powers which antedate and dom-

---

15ff, and the significance of personal patronyms. Cf. the discussion in chap. 8, sec. 1, *below*. And see Harry Slochower, "Incest in 'The Brothers Karamazov,'" in Hendrik M. Ruitenbeek (ed.), *Psychoanalysis and Literature* (New York: Dutton, 1964), especially 309ff: "Grushenka: The Hetaira-Magdalene." Although not directly concerned with Dostoevsky, see also Wolfgang Kayser, *The Grotesque in Art and Literature*, trans. Ulrich Weisstein (Bloomington: Indiana University Press, 1963).

29 Quoted from Matlaw, *Notes from Underground*, 123.

30 According to the Manichaean *Fihrist*, for example, Mani pronounced Jesus a *shaitan* (p. 335, line 8); see A. A. Bevan, "Manichaeism," in James Hastings (ed.), *Hastings' Encyclopedia of Religion and Ethics* (12 vols.: New York: Charles Scribner's Sons, 1928), VIII, 398.

inate any of their specific configurations. The flux of the realm of becoming is concrete and particular, but the august personages and
powers that shape the destiny of man and history tower above existence in massive generality. It is these august *tremenda* that constitute
the great structuring motifs of the Legend, and in this part 3 the "encounter" is between the world-historic personages Christ and Antichrist.

The biblical account is Dostoevsky's ultimate frame of reference,
and the key passage there is Second Thessalonians (2:6–12). The coming of the Inquisitor is the *parousia* of the Antichrist (II Thess. 2:9),
of the "lawless one," the supreme anarchist. The motif of silence is
again enunciated and that of Christ as the *katechon* directly expressed
by the Inquisitor: "be silent. . . . You have no right to add anything
to what you have said of old. Why then are you come to hinder (*me-
shat'*) us? For you have come to hinder us, and you know that." The
silence of Christ is preserved throughout. The formula for the power
of Christ as the One Who silently restrains the power of evil in the
world and prevents the ultimate triumph of Antichrist is the reiterated expression, "Why are You come to hinder us?" Christ is the
divine hinderer or restrainer of the evil power, the *katechon* of II
Thess. 2:7. The symbol of the restrainer is expressed in the neuter
gender in 2:6 and in the masculine in 2:7 in the Greek text and rendered as follows in Dostoevsky's copy of the New Testament: *kto ne
dopuskaet* (2:6) which/who does not allow, *or* permit, *or* which/who
bars and *kogda ne dopuskaiushchego* (2:7).[31] The former may be
understood, not as the old Roman Empire, but as its purified continuator, Holy Russia of the Third Rome. The Christ of the community of true believers is the Russian Christ of the Legend, of the
(true) Orthodox Church, that is, of faith; and this power restrains
Caesar and Rome in its Jesuitical-Socialist incarnation and brings
the eschatology of the Second Epistle to the Thessalonians into harmony with that of the Apocalypse where the Harlot astride the Beast
is Rome, the Antichrist, and its priestly minions.[32]

---

31 *Novyi Zaviet* (1822), 705. See chap. 2, n.58 *above.*
32 The latter passage is cited toward the end of the Legend; see close of part 5.
See Dostoevsky, *The Brothers Karamazov,* I, 264.

4. Political Apocalypse

The evidence indicates the Legend to be a carefully structured political apocalypse, and at this juncture the designation must be clarified and more fully established.

Apocalypse means unveiling or revealing. Each of the Testaments of the Bible contains one book to which this term commonly is applied, Daniel and Revelation: the first of these is the oldest extant specimen of apocalypse, the second has given its name to the genre. Many other books in the Bible contain apocalyptical allusions and passages (notably Mark 13, Matt. 24, 25, and II Thess. 2), and the noncanonical apocalyptical literature is voluminous. It is relatively abundant throughout history—from the intertestamental period to the high and late Middle Ages into the Reformation and post-Reformation periods up to modern times. In the wake of the speculation on the meaning of history of Joachim of Flora (1131–1202), apocalypse evinces increasing preoccupation with the interpretation of political existence. Coincident with the immanentization of Christian eschatology and the rise of radically secular civilization in the West, political apocalypse finds noteworthy expression in various gnostic movements, climaxing after the French Revolution in progressivism, utopianism, and revolutionary activism as incorporated into specific ideological teachings in the nineteenth century.[33]

Generically, apocalypse is characterized by a number of elements. First, it is usually written in times of stress, is frequently pseudonymous, warns of unprecedented suffering and evil, and encourages readers to persevere in faith and righteousness. Second, it speculatively divides history into a sequence of periods, representing it as a battleground between sharply dualistic forces of good and evil—in principle between God and Belial and his successors—simultaneously under the aspects of present and future. Third, it is prophetic as well as eschatological in content; in the biblical context it can be distinguished from other prophecy and eschatology in that (a) apocalyptical prophesying is set in a *temporal* range that is comparatively vast

---

[33] See Eric Voegelin, *The New Science of Politics: An Introduction* (Chicago: University of Chicago Press, 1952), 107–89; J. L. Talmon, *Political Messianism: The Romantic Phase* (New York: Frederick A. Praeger, Inc., 1960), 15–225.

and commonly encompasses the centuries rather than merely the immediate future, and in a *spatial* range that transcends local concerns
to reach cosmic proportions; (b) apocalyptical eschatology not only is
concerned with the ultimate end of history, but, written under a
heightened sense that the End is at hand, it deals specifically with
the events and signs of the final denouement. Finally, apocalypse
represents the dynamics of history as both allowing full play to human
freedom and being decisively determined by divine will, the historical process to culminate in direct intervention by a Messiah to
achieve the Kingdom of God.[34]

Application of these criteria to the Legend results in its clear identification as apocalypse. The spiritual and social ferment out of which
Dostoevsky wrote has been set forth; even the pseudonymous touch,
while not a necessary characteristic of apocalypse, is present in the
Legend's being ostensibly Ivan's poem. That it warns of unprecedented suffering and evil is plain from even a casual reading of the passage, although the details of this must be the subject of subsequent
analysis, as must also be the more obscure question of whether the
Legend is, indeed, an exhortation to perseverence in faith and righteousness and, if so, in what sense. The speculative periodization of
history has already been noticed and must be considered in detail (see
chap. 6, sec. 2, *below*.) The sharp dualism of good and evil is represented in the persons of the Inquisitor (who designates himself to be
the devil's agent) and Christ; that they are portrayed as at present
and for all future time locked in battle for dominion over man, history, and the creation is immediately evident from the text. That the
Legend is apocalyptically prophetic and eschatological can be seen by
considering that: its prophecies reach to the end of history; they are
imputed to a figure of the sixteenth century—that is, the utterances
are dated some three hundred years before they were actually written;

---

34 The present discussion of apocalypse is indebted to H. H. Rowley, *The Relevance of Apocalyptic: A Study of Jewish and Christian Apocalypses from Daniel
to Revelation* (2nd ed.; London: Lutterworth, 1947). See David Winston, "The
Iranian Component in the Bible, Apocrypha, and Qumran: A Review of the Evidence," *History of Religions,* V (1966), 183–216, for the view that Old Testament
apocalypse is of Persian origin, and that it is to Zoroastrianism that the succession
of monarchies in Daniel 2 and 7 and the dualism of biblical and gnostic apocalypse
is traceable. *Ibid.,* 189ff, 200ff, 211.

the tone of the Legend is charged with the imminent expectation of the end of history. These attributes are complemented by the care with which the biblical signs and events of the End have been worked into the text, as will be more fully shown. Lastly, with respect to the dynamics of history, it is evident that the question of human freedom in collision with power is central to the Legend. Whether Dostoevsky intended to affirm the historical process to be predetermined by divine will and—in common with biblical apocalypse—to prophesy divine intervention by the Messiah to establish the Kingdom of God is, however, less than clear on the surface and demands detailed examination.

Therefore, the Legend may firmly be classified as political apocalypse. Yet the source of greatest perplexity for the interpreter remains in the question of the central thrust of this revelation. Perplexity arises especially because the spokesman in the drama is emphatically identifiable with rebellion and the man of lawlessness of Paul's Second Letter to the Thessalonians. This feature differentiates the Legend from biblical apocalypse on principle and suggests its classification as a reverse or evil apocalypse. Even to confirm this identification and go beyond it to perceive that the Inquisitor is the Little Horn of Daniel, to see that his mouth speaks great things, that he has set out to change times and seasons, to wear out the saints and measure himself even against the Most High (Dan. 7:8, 25), that he stands up against the Prince of princes (Dan. 8:25), that he magnifies himself above every god and speaks marvelous things against the God of gods Himself (Dan. 11:36)—even all of this does not dispose of the fundamental question of the Legend considered as indubitably apocalyptic but only renders it more acute. That question is whether the truth of the Legend remains the truth of biblical apocalypse, or articulates a New Word in that tradition, or proclaims a new and radically different truth. Has Dostoevsky incorporated into his Legend the stuff of the ancient apocalyptists and, consonant with their tradition, adapted the experiences, ideas, and symbols of the Bible to the urgent needs of his time in order to utter "a word of power for men in dire need," in order to keep "alive the flame of hope in dark and difficult days?" [35] Or is the truth of the Legend what the Inquisitor tells us it is: the tri-

---

[35] Rowley, *The Relevance of Apocalyptic*, 50.

umphant vision of the coming world of the New Humanism in which
the superstitions of historical infancy and adolescence are surmounted
to enable man to dwell among the endless perfections of his sovereign
essence and know thereby that *his* is the freedom and power of the
Lord of creation? Or has Dostoevsky somehow penetrated radical
doubt and disbelief of the traditional categories of faith and hope,
good and evil to the point of discovering a new "modern" home for
the spirit lying beyond the paradoxical *coincidentia oppositorum* of
the agony of existence, a new truth and faith for post-Christian Modern Man? [36] Only a careful analysis of the text itself can answer these
questions. The procedure will be to present a detailed synopsis of the
Legend with attention to its chief motifs, to identify further its symbolisms and show their functions, and to explore the various possible meanings of the Legend in its parts and as a whole.

---

[36] Cf. Thomas J. J. Altizer, *Mircea Eliade and the Dialectic of the Sacred* (Philadelphia: Westminster Press, 1963), 107ff, 189ff.

CHAPTER IV

LEITMOTIFS

The "Legend of the Grand Inquisitor" is the unwritten poem of the
metaphysical rebel Ivan Karamazov. It is recounted by Ivan to his
cherubic younger brother Alyosha as the two sit together in a tavern
in conversation. Alyosha is one of Dostoevsky's whole men, an accomplished human being who—unlike his brother Ivan, and Raskolnikov,
and Dostoevsky's other "doubles"—has overcome his own division, although the victory appears to be not yet a final one.[1] The decisive
point of the Legend is suggested in Alyosha's first reaction to it; "But
... that's absurd!" he cried, flushing. "Your poem is in praise of Jesus,
not in blame of Him—as you meant it to be" (*The Brothers Karamazov*, I, 267). This response will serve as a guide to the consideration of
the Legend itself.

1. CHRIST: THE PRINCIPLE OF ACTIVE LOVE

Ivan's poem opens with the reappearance, for a moment, of Christ
incarnate. He walks the streets of sixteenth century Seville. The atmosphere is that of Jesus' triumphal entry into Jerusalem on Palm
Sunday. All of the people recognize Him. He is the Christ of the Gospels, the embodiment of Active Love, as the Elder Zosima might have

---

[1] Albert Camus, *The Rebel: An Essay on Man in Revolt*, trans. Anthony Bower
(New York: Random House, Inc., Vintage Books, 1956), 55–104; Nicholas Ber-
dyaev, *Dostoevsky*, trans. Donald Attwater (New York: World Publ. Co., Meridian
Books, 1957), 120.

said.[2] It is the day after a magnificent *auto da fé* which has seen almost a hundred heretics burned to death at the stake at the Grand Inquisitor's direction, *ad majorem gloriam Dei*.[3] Christ walks in silence. His face shines with love and compassion. The people believe as little children and praise His name. A man blind since birth calls to Him from out of the crowd and, suddenly, he is able to see. The people praise Him and worship His name.

He passes before a door of the great cathedral of Seville. Just at that moment a funeral procession bearing the corpse of a little girl of seven is about to enter. The crowd cries to the bereaved mother to ask Christ to raise her. The priest frowns confusedly, but the mother falls at His

---

[2] The figure of the Elder Zosima, like all of Dostoevsky's characters, is a composite. In the main, however, he is based on St. Tikhon Zadonsky (1724–83) whose thought Dostoevsky had meditated for many years and who appears by name in *The Possessed*. The notebooks reveal the depth of the author's interest in this saint and the principle of caritative love he exemplified. See Fyodor M. Dostoevsky, *The Notebooks for "The Possessed"*, ed. and with an intro. by Edward Wasiolek, trans. Victor Terras (Chicago: University of Chicago Press, 1968), especially 52, 156, 345–46, and the entries in the index (p. 430); Dostoevsky, *The Notebooks for "A Raw Youth"*, ed. and with an intro. by Edward Wasiolek, trans. Victor Terras (Chicago: University of Chicago Press, 1969), 425; cf. 445, 491, 513, 518, 523, 533, 538, 541, 552–53; Dostoevsky, *The Notebooks for "The Brothers Karamazov"*, ed. and trans. Edward Wasiolek (Chicago: University of Chicago Press, 1971), 91, 105, 137, 201–204. The idea of "Active Love," the central preachment of Zosima, is directly from Tikhon; see Nadeida Gorodetzky, *Saint Tikhon Zadonsky: Inspirer of Dostoevsky* (London: S.P.C.K. Press, 1951), vii, 181–86; see also Dostoevsky to Apollon N. Maikov, March 25, 1870, in Mayne (trans.), *Letters of Dostoevsky*, 190–91. The name "Zosima" probably was taken from St. Zosima, one of the two founders of the great monastery of Solovki in the fifteenth century. Cf. Fyodor Dostoevsky, *The Notebooks for "The Idiot,"* ed. and with an intro. by Edward Wasiolek, trans. Katherine Strelsky (Chicago: University of Chicago Press, 1967), 201n; cf. 63, 69, 97, 105–106, 129, 143, 198, 205, 216, 228, 236. For understanding the detailed symbolism of *The Brothers Karamazov*, the connection of the Solovki monastery with the Schismatics is of interest. See Serge Bolshakoff, *Russian Nonconformity: The Story of "Unofficial" Religion in Russia* (Philadelphia: Westminster Press, 1950), 70. Tikhon Zadonsky is significant for Dostoevsky also because of his Augustinianism and his anthropology. See George P. Fedotov (ed.), *A Treasury of Russian Spirituality* (New York: Sheed & Ward, 1948), 182, 234–35.

[3] The Latin expression also occurs in the *Diary* in the context of a discussion of Schiller's *Don Carlos* and the Grand Inquisitor; Fyodor M. Dostoevsky, *The Diary of a Writer*, trans. Boris Brasol (2 vols.; New York: Charles Scribner's Sons, 1949), I, 261. The connection of Schiller's drama with the Legend is discussed by Robert Payne in *Dostoevsky: A Human Portrait* (New York: Alfred A. Knopf, Inc., 1961), 357ff. The sources of the Legend are uncommonly varied: see Ralph E. Matlaw, *The Brothers Karamazov: Novelistic Technique* (The Hague: Mouton, 1957), 14ff; also W. Komarovich, *Die Urgestalt der Brüder Karamasoff: Dostojewskis Quellen, Entwürfe und Fragmente* (Munich: Piper, 1928).

feet in adoration and implores Him. In compassion He once again speaks, "Maiden, arise!" The little girl sits up holding the funeral bouquet, refreshed and happy as though waking from a restful sleep. The people feel His burning love as it inundates their souls, and they can but respond by loving Him. They shout "Hosannah!"—*hoshi'ah-nna*, "Save (us) now, we pray!" (Matt. 21:9)—and adore Him. He speaks no more throughout the poem.

This introduction of Christ obviously is indebted to the biblical account of the raising of Jairus' daughter, a miracle which is interrupted by the touch of the hemorrhaging woman who—like the blind man in the crowd in the Legend—is immediately healed through the simple response of faith to the outgoing of divine power (cf. Luke 8:48). These are the last two of four miracles performed by Jesus perhaps on the same day: the first being that of the storm on the lake, and the second—which supplied Dostoevsky's text for *The Possessed*—that of the Gerasene demoniac (cf. Mark 4:35–5:43).[4] In contrast to the biblical account of the raising of Jairus' daughter, however, the little girl of the Legend is not twelve (as it is emphasized that she is in the New Testament accounts) but seven years old.[5] The modification introduces the symbolism of the sacred number[6] into the myth and, together with the other elements of the account, focuses the following aspects of the confrontation of Christ and the world into one picture:

---

[4] Dostoevsky carefully selected these miracles as illustrative in the biblical context of the peculiarly pervasive confidence in Christ which he regards as the principal strength of Russian popular religiousness. That "our people" have "embraced in their hearts Christ and His teachings" he believes equivalent to "*the whole essence of Christianity.*" (Dostoevsky, *Diary*, II, 983; cf. 961–62, 980). A modern biblical scholar makes this comment with respect to the four miracles of Mark 4:35–5:43: "The memorable acts and utterances of Jesus which make these stories unique are all concerned with the maintenance of simple trust in God— a trust that triumphs over natural dangers, demonic powers, disease, and even death." H. G. Wood as quoted in R. McL. Wilson, "Mark," in Matthew Black and H. H. Rowley (eds.), *Peake's Commentary on the Bible* (London: Thomas Nelson & Sons, 1962), 805. Cf. also the account in Matt. 9:27–30 where the blind are healed.

[5] Cf. Mark 5:42, Luke 8:42.

[6] The symbolic significance of the number seven is elaborate. Suffice it to suggest its meaning in Revelation: "The number three means heaven, four means the earth, and the number seven is the blending of these two, or God dwelling with men." N. Turner, "Revelation," in Black and Rowley (eds.), *Peake's Commentary*, 1044.

creation itself, beautiful in life as comes from the hand of God, lies sleeping in the Sabbath of time and history; *mankind,* whose spiritual slumber can be the Heraclitean death of the soul unless quickened through the response of faith; *revelation* of God in Christ as Yahweh: the One Who Is Who reveals Himself (cf. Exod. 3:14) ; *redemption* through grace which the sin of man calls forth as the substance of divinity to climax in the mission of the suffering Savior (cf. Exod. 3:13–17; 14:30; Isa. 59:20; John 1:29; Rom. 1:16; 3:21–25; 8:2). The perfection of the creation-rest of God (Gen. 2:4) has its complement in the perfection of the redemption-rest of the faithful in Christ (Heb. 4:1–11); *resurrection* and beatitude as the portion of those who respond to grace by faith; and *death* and destruction as the fate of faithless souls who ignore revelation and resist grace to persevere in the vain pretense of self-sufficiency which is the pride of life (I John 2:16) and the first and chief one of the seven deadly sins of tradition.

Thus, not in terms but by a stunning artistic picture, which is a masterstroke, Dostoevsky emblazons the divine affirmation across the firmament in the poem's first moment: Christ's identity is established with the people by an act of faith. The communion in God *(sobornost')*[7] of the opening of Ivan's poem is coupled with the kiss

---

7 *Sobornost'* "is the key theological concept of Russian Orthodoxy." Ernst Benz, *The Eastern Orthodox Church: Its Thought and Life,* trans. Richard and Clara Winston (Chicago: Aldine Publ. Co., 1963), 153. This term (or *sobornyi*) was originally the Old Church Slavonic translation of *ekklesia* (church) as catholic (*katholike*) or "universal" used by Cyril and Methodius in their mission to the Slavs. It denotes both the external church as well as the Church as the Mystical Body. In particular, it links personalism and freedom of faith with the notion of a community of brotherly love: "love being an act of freedom and creative spontaneity upon the part of redeemed man." *Ibid.,* 158. A. S. Khomyakov (see his *The Church Is One* [London, 1948]), used the term to designate the "organic unity of all in love and freedom as the essence of the Church." Nicholas V. Riasanovsky, "Khomyakov on *Sobornost',*" in E. J. Simmons (ed.), *Continuity and Change in Russian and Soviet Thought* (Cambridge: Harvard University Press, 1955), 185. Khomyakov is close to the Dostoevsky of the Legend in this conception of the Christian community, and in the further respect that, as a fervent advocate of Christian personalism, he charged the "atheistic West with annihilating human personality." Benz, *The Eastern Orthodox Church,* 159. For the origin of the representation of the church as "catholic" in Philo's description of the entire Jewish nation of his time by the expression "more universal polity" (*he katholikotera politeia*), see H. A. Wolfson, *Faith, Trinity, Incarnation,* Vol. I of *The Philosophy of the Church Fathers* (1 vol. to date; rev. ed.; Cambridge: Harvard University Press, 1964), 495ff.

placed by Jesus upon the lips of the Grand Inquisitor, which closes the poem in an act of love, to symbolize the communalism and personalism of Christian faith. The tension of faith in Christ as the affirmation of the essence of eternal Being Who *is* Love and Freedom and Truth is the feeling-idea which dominates the Legend and which makes this piece of writing *itself* the climax of Dostoevsky's Christian metaphysics. Christ demands the free response of men to His truth, and freedom is the Legend's leading theme. The experience of faith in the free response of the people of the poem to the person of the God-man is crucial to Dostoevsky's meaning. The deluge of negation and rebellion which constitutes the body of Ivan's poem is bracketed by affirmations of the reality of transcendent being and an anthropology of its apprehension which are granted the status of facts. They hold equal standing with the facts of evil and suffering in human experience recounted by Ivan in the conversation preliminary to his recitation of the poem and by the Inquisitor in his confrontation with Christ.

The ontological and existential dimensions of faith must again be stressed. Only if faith is understood as a real experience, the reciprocal interpenetration of man and God, can the Legend be grasped. Such faith structures existence, assuages sorrow, appeases suffering, and makes otherwise meaningless life meaningful. The conception is given pungent expression by Dostoevsky in a sentence about St. Tikhon Zadonsky: "The most important thing about Tikhon is Tikhon." [8] Likewise, the most important thing about Christ is the *fact* of Christ Himself.[9] In a decisive sense, the fact of revelation is its

---

[8] Quoted in Gorodetzky, *Saint Tikhon Zadonsky*, 193; cf. n. 2, *above*.

[9] For Dostoevsky's view of Christ, see Nicolas Zernov, *Three Russian Prophets: Khomyakov, Dostoevsky, Solovyov* (London: S. C. M. Press, 1944), 106ff. The significance of Vladimir Solovyov for Dostoevsky's conception of Christ and the God-man and man-god relationship is probably considerable. Cf. V. Solovyov, *A Solovyov Anthology*, ed. and with an intro. by S. L. Frank, trans. N. Duddington (London: S. C. M. Press, 1950), 35ff; also, Vladimir Seduro, *Dostoevski in Russian Literary Criticism, 1846–1956* (New York: Columbia University Press, 1957), 310–11. The personal relationship of Solovyov and Dostoevsky is set forth in E. H. Carr, *Dostoevsky* (London: Allen & Unwin, 1931), 277ff. Solovyov is also of interest for the gnostic influences in Dostoevsky's work. (See chap. 5, sec. 1, *below*.)

content.[10] The divine truth manifested in the climax of revelation in Christ is empirically evinced in the lives of the saintly individuals of all the ages. "*Keep* the image of Christ and if possible picture him in yourself," Dostoevsky wrote in the notes; he then drove home the linchpin: "What is the Truth? It stood before him, Truth itself." [11] It is the absence of faith thus strictly understood from the experience of Ivan which tragically flaws his character and makes him precisely what he is.

The terrible truth of man's existence is that freedom is for both good and evil, as Plato long ago pointed out (*Republic*, 557ff). The trouble with Christianity, the Inquisitor bitterly remarks, is that the "words of Saint Peter—'Thou art the Christ, the Son of the living God'—must burst from the spirit and from an unconstrained conscience." [12] Dostoevsky's faith, as one can surmise from a perusal of his artistic production (and as he often directly says), was not easily won. He gained it through a lifetime of torment—a veritable *Via Crucis*—shaped by the suffocating experience of imprisonment and political exile in Siberia (1849–59), chronic illness and susceptibility of epileptic seizure, and a burden of conscience that evoked nightmarish confrontation with the devil as the indwelling other half of his divided soul. In a late issue of the *Diary* he wrote:

> The dolts have ridiculed my obscurantism and the reactionary character of my faith. These fools could not even conceive so strong a denial of God as the one to which I gave expression [in *The Brothers Karamazov*]. . . . The whole book is an answer to *that*. You might search Europe in vain for so powerful an expression of atheism. Thus it is not like a child

---

10 This view of revelation is reflected in Dostoevsky's work, and he indicates that in the notes with such expressions as "the truth is the truth even *without me*" (*The Notebooks for "A Raw Youth"*, 71, italics Dostoevsky's), and "What is the Truth? It stood before him, Truth itself" (*The Notebooks for "The Brothers Karamazov*," 102) . See Voegelin, *The New Science of Politics: An Introduction* (Chicago: University of Chicago Press, 1952), 78; and H. Richard Niebuhr, *The Meaning of Revelation* (New York: Macmillian Co., 1941), chap. 3.

11 F. M. Dostoevsky, *The Notebooks for "The Brothers Karamazov*," 100, 102. The quoted passages are from the notes for bk. 6.

12 Berdyaev, *Dostoevsky*, 80.

that I believe in Christ and confess Him. My Hosanna has burst forth from a huge furnace of doubt.[13]

Dostoevsky discovered the important principle of political philosophy that the sufferings of mankind are in large part due to "the fact that man is born a free spiritual creature" and, that, being of this nature, he "may prefer to go hungry than to lose his freedom of spirit and be enslaved to material bread." [14] This observation provides the ultimate refutation of the Grand Inquisitor's "Euclidian" reasoning at the empirical level.

2. CONFESSIONS OF FAITH

Before addressing in detail the Inquisitor's argument, one must be reminded of the background of spiritual, or metaphysical, rebellion expressed by Ivan. In his rebellion God Himself is put on trial. Both the creation and divine revelation are rejected. Ivan's rebellion begins in outrage and indignation rooted in humanitarian pity for his fellow men, particularly for the guiltless, the children who are innocent and unblemished by sin.[15] The suffering of children introduces the theme

---

[13] Quoted in Henri de Lubac, *The Drama of Atheist Humanism*, trans. E. M. Riley (London: Sheed & Ward, 1949), 180. Ernest J. Simmons' reaction to this statement that Dostoevsky "seems more proud of Ivan's Negation of God than Zosima's faith in Him" is unfortunately misplaced. But, then, this distinguished critic has great trouble in ever supposing Dostoevsky's Christianity to be much more than verbal incantation. Simmons, *Introduction to Russian Realism* (Bloomington: Indiana University Press, 1965), 133; cf. *ibid.*, 114, 121, where the author's Christianity is mentioned and slurred. Contrast the assessments of A. Steinberg, *Dostoevsky* (New York: Hillary House, Publ., 1968), 31, 38 and chaps. 3 and 4; and Konstantin Mochulsky, *Dostoevsky: His Life and Work*, trans. and with an intro. by Michael A. Minihan (Princeton: Princeton University Press, 1967), 566–78, 617–23, 633–48.

[14] Berdyaev, *Dostoevsky*, 144.

[15] It is evident from Dostoevsky's handling of the victimization of children that he (or at least Ivan) identifies them with the innocent and blameless in a theological sense. This impression of his meaning is not simply symptomatic of heretical naturalism as an aspect of Rousseauism or a lapse back into folk religiousness, but it enjoys support from the Eastern Orthodox conception of original sin, which is not equivalent to Roman Catholicism's more rigid view that a sinful nature is flatly present in the human creature from the first moment of life. Rather, Orthodoxy holds original sin to mean an unnatural propensity toward defection from the will of God, or imperfect participation in grace because of the mortality and corruptibility of human nature (*not* because of radical moral depravation). One

of kenosis and the holy "passion-sufferers." [16] He reasons, from effect
to cause, that their suffering arises from the necessity of suffering in
God's creation so that man may be permitted a free choice between
good and evil: it is only through free choice of the good that salvation
and the kingdom of God (the "final harmony") can be achieved. To
God he opposes the principle of justice, suggesting the transformation
of religion into a positivistic religion of humanity. All he knows, he
says, is that there is suffering where there is no guilt. This is decisive.
In a particularly poignant passage, he recounts the most horrifying
atrocities perpetrated on children and then almost savagely turns to
his stricken brother, Alyosha, with the question which mysteriously
transfigures the humanitarian into the man-god charged with judging
God and correcting the order of creation:

> Imagine that you are creating a fabric of human destiny with the object
> of making men happy in the end, giving them peace and rest at last, but
> that it was essential and inevitable to torture to death only one tiny
> creature—that baby [the one smeared and choked with its own excrement

reason for this important difference in the conception of original sin in the East,
as opposed to the Catholic West, is that the Augustinian doctrine of the Fall
"which has determined the whole theological development of the Christian West"
remained completely strange to and ignored by the Christian East. "Not one work
of Augustine was translated into Greek." George P. Fedotov, *The Russian Religious Mind: Kievan Christianity; The Tenth to the Thirteenth Centuries* (New
York: Harper & Row, Publ., Torchbooks, 1960), 222; cf. Vladimir Lossky, *The
Mystical Theology of the Eastern Church* (London: James Clarke & Co., 1957),
130ff. Hence the fatal consequence of Adam's fall was his mortality and corruptibility. The conception entered Russian thought through the Slavonic translation of Methodius of Olympus' *On Freedom of Will*. Every "Russian scholar knew
and repeated that man is 'free' or 'master of himself,' *samovlasten*." A Russian
formulation of the twelfth or thirteenth century puts the matter concisely: "Man
was created in the image of God, that is, free for better or worse." Fedotov, *The
Russian Religious Mind*, 222. The summary of this doctrine is that man sins freely:
his *natural* disposition is toward God, and no idea of "supererogatory grace" added
to human nature is to be found in Eastern theology as the explanation of the
orientation toward God. "The decadence of human nature is the direct consequence of the free decision of man" who by willful act deprives himself of grace
(Lossky, *The Mystical Theology*, 132). But cf. Mochulsky, *Dostoevsky*, 616–17.

[16] That is, the idea of the moral perfection of those who suffer and meet death in
purity and nonresistence *in* (if not *for*) Christ. Cf. Fedotov, *The Russian Religious
Mind*, 104–105, for specific mention of the death of children. Those who meet
death passively and in Christ are sanctified and called "passion-sufferers" (*strasto-
terptsy*). See Michael Cherniavsky, *Tsar and People: Studies in Russian Myths*
(New Haven: Yale University Press, 1961), 7ff, 14, 16ff, 23.

and forced to spend a frosty night in a privy by its mother because it would not ask to be taken up at night] beating its breast with its fist, for instance—and to found that edifice on its unavenged tears, would you consent to be the architect of those conditions? Tell me, and tell the truth.

"No, I wouldn't consent," said Alyosha softly. (*The Brothers Karamazov*, I, 250–51.)

Here is the problem of theodicy in its most urgent terms, and Dostoevsky's whole being grapples with it.[17] God's creation is rejected and Ivan returns his "entrance ticket" to the promised eternal harmony. Reason and justice command this rejection. But so also does the irrational religious consciousness of the humanitarian-socialist-rebel: "I don't want harmony. From love of humanity I don't want it. I would rather remain with my unavenged suffering and unsatisfied indignation, *even if I were wrong.*" Camus observes that the *even if* is decisive. With it Ivan becomes a religious founder, and he founds the City of Satan and formulates the ideology of the "Legend." He denies divine will and sets in its place self-will. If there is no God, or even if there is one whose creation and revelation are rejected, then men must become gods. And because a god is a law unto himself, whatever the man-god or superman wills is lawful: hence Ivan's dictum, "All things are lawful." Without belief in the operative reality of Providence and in revelation, participated in through loving reciprocity by man as an immortal being created in the Divine image, Ivan's "Everything is lawful" (*Vse pozvoleno*) becomes the basis of social order—such as there exists in the state of disorder.

The anthropology of atheistic humanism and the politics of messianic socialism are the content of the Grand Inquisitor's monologue. It is cast in the form of a prophecy. One need not dwell upon the prophetic quality of Dostoevsky's thought in order to acknowledge the fascinating and profound portrayal of spiritual rebellion and totalitarianism that he gives. The impact of rebellion upon the psychic

---

17 The problem of theodicy in Ivan's presentation of it is, in fact, not so "unassailable" as Dostoevsky believed it to be. See the remarks of Eric Voegelin, *The World of the Polis* (Baton Rouge: Louisiana State University Press, 1957), Vol. II of Voegelin, *Order and History* (3 vols. to date; Baton Rouge: Louisiana State University Press, ——), 255.

and physical being of Ivan himself, as he seeks to live with his "logic" hypostatized into a religious obsession, is instructive. Rebellion is not against God but against His creation. The gnostic complexion of this doctrine seems patent. Underlying the statement would seem to lurk a conviction that the power Who created the world is evil and that the God of Light is completely divorced from the intrinsically evil world in which man must live and surely suffer. But there is ambivalence here no less than elsewhere in the Legend, so that a flat judgment of the kind can scarcely be made. Is this gnosticism or something quite different? The ambiguity of the Wanderer comes to mind. Ivan's rejection of the world subtly approaches identity with that of the mystic who seeks God in the apophatic attitude, who (following Dionysius Areopagita) *refuses* to accept being as such because it obscures divine nonbeing, and whose renunciation of the creation is motivated by the desire to gain access to the "Darkness which is beyond Light." [18] The consummate skill of the characterization of Ivan is breath-taking. Ivan is a sincere man who acknowledges that he is a believer. No one who has read the culminating passage of "Rebellion" can doubt the sincerity of his conviction, whose statement climaxes in the assertion—so profound is his love for the suffering and so outraged his thirst for divine justice—that, unless the wrongs of the earth somehow are righted, the undeserved tears atoned for in a rationally comprehensible way, then he must reject the promised future harmony of union with God. "I don't want harmony. From love of humanity I don't want it." The power of this is undeniable and it has been seen to echo sentiments expressed by Belinsky. Yet it comes as a thunderbolt to discover that both Belinsky and Ivan have taken their thoughts, nearly their lines, from perhaps the greatest of the Greek mystics, St. Simeon the New Theologian! For Ivan is heir to the spirit that breathes in all "humanism," the Christian awareness that one's personal well-being, happiness, and perfection are intimately bound up

---

[18] Pseudo-Dionysius the Areopagite, *"The Mystical Theology,"* chap. 2, in C. E. Rolt (ed. and trans.), *Dionysius the Areopagite "On the Divine Names" and "The Mystical Theology"*, Translations of Christian Literature, Series I: Greek Texts (London: S. P. C. K.; New York: Macmillan Co., 1920), 194; cf. Lossky, *The Mystical Theology*, 38. See chap. 2, sec. 4, *above*.

with the salvation of all men; that the love of God is somehow intricately and necessarily emmeshed with the love of one's fellow men.

> I know a man who desired the salvation of his brethren so fervently that he often besought God with burning tears and with his whole heart, in an excess of zeal worthy of Moses, that either his brethren might be saved with him, or that he might be condemned with them. For he was bound to them in the Holy Spirit by such a bond of love that he did not even wish to enter the kingdom of heaven if to do so meant being separated from them.[19]

The spiritual fervor of Ivan and his kin can be judged by the similarity of their declarations with this one. However, the explanation of Ivan as a gnostic is not destroyed by the discovery that he is a man of ardor and conviction. This was known before and the proposed explanation remains the correct one. For Ivan must "see," he must "know" in the concrete and phenomenal way; and he burns with the enthusiasm of the apophatic mystic without ever knowing his faith. By this tragic flaw alone is Ivan separated from the great mystics of which he is potentially one in Dostoevsky's magnificent representation of him.

Personally and concretely—apart from his "fantasy" of theocratic socialism that *everything is lawful*—the theoretical principle of "Karamazov baseness," has its pragmatic issue in parricide: the murder of Fyodor Pavlovich Karamazov by Smerdyakov, the moral Caliban, biological half-brother and spiritual son of Ivan. This "direct attack against nature and procreation" [20] upon a despicable man whose voluptuous nature is implanted in an intellectual way in Ivan's own and keeps him from the God of Alyosha (but who is nonetheless his father and a man) drives Ivan insane. Ivan apparently rebels out of humanitarian pity because of outrage at suffering, because of revulsion to killing. But he finds, following his "humanitarian" solution, after the supreme crime of deicide—the Nietzschean murder of God—there can only follow parricide. The contradiction of his own apotheosis of

---

19 Lossky, *The Mystical Theology*, 214; cf Fedotov, *The Russian Religious Mind*, 153, 388. St. Simeon the New Theologian (tenth century) was known in Russia from the fourteenth century when mysticism first developed there.
20 Camus, *The Rebel*, 59n.

"thirst for life" and realization that the cure was worse than the disease drove Ivan mad. The murder of God entails the equally certain annihilation of man as well.[21]

3. THE GRAND INQUISITOR:
THE PRINCIPLE OF NEGATION AND REBELLION

The Grand Inquisitor is not himself the devil, but he is of like mind with him.[22] The essentiality of the devil is that he is the spirit of pure negation whose goal is simply annihilation, as Dostoevsky makes clear in the later chapter of the novel, entitled "The Devil. Ivan's Nightmare" (bk. 11, chap. 9). But if the Grand Inquisitor is to be distinguished from the devil himself, where does the difference lie? Both are portrayed as loving humanity, and of loving it in an identical sense—that is, they wish above all for mankind's earthly happiness and will pay any price for it. This is the attractive fire burning in their breasts. The ninety-year-old cardinal of the Roman Catholic church is not the devil himself, but he is actuated by the same principle of negation which is the devil pure and simple. He brings to this a human quality, however, one which the devil as a purist ridicules. For, although the devil speaks of *his* truth and of the *other* truth (about which, as he admits, he can know nothing because he is pure negation) and says of it that which of the two is the better will be decided only at the end of the world, he is an honest swindler in that he does not himself know the secret of the truth of existence.

The Inquisitor as mortal man, on the other hand, is a swindler of

---

21 See *The Notebooks for "The Brothers Karamazov,"* 71–73, 218.
22 Temira Pachmuss has drawn an important distinction between the Inquisitor's "Satan" and Ivan's "devil" which she believes Dostoevsky intended to contrast. See her *F. M. Dostoevsky: Dualism and Synthesis of the Human Soul* (Carbondale: Southern Illinois University Press, 1963), 108, 110, 129–30. The distinction does not seem cogent because, whatever the full meaning of the author's demonology, the pettifogging little bourgeois devil of Ivan's nightmare operates with precisely the same doctrine as does the Inquisitor's ominous *him*: the negation of being by destruction of man's awareness of God. See, in this connection, Charles E. Passage who traces to Hoffmann's *Die Elixiere des Teufels* Dostoevsky's characterization of Ivan and his two "doubles" (Smerdyakov and the Devil): Ivan=Medardus, Smerdyakov=Viktorin, the Devil=Belcampo. That the Grand Inquisitor is yet another "double" has not been noted. Passage, *Dostoevsky the Adapter: A Study in Dostoevsky's Use of the Tales of Hoffmann* (Chapel Hill: University of North Carolina Press, 1954), 170ff.

a different stripe. The grandiose scheme which he unfolds in the course of his monologue is built upon the psychologically solid ground of a moral sanction in the form of a caricature of Christianity. The Inquisitor knows God *is*. Dostoevsky makes this abundantly clear by having him confront the Prisoner face to face and address Him as the divinely omniscient Christ of the Gospels. Simple atheism is not his true affliction, if, indeed, it is the affliction of any man: men always worship God, and if they cannot relate themselves to the transcendent ground of being, then they must inevitably fall back upon substitute grounds. This insight is a major strength of Dostoevsky's analysis of the theoretical structure, not only of Ivan's psychological plight, but of modern ideological movements in general and of their relationship to traditional religious experiences and doctrines.

Whether the revolt of Ivan is accountable in terms of assertion of Max Stirner's principle of the Ego (which, as a position derived from Hegel and Feuerbach, Masaryk is doubtless correct in suggesting as an ingredient) as the substitute ground of being, or whether the structure of the rebellion is more complex demands careful analysis. For the moment it is important not to oversimplify the position articulated by the Inquisitor. His pathology is such that he knowingly rebels against God as revealed through Christ, the God-man; but, knowing also that all of mankind is aware of God and that the Christian world equates Him with the Holy Trinity revealed through Christ, he sees no practical alternative to usurping the role of the historical Christ in the church and perversely playing it himself as the means of securing earthly dominion and peace. Thus the awful but at least partly well-intentioned swindle is perpetrated. The Inquisitor both knows God to be and that he is neither himself God nor His agent; but he confesses to Christ that he rejects revelation as irrational, unrealistic, and too noble for the pitiable race of men. The experiential basis of the swindle is, however, not so simple and clear as this. Man is so in love with truth that he must have a moral sanction in order to swindle, the devil later tells Ivan. Human swindlers must know the truth—even if they have to invent it themselves out of the whole cloth of Cartesian doubt and intellectual pride. Ivan and the Inquisitor long again for the Old Covenant of the Law to

which submission was so clear and which provided so firm a foundation for order; Feuerbach augmented Descartes by arguing that men
have always invented their gods, and better to live in the half-
conscious deceptiveness of this peculiarly modern idolatry, in the
simplicity of clear duty to obedience to rule, than to attempt to foster
among lowly men the seductions of the loving God of the Gospels.
Christ demands too much, aims too high. They seek, in short, to
eradicate through brutal misrepresentation the revelation of the
God of Love Who elevated freedom of conscience in the knowledge of
good and evil before mankind by disclosing Himself in the image
of Christ, the ultimate Truth and only Redeemer. "Reason" thereby
drives a wedge into being which absolutely sunders truth from
existence.[23]

Dostoevsky has spared neither himself nor his readers in drawing
the portrait just sketched. He has laid his finger precisely upon the
center of the existential problem which is also of decisive moment in
technical philosophical speculation. Man (and this means *all men*)
knows himself to participate in a reality ontologically superior to
himself to which he owes his being. The awareness of this participation, and of man's dependence, immediately precludes his mistaking
himself for God. That this awareness of man's must be obliterated
underlies Ivan's (and his puppets') proposals that the idea of God
be destroyed—for then one can swindle with impunity, because without God and immortality the ethical and political orders collapse;
or, if this solution is too strenuous (as the idea of God is too well
rooted in the minds of men), then one can proclaim himself God and

---

[23] To have *no* awareness of God is a psychopathic condition. Lossky writes: "Just
because it is light grace, the source of revelation, cannot remain within us unper-
ceived. We are incapable of not being aware of God, if our nature is in proper
spiritual health. Insensibility in the inner life is an abnormal condition." Lossky,
The Mystical Theology, 225. Cf. Dostoevsky, *The Notebooks for "The Brothers
Karamazov,"* 84. Ivan says (p. 76) in the notes: "I will accept God all the more
readily if he is the eternal old God who cannot be understood. And so let it be
that God." For Masaryk's remarks see the recently published volume which com-
pletes his important study of Russian thought as it climaxes in Dostoevsky: Thomas
G. Masaryk, *The Spirit of Russia: Studies in History, Literature and Philosophy*,
Vols. I and II, trans. Eden and Cedar Paul (2nd ed.; New York: Macmillan Co.,
1955); Vol. III, ed. George Gibian, trans. Robert Bass (New York: Barnes & Noble,
Inc., 1967), III, 11. Descartes' *"Je pense, donc je suis"* is quoted by the devil in
Dostoevsky, *The Brothers Karamazov*, bk. 11, chap. 9.

become a law unto himself—thereby sanctioning his swindling with the halo of divinity; or, if this is likely to be unpalatable to the remainder of mankind (the slave-men), then one can pervert the representation of the true God to one's own purposes while pretending to be a faithful servant, as the Inquisitor with his utilitarian motivations has done. Swindle and lust are equally characteristic of each "solution" to the problem, however well this is obscured by the "moral sanction" so derided by the devil. There is, then, the critical task of so anesthetizing the spiritual consciousness with the propaganda of atheism, scientism, and political activism that the discovery of the swindle cannot occur as a socially effective phenomenon.

All of these considerations are present in Dostoevsky's characterization, where the fundamental philosophical issue is brilliantly perceived. One may take, in this connection, the formulation by St. Thomas Aquinas as authoritative for the metaphysics of transcendence as argued from the time of Plato. He maintains that

everything, that in any way is, is from God. For whatever is found in anything by participation must be caused in it by that to which it belongs essentially, as iron becomes heated by fire. Now it has been shown . . . that God is self-subsisting being itself, and also that subsisting being can be only one; just as, if whiteness were self-subsisting being, it would be one, since whiteness is multiplied by its recipients. Therefore all beings other than God are not their own being, but are beings by participation. Therefore, it must be that all things which are diversified by the diverse participation of being, so as to be more or less perfect, are caused by one First Being, Who possesses being most perfectly.[24]

When Marx, in a rebellion intellectually analogous to Ivan's, found himself compelled to negate the central conclusion of existential awareness and of transcendental philosophy (man's participation in Being) because of his desire to establish that "man owes his existence [only] to man" and to prove the "entire so-called history of the world

---

24 *Summa Theologica*, I, 47, 1; quoted from Anton C. Pegis (ed.), *Basic Writings of Saint Thomas Aquinas* (2 vols.; New York: Random House, Inc., 1945), I, 427. Cf. Etienne Gilson, *History of Christian Philosophy in the Middle Ages* (New York: Random House, Inc., 1955), 373.

is nothing but the creation of man," he virtually recapitulated Aquinas' argument.

> A *being* [*Wesen*] only considers himself independent when he stands on his own feet; and he only stands on his own feet when he owes his *existence* to himself. A man who lives by the grace of another regards himself as a dependent being. But I live completely by the grace of another if I owe him not only the maintenance of my life, but if he has, moreover, *created* my *life*—if he is the *source* of my life. When it is not of my own creation, my life has necessarily a source of this kind outside of it. The *creation* is therefore an idea very difficult to dislodge from popular consciousness. The fact that nature and man exist in their own account is *incomprehensible* to it, because it contradicts everything *tangible* [*Handgreiflichkeiten*] in practical life.

This remarkable passage poses the same problems faced by Ivan and the Inquisitor, and answered by man's common sense by virtue of participation in being, and by Aquinas philosophically. The key question is: If this is the creation, and if I am a creature, then Who is the creator of my being? Or, in Marx's words: "Who begot the first man and nature as a whole?" The passage was quoted earlier, so only the nub of Marx's answer need be given. To ask such questions is to abstract from present reality, and this is nonsensical; a "reasonable man" does not ask such questions: "I cannot reply. . . . Don't think, don't ask (*Denke nicht, frage mich nicht*)." Even to *deny* the existence of God (atheism) is no longer necessary; it is best simply to affirm socialist reality.

The solution is akin to Ivan's, although the passage from Marx could not have been known to him because it was first published in 1932. The Inquisitor is the emblem of bad faith (in Sartre's sense) whose thirst for power and certitude overwhelms his awareness of the divine to become existentially controlling; he therefore willfully *knows* God does not exist, even as he rebels against Him, and this "knowledge" is plausibly supported by instrumental rationality (Euclidian reasoning). But he does not assert atheism; rather he proclaims the dogma of divinity as a screen and so rules that the citizenry, preoccupied with the rites and diversions of their treadmill existence, do not apprehend the lie or perceive the Abomination of Desolation standing in the Holy Place. While no less a swindler nor less guilty of bad faith, Marx is perhaps more forthright in that he boldly prohibits the asking of questions and even the thinking of atheism. "*Atheism*, as the denial of this unreality, has no longer any meaning, for atheism is a negation of God, and postulates the *existence of man* through this negation; but socialism as socialism no longer stands in any need of such a mediation. It [begins] from the *practically and theoretically sensuous consciousness* of man and of nature as the essence [*Wesens*]." [25] Like Ivan, who flatly says in the notes, "I would like to destroy completely the idea of God," Marx suggests that to affirm that man is god, the denial of the existence of God has in the past been necessary.[26] But to deny the existence of God is to stir the ashes of experience, pay worship to Him, and perhaps rekindle awareness of a higher and nobler Being than the self-announced earthly god. The prudent course is to desist from proclamation of atheism, to accept as undisputed fact that essence lies in the absorption of consciousness into the sensuous movement of the historical process as a dimension of unfolding nature, to know with dogmatic certainty that the highest being for man is man himself.

However, the solution can be even moderately satisfactory only for intellectuals who are, in any event, because of their distancing from common sense and from social tradition, most susceptible of existential disorders; and it can suffice only for such of them, as Marx himself, for example, who are already far gone in metaphysical rebellion. Dostoevsky proves himself perhaps both a better psychologist than and a superior philosopher to Marx in perceiving that naked rejection of transcendence is nothing but nihilism and must, inevitably, end in suicide, insanity, and anarchy. Even Ivan, the intellectual par excellence, could not bear the thought; Albert Camus' whole study, *L'homme révolté*, supports this view. If no individual, then certainly no mass movement can foot upon the void of existential nothingness—and achieve a following, much less stable dominion over the hearts and minds of entire societies. Be-

---

25 Karl Marx, *Economic and Philosophic Manuscripts of 1844*, ed. Dirk J. Struik, trans. Martin Milligan (New York: International Publ., 1964), 144–46.
26 *The Notebooks for "The Brothers Karamazov,"* 72.

cause Marx's writings themselves became (in the hands of the Inquisitor's Russian successors) the Koran of the most successful ideological mass movement in history, it follows that Marx's perverse asceticism in refusing to entertain ontological questions (even in the solitude of his meditations) finds social expression in the corollary of terror of both a psychological and physical kind. It follows also that, not content with his dogma of 1844, he elaborates in the *Communist Manifesto* three years later the speculative scheme of universal history which is (as Karl Löwith proved), in its every key aspect, an apocalyptical immanentization of the principal faith symbolisms of Christianity which breathes the very fire of Old Testament prophetism. He thereby both screened himself from the fall into absolute nothingness and simultaneously laid the groundwork for success of the revolutionary movement which he founded and fostered till the end of his life. The Inquisitor's and Marx's enterprises, thus, display important parallels and analogies; and there is little doubt that Dostoevsky did know the *Manifesto*. The parallels in the logic of the Legend and of the early Marx are not, then, simply fortuitous. Dostoevsky both drew from the milieu of which Marx was a part and knew something of his doctrine. The modes of thought of Ivan and Marx are the same. They are apocalyptical gnostics who envision (in the name of knowledge and scientific prediction) a radically immanentized paradise for a transformed and dehumanized mankind as the final stage of history. The troublesome "tangible" experience of universal mankind no more deflects their convictions concerning future history than it influences their repudiation of traditional theology.[27]

---

[27] The insensibility of the modern apocalyptical gnostic to *facts* (including phenomenal facts) has been insufficiently noticed. It must be accorded a prominent place in any description of his psycho- or pneumatopathology. For not only is his conception of reality distorted by radical closure against transcendent Being, but he is highly selective and perversely willful with respect to the elements of phenomenal reality accepted as substantial. There is, thirdly, distortion in ratiocination of a wholly unconscious kind. All of these types of deformation are illustrated in the passage from Marx's *Economic and Philosophic Manuscripts of 1844* just considered: the dogma is to be maintained whatever the cost: (1) tangible experience that brings it into question must be ignored; (2) questions that are raised which cannot be coped with must be dropped because the doctrine is otherwise endangered (and, in real life, if someone insists on asking the questions anyway

The Grand Inquisitor's monologue with Christ is a critical explanation of the following: wherein God has erred in understanding His creature man; what is the true nature of man; the principles upon which order in society must be based if an ecumenical society ever is to be realized; and the nature of the eventual worldwide society of the future. It is built around the three proposals of the devil in the Gospel account of the temptation of Christ in the wilderness.

The Inquisitor speaks to his Prisoner in the capacity of one who also loves humanity and whose dedication it is to bring men into the fold of the true believers. He, too, is a child of Light.

(a) Thou hast erred

Only yesterday the Inquisitor has ordered burned almost a hundred heretics. It is God's fault that things are in such a bad way.

---

he may well be liquidated); (3) the consideration of the reality of God must be prohibited to the point that neither affirmation *nor* denial of this sector of reality is to be permitted. This mentality can be seen at work in the leading sentence of part 1 of the *Communist Manifesto*: "The history of all hitherto existing society is the history of class struggles." Eric Voegelin and Karl Löwith, in particular, have shown the religious quality of the *Manifesto*, and the expectation of a radical change in being there anticipated has been designated "metastatic faith." There is a further point relating to the data of experience. It is illustrated in a significant way by the fact that Marx can affirm in the sentence quoted (1) that all available evidence points to a constant to be found throughout the whole range of human history as the primary causal factor in the dynamic of the historical process; and (2) in the very next breath put forward as a *scientifically grounded prediction* the view that what has always heretofore been the case without exception (class antagonisms) is soon to be abolished from the face of history (in the classless society). That *this* prediction can be made as "scientific" on the basis of *that* evidence defies belief. But equally incredible is that a substantial number of people still wish to discuss Marx's "scientific socialism"! It should by now be evident that one is here confronted with, not *science*, but *obsession*. See in relation to the foregoing, Eric Voegelin, "The Formation of the Marxian Revolutionary Idea," *Review of Politics*, XII (1950), 275–302; repr. in M. A. Fitzsimons, *et al.* (eds.), *The Image of Man* (Notre Dame: University of Notre Dame Press, 1959), 265–81; Voegelin, *Wissenschaft, Politik und Gnosis* (Munich: Kösel, 1959); Voegelin, *Israel and Revelation* (Baton Rouge: Louisiana State University Press, 1956), Vol. I of Voegelin, *Order and History* (3 vols. to date; Baton Rouge: Louisiana State University Press, 1956——), especially 450ff; also, Karl Löwith, *Meaning in History* (Chicago: University of Chicago Press; Phoenix Books, 1949), chap. 2; J. L. Talmon, *The Origins of Totalitarian Democracy* (New York: Frederick A. Praeger, Inc., 1952); Talmon *Political Messianism: The Romantic Phase* (New York: Frederick A. Praeger, Inc., 1960), especially 221–28.

God's cardinal error was in exalting freedom and the bread of heaven above everything else during the time He spent on earth as the Christ. He sought man's faith through free love and gave him only His image as a guide. The effect of this has been, in fact, to create man a rebel, and rebels can never be happy. Freedom was granted as God's greatest gift, but fifteen hundred years of history attest that it has been the bane of mankind. "Thou didst crave for free love and not the base raptures of a slave," the Inquisitor says, but "I swear, man is weaker and baser by nature than Thou hast believed him!"

(b) The devil's appreciation of man

God was warned of the true nature of man by the devil, that "wise and dread spirit, the spirit of self-destruction and non-existence," during Christ's temptation in the wilderness. The secret of human nature was made known there, but it was ignored because God would not deprive men of freedom. The promised bread of heaven can never compare with "earthly bread in the eyes of the weak, ever sinful and ignoble race of man." The "secret" and fundamental axiom of the devil is, then, that mankind worships its belly.

But this bald fact must be dressed up a bit. The devil sees that there is a universal and everlasting craving of humanity to find *"community* of worship." Whatever is to be worshipped must, however, have certain characteristics: it must be established so that there is no disputing about it and all can agree, so that all can be together in it and satisfy the pungent craving for community of worship which is the chief misery of every man singly and of all humanity generally from the beginning of time. Earthly bread fills these qualifications better than anything else. Man's greatest anxiety is to be rid of his freedom. He can dupe himeslf into surrendering it, however, only to those who are skillful enough to appease his conscience. Freedom is God-given. So those who take it from man must give him in return a stable object which will permit him to continue to believe life is worth living; otherwise, man will destroy himself. Man seeks peace and prefers even death rather than the torments of freedom of choice in the knowledge of good and evil.

Men, then, essentially are slaves incapable of free love. Their God-given freedom most often and in the generality of mankind manifests itself as self-destructive rebellion. Their implacable yearning as social beings is for a universal state so ordered as to promote free indulgence of the passions without the risk of physical or spiritual suicide. Beauty is the twin ideal of Sodom and the Madonna. As another poet has since said:

> They constantly try to escape
> From the darkness outside and within
> By dreaming of systems so perfect that
>   no one will need to be good.
> But the man that is will shadow
> The man that pretends to be.[28]

The sum of human aspiration is to have "someone to worship, someone to keep his conscience, and some means of uniting all in one unanimous and harmonious ant-heap, for the craving of universal unity is the third and last anguish of men."

In a thousand years, the Inquisitor promises, in the last stage but one in human history, freedom, free thought, and science will have led mankind into such straits and confronted them with such marvels and insoluble mysteries that the varieties of human nature will separate out of the mass and the unadjustable types will perish. The "fierce and rebellious" will destroy themselves; the "rebellious but weak" will destroy one another; and the remaining multitude, the "weak but unhappy," will surrender their freedom and ask to be saved from themselves. This last paroxysm paves the way for the rise of the ideal society of the future, an existence purged of freedom.

Even the devil's appreciation of human nature does not, however, totally disallow the individual integrity and the soul's accessibility to God. At the moment of final despair, when men unwittingly blaspheme God by saying, "*He must have meant to mock me by endowing me with freedom,*" this accusation "will make them more unhappy still, for man's nature cannot bear blasphemy, and in the

---

[28] T. S. Eliot, in "Choruses from 'The Rock'" in *Collected Poems 1909–1935* (New York: Harcourt, Brace, Inc. 1936).

end always avenges it on itself." Again, even when surviving mankind shall have become convinced that of themselves they never can be free—for they are weak, vicious, worthless, and rebellious, and shall have entrusted their total being to the ultimate society of the future—there will still arise conflicts between dictates of conscience and the instructions of those who have undertaken the ordering of their existence. By these hints the devil acknowledges that disorder in the soul will forever remain existentially troublesome and grudgingly affirms the indestructibility of the human person.

(c) The church and foundations of the new order:
apocalyptical arrogance

The old man speaks to Christ as an equal. He has seen all, understood all, and has wisely chosen for mankind. He unflinchingly states his qualifications to the Prisoner, Who listens throughout in silence, gently searching the old man's face with an expectant gaze.

> Know that I fear Thee not . . . that I too was in the wilderness, that I too have lived on roots and locusts, that I too prized the freedom with which Thou hast blessed men, that I too was striving to stand among Thy elect, the strong and powerful. . . . But I awakened and would not serve madness. I turned back and joined the ranks of those *who have corrected Thy work*. I left the proud and went back to the humble, for the happiness of the humble. What I say to Thee will come to pass, and our dominion will be built up.[29]

The Inquisitor's language is theologically precise without being pretentious and is indebted to St. Tikhon Zadonsky. The turning back from God is the reversal of conversion, in which the soul ceases to live from the spirit and begins to live with the life of the body. The passions thereby revived absorb the life of the person who spiritually dies.[30] The Inquisitor's attack is even stronger in the

---

[29] Cf. Mark 1:6.

[30] Tikhon wrote: "The human soul is a spirit created by God, and only in God, who has created it in His own image and likeness, can it find contentment and rest, peace, consolation and joy. Once separated from Him, it seeks for satisfaction among created things, and feeds itself on passions, on husks, food for pigs; but finding not its true repose, nor its true satisfaction, it dies at length of hunger. For spiritual food is a necessity to the soul." St. Tikhon, *Works,* II, 192, as quoted in Lossky, *The Mystical Theology,* 127–28.

notes: "I have only one word to say to you [Christ] that you have been disgorged from Hell and are a heretic, and that the very people who fell down before you will rake up the coals tomorrow—." [31]

(1) The church as the state   The church already has begun establishment of the new social order based upon the devil's appreciation of man. The unfailing banner of the new society is "earthly bread for all." The new morality points to a time when there will be no crime and no sin; only hunger will endanger order. We must first feed men and then ask virtue of them, the Inquisitor confides, thereby voicing the recurrent theme in radical literature: "Erst kommt das Fressen, dann kommt die Moral." [32] Submissiveness is the prime virtue of the new race of men. Another thousand years of history and the building of a new Tower of Babel lies before mankind. But in desperation, they will at last come to the church. It will feed them, complete the tower, and falsely declare everything is done in God's name.

The only effective means of controlling the consciences of the impotent rebels constituting the remainder of humanity, the Inquisitor says, is through means which Christ Himself expressly rejected: miracle, mystery, and authority. Christ thereby doomed His cause. Miracle was an especially unfortunate loss, yet He refused to prove miraculously His divinity to the whole world for all time by casting Himself down from the pinnacle of the temple during the temptation and disdained coming down from the cross as the mocker urged Him to do during the crucifixion. Yet, the Inquisitor notes, the miraculous is essential to mankind; man cannot be without it, and if he is, then he will invent miracles of his own and worship them. "When man rejects miracle he rejects God too; for man seeks not so much God as the miraculous."

(2) Joyous lies unto oblivion   The church will order man's existence

---

31 Dostoevsky, *The Notebooks for "The Brothers Karamazov,"* 78.
32 Berthold Brecht, "Dreigroschen Oper," in Brecht, *Stücke,* ed. Elizabeth Hauptmann (14 vols.; Berlin: Aufbau-Verlag, 1955–67), III; see Philip Rahv, "The Legend of the Grand Inquisitor," *Partisan Review,* XXI (1954), 261n.

on the basis of the principles miracle, mystery, and authority by persuading mankind of the truth of certain judicious lies. The essential lies are five in number, namely: *First*, the church's freedom is the same granted men by God: "We shall persuade them that they will only become free when they renounce their freedom to us and submit to us. And shall we be right or shall we be lying?" *Second*, earthly bread is the spiritual bread of life. *Third*, the church serves God and rules man in His name. *Fourth*, "it is not Love that matters, not the judgment of their hearts," but a mystery which we hold before them and in which they must blindly believe even against their consciences. *Fifth*, eternal salvation is the reward of the obedient.

(3) The "mystery" dispelled The secret of the church as state and propagator of the New Order is its alliance, not with God, but with the devil: "We are not working with Thee but with *him*—that's our mystery. It's long—eight centuries—since we have been on his side and not Thine."

By these words from the mouth of the Inquisitor a formal if impenitent confession is given of the heresy of Roman Catholicism after the Seventh Ecumenical Council (Nicaea II), held in 787—the last council accepted as genuinely ecumenical by the Eastern Orthodox Church. The iconoclastic controversy of that century and the championship of the veneration of images by St. John of Damascus, who is mentioned in Dostoevsky's notes to the Grand Inquisitor,[33] supplied part of the background for the estrangement of the Christians of the East and West which finally resulted in the Great Schism of 1054. The specifically political allusion appears to be to the revival of the Roman Empire in the West by the papacy through alliance with the Frankish Empire, the union receiving formal sanction in the coronation of Charlemagne at St. Peter's on Christmas day, 800, by Pope Leo III. The real basis for this dating in the Legend, however, is that it was reputedly by act of the emperor, Charlemagne,

---

[33] See Komarovich, *Die Urgestalt der Brüder Karamasoff*, 545; *The Notebooks for "The Brothers Karamazov,"* 74. See John of Damascus, *Writings* [*The Fount of Knowledge*], trans. Frederic H. Chase, Jr. (New York: Fathers of the Church, Inc., 1958), 160; also, Francis Dvornik, *The Ecumenical Councils* (New York: Hawthorn Books, Inc., 1961), 36–40.

that the doctrine of the Holy Trinity of the original Nicene Creed was modified by insertion of the word *filioque* (and the Son). The effect was that the West thereafter confessed that the Holy Spirit proceeded from the Father *and the Son*, rather than from the Father alone. In the view of the Eastern Orthodox Church, this revision perverted the Christianity of the West and comprised "an assault upon the innermost substance of the religion itself." [34] Done at the instance of the political sovereign, it was undeniable proof that Roman Catholicism had, indeed, become the religion of "Rome" and had succumbed to the third temptation rejected by Christ in the wilderness. The politicizing of the Roman Church, finally, may also have been seen by Dostoevsky in the innovation of the *missi dominici* and the establishment of the theocracy of the Frankish Empire, a device whereby a bishop and a count appointed by Charlemagne were utilized as the principal supervisors of financial, judicial, and clerical administration in respective districts of the Empire and were impowered to dismiss other functionaries. The Photian controversy and other aspects of the breach between the Greek East and the Latin West, the modern history of the West including the establishment and eventual collapse of the *Christianitas*, the Reformation, fragmentation of the West into contending nation-states, and the Counter Reformation all are seen by Dostoevsky as historical consequences and manifestations of the apostasy confessed by his Inquisitor. The Church of Rome took from *him* what Christ in the temptation had scorned: "Rome and the sword of Caesar, and [we] proclaimed ourselves sole rulers of the earth. . . . We have rejected Thee and followed *him*. . . . And we shall sit upon the beast, [the State, Leviathan; mankind wearied of its freedom] and raise the cup, and on it will be written *Mystery*."

(4) Negation's millennium: ecumenical abjection Millions and thousands of millions of happy subjects will be ruled by a hundred thousand who are the keepers of their consciences, their masters in the church become the state. The ruled compose a chastened man-

---

34 Benz, *The Eastern Orthodox Church*, 57.

kind who have found and know "too, too well" the value of total submission. They will be happy. They will receive their own bread from the rulers without any miracle but will be grateful to have it. They will be persuaded not to be proud and will be taught the humility befitting weak, pitiful creatures. They will be timid and fearful and will marvel and be awestricken at those who rule them with such omniscience. They will tremble before the wrath of their sovereigns. They will be quick to weep. They will be set to work, and leisure too will be organized so that it is like a child's game. Even sin will be allowed, and they will be told that every sin is expiated if it is done with the permission of the church. "Oh," the Inquisitor raptures, "they will love us for allowing them to sin!"

The rulers will be looked upon as saviors and believed to have assumed the people's sins before God. Men will have no secrets from the church. Privacy will disappear. Subjects will be allowed or forbidden to live with wives and mistresses, to have or not to have children on the basis of their record of total subservience and submission. They will carry out such decisions cheerfully. The deepest secrets of the conscience will be confessed, every problem be told, and each have an answer which this purged, abject mankind will be glad to learn and abide by. It will save them from the "great anxiety and terrible agony they endure at present in making a free decision for themselves." Dostoevsky thus characterizes in all its psychological subtlety that monstrosity of the twentieth century—the confessional state and its extravagant promises of human perfection. The primordial innocence of Eden is restored through sacrifice of freedom and the knowledge of good and evil which first constituted historical existence in the wake of the Fall. Through his own grace man redeems himself, the Inquisitor says in concert with Nietzsche.[35]

(5) The agony of the hundred thousand: suffering saviors   Only the hundred thousand who rule will be unhappy in this society, for

---

[35] "Love yourself through grace, then you are no longer in need of your God, and you can act the whole drama of Fall and Redemption to its end in yourself." Nietzsche, *Morgenröte*, sec. 79.

these alone will know good and evil and so be keepers of the Mystery. All of mankind except these few will live and die in Christ's name, in expectation of eternal blessedness and heavenly life. Ivan's blasphemy climaxes in the notes in this statement, apparently to Alyosha:

> That religion is inappropriate for the overwhelming majority of people, and therefore cannot be called the religion of love, that he had come only for . . . the chosen, for the strong, and mighty, and that those who suffer his cross will not find anything that has been promised exactly as he himself [Christ] had found nothing after his cross. (That's your) Unique Sinless One, whom you have championed. And consequently the idea of slavery, servitude, and mystery—the idea of the Roman church and perhaps even of the Masons is much more true for the happiness of people, even though based on universal deception. That's the significance of your Incomparable Sinless One.[36]

Beyond the grave, then, men will find only oblivion. "Though," the Inquisitor scornfully adds, "if there were anything in the other world it certainly would not be for such as they." Dostoevsky reminds himself in the notes, *"Those who love men in general* hate men in particular," a point enforced not only by the Inquisitor's repudiation of mankind along with God, but also by having Ivan say to Alyosha: "What am I the keeper of my brother? (Cain's answer)." The attitude is integral to the scathing characterization of the paradigmatic New Humanitarian as a hypocrite who sets out to save mankind out of "love" yet despises his fellow men as persons, even his brothers.[37]

Only the hundred thousand who rule will know mankind is being led to death. Their critical task will be to keep the slave-men happy on the way so they will not notice in which direction they are being led.

(6) The apocalyptical arrogance of megalomania But the saviors will have suffered even more than the Grand Inquisitor will say, for they cannot be oblivious, as can the devil, to transcendent truth. Therefore, the answer to the accusations against them on the last day,

---

[36] Dostoevsky, *The Notebooks for "The Brothers Karamazov,"* 82.
[37] *Ibid.,* 33, 71, 240–42.

when the final trump has sounded and Christ and His chosen appear for the Judgment, has already been thought out by the Inquisitor. He will tell the Heavenly Host that they have saved only themselves, whereas the Church has saved all, "thousands of millions of happy children who have known no sin." The hundred thousand will stand before the Judgment at the final day and challenge Him: " 'Judge us if Thou canst and darest.' Know that I fear Thee not."

The Holy Prisoner looks intently but gently at the old man as he speaks these last words. A few silent moments pass, and He suddenly comes forward and kisses the Inquisitor's withered lips. The old man shudders, opens the cell door and points: "Go, and come no more . . . come not at all, never, never." The Prisoner disappears into the darkness.

CHAPTER V

THE TEMPTATION:
TRIAL AND
APOCALYPSE

The use of Christ's temptation in the wilderness as a theme by
Dostoevsky reaches the level of "universal generalization" in the
Legend, but its literary history can be traced in his writings in many
places, particularly in the "Dream of a Ridiculous Man." (1877), in
the confession of Versilov in *A Raw Youth* (1875), and in the confession of Shatov in *The Possessed* (1871).[1] The temptation is explicitly indicated by Ivan as the chief part of the Legend; hence,

---

[1] Cf. A. S. Dolinin (ed.), in Fyodor M. Dostoevsky, *Pis'ma* (4 vols.; Moscow-
Leningrad: Academia, 1928–56), III (1934), 362. This short story appeared in the
Diary (April, 1877, ii); see Fyodor M. Dostoevsky, *The Diary of a Writer*, trans. Boris
Brasol (2 vols.; New York: Charles Scribner's Sons, 1949), II, 672–90. The return to
earth of Christ and confrontation with mankind is a theme Dostoevsky developed
already in the notes for his first great novel, *Crime and Punishment* (1866), where
the text is quite similar to portions of the Inquisitor's monologue; see Fyodor M.
Dostoevsky, *The Notebooks for "Crime and Punishment"*, ed. and trans. Edward
Wasiolek (Chicago: University of Chicago Press, 1967), 85–86, 230. The temptation
of Christ in the wilderness appears in Fyodor M. Dostoevsky, *The Notebooks for
"The Idiot"*, ed. and with an intro. by Edward Wasiolek, trans. Katherine Strelsky
(Chicago: University of Chicago Press, 1967), 106, 230, and is thoroughly explored
in Fyodor M. Dostoevsky, *The Notebooks for "A Raw Youth,"* ed. and with an
intro. by Edward Wasiolek, trans. Victor Terras (Chicago: University of Chicago
Press, 1969), 70, 148, 150, 219, 252, 449, as is also the theme of the humiliated and
rejected Christ: "they reenacted Christ's trial in England and decided that he was
guilty." *Ibid.*, 251; cf. 246, 367.

any interpretation must be attentive in the utmost degree to its meaning and symbolism. Dostoevsky's intentions, insofar as these can be penetrated, will be the foundation of the interpretation.[2] Pertinent passages found elsewhere in Dostoevsky are, however, also to be utilized. The biblical account of the temptation (especially in the Gospel According to St. Matthew) may readily be accepted as Dostoevsky's primary source for this episode, and reliance is placed upon the Bible as a principal source of the substance of the Legend.

1. DOSTOEVSKY AND SOLOVYOV

The question of the relationship of the Legend to Solovyov's *Lectures on Godmanhood* (*Chtenie o Bogochelovechestve*) must be clarified at the outset. No reader of both Solovyov's Lecture XI–XII and of Dostoevsky's Legend can fail to perceive the close and illuminating connection of the two works. The intimate friendship between the authors of these works in the period from 1873 until Dostoevsky's death in 1881 and their known intellectual and spiritual affinity warrant a keen interest in the final lecture as a discursive theoretical elaboration of the central passage of the Legend. That Dostoevsky himself is known to have attended Solovyov's lectures in the spring of 1878, however, raises the question of the relationship between the

---

2 The significance of the temptation to the Legend has not been seriously explored in the critical literature so far as I know. Some attention is paid it in the recent study by Roger L. Cox, *Between Earth and Heaven: Shakespeare, Dostoevsky, and the Meaning of Christian Tragedy* (New York: Holt, Rinehart & Winston, Inc., 1969), chap. 9.

We speak of Dostoevsky's "intentions" as controlling because his mastery of both the material and his craft was such that there is very little "intentional fallacy" at work in his pages: as complex and varied as is the subject matter of the Legend or of *The Brothers Karamazov*, it was precisely Dostoevsky's genius to have intended it *all*. Cf. a similar judgment in E. J. Simmons, *Introduction to Russian Realism* (Bloomington: Indiana University Press, 1965), 111, 131–32; also Edward Wasiolek in the Introduction to Dostoevsky, *The Notebooks for "The Brothers Karamazov,"* ed. and trans. Edward Wasiolek (Chicago: University of Chicago Press, 1971), 2, 13, 18. For a discussion of the "intentional fallacy" see W. K. Wimsatt, Jr., *The Verbal Icon: Studies in the Meaning of Poetry* (Lexington: University of Kentucky Press, 1954), 3ff; cf. Robert L. Belknap, *The Structure of "The Brothers Karamazov,"* Slavistic Printings and Reprintings, LXXII, ed. C. H. van Schooneveld (The Hague and Paris: Mouton, 1967): "A work completely free of its author's intent is called delirium. A work with no identity beyond his intent is called propaganda. The interplay's the thing (16; cf., 110)." As a great artist, Dostoevsky also intended the "interplay."

significance of the temptation in the Legend and its exposition in the lecture.

More than one commentator has spoken of Solovyov's influence on the work of Dostoevsky. At least one writer, Vladimir Szylkarski, has asserted that Dostoevsky gained his conception of the Roman Catholic church's succumbing to the three temptations in the course of history from Solovyov's presentation in the final lecture of the series. *"Both* friends perfectly see the transfer" of the temptations to the historical work of the Catholic church, "but the younger man does this *before* the older one." Both agree that Rome and the West manifest the "power of evil" and that the

> light of the pure faith burns only in the East, that the Russian people must therefore take care that this Holy Light, which alone can bring deliverance and salvation to mankind, is not extinguished. When one keeps firmly in mind this fundamental conviction which the youthful Solovyov developed with unsurpassed philosophical and artistic conceptual power, he then has in his hand the key to Dostoevsky's most famous creation, his "Grand Inquisitor." [3]

Valuable as the Solovyov exposition undoubtedly is for the student of the Legend, Szylkarski's view is insupportable. Apart from the consideration of Dostoevsky's interest in the temptation years before his acquaintance with Solovyov and his longtime opinion of Roman Catholicism as evil and the West as corrupt, there is a decisive fact: Solovyov's published Lecture XI–XII and the oral presentation "have nothing in common" with one another.[4] The lectures as given in 1878 had a distinctly eschatological and apocalyptical tone, "including the theme of the *'apocatastasis ton panton'* and universal

---

[3] Vladimir Szylkarski, "Messianismus und Apokalyptik bei Dostojewskij und Solowjew: ein Nachwort" in Antanas Maceina, *Der Grossinquisitor: Geschichtsphilosophische Deutung der Legende Dostojewskijs* (Heidelberg: Kerle, 1952), 300–301.

[4] The fact is noted by Georges Florovsky, "Reason and Faith in the Philosophy of Solovyov," in Ernest J. Simmons (ed.), *Continuity and Change in Russian and Soviet Thought* (Cambridge: Harvard University Press, 1955), 285n. Dostoevsky's convictions about Roman Catholicism and the West find expression, for example, in his writings of 1862, *Winter Notes on Summer Impressions* (New York: Criterion Books, Inc., 1955). See chap. 5, "Baal," the meaning of the expression (p. 91), the allusions to the Catholics (pp. 97, 131).

salvation." The program for the two final lectures, as advertised in the *Pravoslavnoe obozrenie*, was as follows: "XI—The Church as a Divine-human organism or the Body of Christ. The Church, visible and invisible. The growth of man 'into the fullness of the stature of Christ.' XII—The Second Coming of Christ and the Resurrection of the dead (the redemption of restitution of the world of nature). The Kingdom of the Holy Spirit and the full revelation of the Godman-hood." [5] The printed version of the lectures was composed only in 1881—well after publication of the Legend, in fact after Dostoevsky's death. Solovyov, in a letter to his editor which accompanied the revised version, expressed his satisfaction with the manuscript as "the best of all my writings up to this time" and asked that it be published "not divided" in the next number of the magazine. He continued: "what I read three years ago about 'final things,' I decided not even to mention, since this would carry too far." [6] N. N. Strakhov attended the final lecture and summarized it in a letter to Tolstoy dated April 9, 1878; no mention is here made either of the theme of the temptation or of the Roman Catholic church:

This lecture was very effective. With great heat he spoke a few words against [the doctrine of Hell],[7] the dogma of everlasting torment. Doubtless he was ready to preach many other heresies, but evidently lost his courage, and chose this dogma in order to show his intentions fully and clearly. Considering now all of his lectures, I see that he wished to make a synthesis of East and West, to mix in one system atomism, Darwinism, pantheism, Christianity, *etc.* To give all of his positions is a good prob-

---

5 Quoted from Florovsky, "Reason and Faith in the Philosophy of Solovyov," 285. On the subject of *apokatastasis* (cf. Acts 3:21) or the transformation of the world to restore "the Garden of Eden" in Orthodox thought, *see* Jon Gregerson, *The Transfigured Cosmos: Four Essays in Eastern Orthodox Christianity* (New York: Frederick Ungar Publ. Co., 1960), 72ff.

6 Vladimir S. Solovyov to P. A. Preobrazensky, Letter No. 4, 1881, between April and September, in Vladimir S. Solovyov, *Pis'ma*, [Vol. IV, Supplement] ed. E. L. Radlova (St. Petersburg: Izdatel'stvo Vremia, 1923), 233.

7 Ellipsis as in the published version of Strakhov's letter. That the scandal here implied pertained to the treatment of the doctrine of hell is clear from Solovyov's letter to Olga A. Novikov some six weeks later which says in part: "One person said of me 'Here is this Nihilist.' And another person, meeting me on Nevskii, solemnly reported to me through 'astonished Petrograd,' that to deny eternal hell fire is much worse than to deny the existence of God." Letter No. 8 from Vladimir S. Solovyov to Olga A. Novikov, May 22, 1878, in Solovyov, *Pis'ma*, IV, 163.

lem, but, firstly, it cannot be done, and, secondly, you don't see even a shadow of the original meaning which you hope to be able to do. The Divinity, starting basically, reaches its full realization in man. Now we are found in the process of this realization; humanity has left its basic principles, but must presently return to them, to be reconciled with God, then He will be fully realized—and God will be all-in-all (Ap. Pavel). Sin and matter—necessary conditions of this process. To leave [The result is] pantheism completely similar to Hegel (*Gegelevsky*), only with the Second Coming in front. Kabbala, gnosticism, and mysticism—play their part here. But all of this was scattered like smoke, and not one idea from the whole lecture stayed with me.[8]

Szylkarski's contention rests squarely on a *post hoc* argument, which is dubious ground enough without the clear implication of Strakhov's letter: the key insights of the published lecture did not even find mention in the oral presentation, the only version known to Dostoevsky.

2. APOCALYPSE AND HISTORY

The significance of the temptation as incorporated in the Legend is, at once, diagnostic, speculative, and apocalyptic. Moreover, it cuts two ways: it is at once blasphemy and hosanna, negation and affirmation, rebellion and vindication of the faith.

At the core of the presentation is the diagnostic analysis of evil as manifested in spiritual disorder and social corruption done in terms of the Christian conception of sin. Specifically pointed toward the rationalist-gnostic *knower* and his assertion of satanic "truth," the emphasis is on sin as error or ignorance about what ought to be known (*agnoematon;* Heb. 9:7). The characterization of Ivan as one for whom, hypothetically, "all things are lawful" finds mythopoetic projection through an ostensible creation of his diseased psyche: the blatantly sinful and rebellious Grand Inquisitor. The formulation in the First Epistle of John (I John 3:4) is fundamental: "Everyone that practices sin also lawlessness practices; and sin is lawlessness (*hamartia estin he anomia*)." The profundity of Ivan's position is to be noticed. His watchword as man-god, "All things are lawful,"

[8] Letter No. 76, N. N. Strakhov to L. N. Tolstoy, April 9, 1878, in Vladimir G. Chertkov and Nikolai N. Gusev (eds.), *Tolstoi i o Tolstom: Novye Materialy* (2 vols.; Moscow, 1924), II, 160–61.

always occurs in quotation marks for the good reason that it *is* a quotation. John of Damascus, in *The Fount of Knowledge*, identifies barbarism as the primordial heresy, the first of 103 heresies which he enumerates:

> The parents and archetypes of all heresies are four in number, namely: (1) Barbarism; (2) Scythism; (3) Hellenism; (4) Judaism. Out of these came all the rest.
>
> 1. *Barbarism* is that which prevailed from the days of Adam down through ten generations to the time of Noah. It is called barbarism because of the fact that in those times men had no ruling authority or mutual accord, but every man was independent and a law unto himself after the dictates of his own will.[9]

The scriptural source (not cited by John) yields the phrase verbatim. It is taken from Paul in I Corinthians 6:12, where it occurs twice (to be twice more repeated in I Cor. 10:23): *Panta moi exestin* ("Everything is for me permissible or lawful"). The phrase is used polemically by Paul as the presumed assertion of a certain faction in the church at Corinth which has misunderstood the meaning of Christian freedom and perverted it. Indeed, the man in Christ *is* in truth and is freed; all things are lawful but not expedient and none tyrannizes him. But this is precisely spiritual freedom: a release from the bondage of the passions and of the world, on one hand, and a free access into infinite perfections of life in the Holy Spirit, on the other hand (cf. Gal. 5:13, 16). Hence, the reproof fits Ivan well. For he understands that sanctification carries with it unlimited freedom, but he persists in his failure to acknowledge this uncircumscribed freedom of the spirit attuned to divine Truth to be perverted into diabolical evil when it becomes disoriented toward self-gratification and idolatry. By this perversion freedom becomes license and sin in the technically exact meaning of the term, foundation of a heretical doctrine whose performance plunges human existence back into antediluvian barbarism.

But from Ivan's characterization it is clear that spiritual obtuseness cannot be the complete explanation. After all, he has written a

---

9 John of Damascus, *Writings* [*The Fount of Knowledge*], trans. Frederic H. Chase, Jr. (New York: Fathers of the Church, Inc., 1958), 111.

treatise on church law, says he believes in God but rejects the eternal harmony, and his Inquisitor states he is in league with Satan. The only available existential alternative is a fall from faith into heretical gnosis. The nihilistic streak in Ivan is a counterpart of his knowledge that the Christian God is not really the good God, rather man is the God of history whose true communion is with the traditional Satan. This transfiguring knowledge ranks Ivan with the gnostic pneumatics, for whom all things are lawful.[10] It carries with it the obligation to destroy the moral and metaphysical order of the world because the world is evil and imprisons the spirit. This shifting back and forth among the various levels of symbolism is one reason for the obscurity of Ivan's position, a second reason being Ivan's agonizing uncertainties as to where truth lies. Yet, the cardinal point must be made crystal clear because it supplies the key to the modern political mind: to the apocalyptical gnostic-ideologue the inevitable prelude to freedom and salvation is nihilistic destruction of the world.[11] Destruction is therefore undertaken as a high religious calling, an ineluctable mission, the prelude to justice and perfect happiness.

The sweeping conception of sin as a combined missing of the mark (*hamartia*), whatever the cause, and an attendant contemptuous lawlessness, meaning thought and action contrary to the divine Law (*anomia*),[12] prepares the way for the definition of the devil's truth

---

[10] Cf. Hans Jonas, *The Gnostic Religion: The Message of the Alien God and the Beginnings of Christianity* (2nd ed., rev.; Boston: Beacon Press, 1963), 46, 320ff. The state of mind of those for whom "all things are lawful" is illustrated by the gnostic Messalian sect: "The Messalians . . . held that strict asceticism was necessary for the ordinary 'believers,' while free indulgence in sexual intercourse was a prerogative of those who had succeeded in driving out the demon from within them and who were thus perfect." Dmitri Obolensky, *The Bogomils: A Study in Balkan Neo-Manichaeism* (Cambridge: Cambridge University Press, 1948), 129n. The Messalians' alternative names were *Satanists* and *Euchites*, and John of Damascus devotes considerable attention to them; cf. *The Fount of Knowledge*, 131–37. On the Messalian relationship to the Khlysty, see Karl K. Grass, *Die russischen Sekten* (1907–14; 2 vols.; repr. ed.; Leipzig: Zentral-Antiquariat, 1966), I, 491, 635, 644–48.

[11] That is, "human existence"—the primary meaning of *world* in the English language. Cf. Eric Voegelin, "World-Empire and the Unity of Mankind," *International Affairs*, XXXVIII (1962), 177ff.

[12] Cf. George R. Berry, "New Testament Synonyms," in Berry, *A New Greek-English Lexicon to the New Testament* (Chicago: Wilcox and Follett, 1948), sec. 2, pp. 117–18.

by a careful correlation of the three "truths" of the temptation with the cardinal triad of worldly concupiscence. This triad is articulated as the three "anguishes" of man in the psychology of the Inquisitor. The trilogy of faiths and triad of anguishes are coordinate in the Legend and may be identified with the scriptural formulation of I John 2:16: (1) the lust of the flesh (*epithymia tes sarkos*); (2) the lust of the eyes or mind (*epithymia ton ophthalmon*); and, (3) the empty, swaggering, insolent assurance (pride) of life (*alazoneia tou Biou*).[13]

Indeed, the symbolism of *threeness* pervades the Legend.[14] Evocative of the Holy Trinity in its positive aspect, as symbolic of negation it represents the "trinity of evil" [15] of the Apocalypse: the dragon, the beast, and the false prophet (Rev. 20:13). The intricacy of the symbolism can be seen by unravelling its principal threads. The temptations are three: (1) Turn these stones into bread; (2) Cast Thyself down from the pinnacle of the temple; and (3) Worship Satan and receive dominion over the kingdoms of the earth. The categories of temptation are threefold, as just indicated. The rejection of the temptations by Christ secures the constitutive forces

---

13 Following Thayer, the meaning is *life* in extension. Cf. Joseph H. Thayer, *A Greek-Lexicon of the New Testament: Being Grimm's Wilke's Clavis Novi Testamenti*, translated, revised, and enlarged (corrected ed.; New York: American Book Company, 1889), 102. The phrase according to more recent authority, however, is understood to mean *pride in one's possessions*. Cf. Walter Bauer, *Greek-English Lexicon of the New Testament and Other Early Christian Literature*, ed. and trans. by W. F. Arndt and F. Wilbur Gingrich (Chicago: University of Chicago Press; Cambridge: Cambridge University Press, 1957), 34. For the meaning of the three lusts in Western spirituality, see St. Augustine, *Confessions*, bk. 10, chaps. 31–41.

14 The symbolism of threeness in *The Brothers Karamazov* has been noticed by Harry Slochower, who finds it the "leading motif." Cf. Slochower, "Incest in 'The Brothers Karamazov,'" in Hendrik M. Ruitenbeek (ed.), *Psychoanalysis and Literature* (New York: E. P. Dutton & Co., 1964), 318n8: "The number 3 is a leading motif in *The Brothers Karamazov* as it is in the Oedipus dramas, the *Divine Comedy, Don Quixote, Faust*, and other mythopoesis. In Dostoevsky's novel, it has a diabolic sign (the violence of the 3 brothers, the abandonment of Mitia when he was 3 years old, the 3,000 rubles, the 3 blows with which Smerdyakov kills Fyodor, Ivan's 3 interviews with Smerdyakov, and the devil's 3 visits with Ivan); and its resurrectory sign, his [*i.e.* Dmitri's] 3 ordeals, his arrest on the 3rd day of his struggle to save himself." Cf. Belknap, *The Structure of "The Brothers Karamazov,"* 55.

15 N. Turner, "Revelation," in Matthew Black and R. H. Rowley (eds.), *Peake's Commentary on the Bible* (London: Thomas Nelson & Sons, 1962), 1057.

which order the creation in accord with the threeness of the New Dispensation: (1) the freedom of the will (hope); (2) the free verdict of the heart (faith); and (3) the power of the Spirit (love). The powers or forces proffered in the temptation and accepted by the Inquisitor as the Paraclete of the Antichrist are three: (1) the miracle of earthly bread; (2) the mystery of salved conscience; and (3) the authority of the sword of Caesar. By implication, these powers are pointed toward the trichotomy of *human nature*: (1) body or life force (*soma* or *bios*); (2) soul (*psyche*); and (3) spirit or mind (*pneuma, nous*).[16] The typology of human characters under the aspect of rebellious man is threefold: (1) the fierce and rebellious; (2) the rebellious but weak; and (3) the weak and unhappy: the human material for the building of the future harmony. The anguishes of man are three: (1) the desire for someone to worship; (2) the desire for someone to keep his conscience; and (3) the craving for universal unity or a universal state. The institutional satisfaction of these lusts is represented by three symbols: (1) the Tower of Babel—the ideal society of the revolutionary wishing to insure without God the happiness of mankind: the symbol of idolatry; (2) the Crystal Palace—society illumined from within by the power of human reason but opaque to the light of faith which is rejected, together with tradition, as irrational mystery: rationalism, symbol of the pride of mind;[17] and (3) the Ant Heap—the future ecumenical society of man devoid of humanity and reduced to the level of an insect in the name of humanitarianism: the symbol of the end of secular history.[18] There is finally the speculative division of all history into three ages, with

---

[16] Cf. Vladimir Solovyov, *Lectures on Godmanhood*, trans. Peter Zouboff, (London: Dennis Dobson, 1948), 194. Also, Vladimir Lossky, *The Mystical Theology of the Eastern Church* (London: James Clarke & Co., 1957), 127–28, where Tikhon Zadonsky is quoted.

[17] Not made explicit in the Legend, but implied. Cf. Henri de Lubac, *The Drama of Atheist Humanism*, trans. E. M. Riley (London: Sheed & Ward, 1949), 188.

[18] The term probably derives from Alexander I. Herzen, *From the Other Shore and The Russian People and Socialism, an Open Letter to Jules Michelet*, trans. Richard Wollheim, with an intro. by Isaiah Berlin (New York: George Braziller, Inc., 1956). See Fyodor M. Dostoevsky, *Notes From Underground*, ed., trans., and with an intro. by Ralph E. Matlaw (New York: E. P. Dutton & Co., 1960); also Joseph Frank, "Nihilism and *Notes from Underground*," Sewanee Review, LXIX (1961), 17.

emphasis upon the third as something of a diabolical obversion of
Dostoevsky's dream of the free universal theocracy of Moscow the
Third Rome. The ages in the Legend are (1) the Age of the Father,
expressed as that of the "Ancient Law"—that is, up to the advent of
Christ; (2) the Age of the Son and of faith, which begins with "suffering in freedom" and traverses a course of twenty-five hundred years
marked by rejection, denial, rebellion, and collapse of authority ending in "cannibalism," the "barbarism" of John of Damascus; and (3)
the final Age of the Spirit and of peace and happiness attained
through the universal dominion of the great seducer, the Antichrist,
with whom the Inquisitor identifies himself. While not calculated
in time, this epoch is said to include "thousands of millions of babes"
who have "known no sin," and the imagery suggests the completion
of the cycle bringing mankind to a new infancy, reminiscent of
Nietzschean nihilism and the eternal return. Outside of this cycle,
beyond the third age, lies the *parousia* of Christ in victory and the
Last Judgment at the end of history conceived teleologically as
fulfillment.

The elaborate symbolism of threeness can be summarized and to
a degree coordinated in tabular form in figure 2.

The assertion that "in those three questions" of the temptation
"the whole subsequent history of mankind is, as it were, brought
together into one whole, and foretold, and in them are united all
the unsolved historical contradictions of human nature" indicates
the dual thrust of the temptation in the Legend in the dimensions
of prophecy and metaphysics. The periodization of history, therefore, as well as the unfolding of the nature of man in time, properly
command further attention. The philosophical anthropology of Dostoevsky requires detailed investigation, therefore this topic will be
set aside for the moment in order first to consider the theory of
history.

George Fedotov remarked that the surge of lay religion in the
seventies was "an exodus, if not into the Thebaid, at least into the
Montanist Phrygia." [19] Dostoevsky himself is regarded by some to

---

19 E. Bogdanov (G. P. Fedotov), "Tragediia intelligentsii," *Versty*, no. 2 (Paris,
1927), 171ff. Quoted by Florovsky, in Simmons (ed.), *Continuity and Change*, 289.

FIGURE 2

Table of *Threeness* in the Legend

	(Desires)	*(Anguishes)*	*(Powers & dominions)*
First temptation	Lust of the flesh	Desire for someone to worship	Bread (*soma*)=body (*bios*)=life force
Second temptation	Lust of the eyes	Desire for someone to keep conscience	Conscience (*psyche*)=soul
Third temptation	Pride of life	Desire for universal harmony	Sword *pneuma*=spirit *nous*=reason, mind

or (alternatively)
1. Sensuality
2. Pride
3. Ambition

(*continued*):

(Powers on principle)	*(Symbols)*	*(Ideologies)*	*(True virtues)*	*(Pseudo-virtues)*
Miracle	Tower of Babel	Socialism	Hope	Certainty
Mystery	Crystal Palace	Rationalism	Faith	Peace & happiness
Authority	Ant Heap	Imperialism	Love	Coercion

(*continued*):

(Human typology)	*(Trinitarian periodization)*	*(Forces in the soul)*
Fierce and rebellious	Age of the Father: Law	Freedom of the will
Rebellious but weak	Age of the Son: Faith	Free verdict of the heart
Weak and unhappy	Age of the Spirit: Bliss	Power of the Spirit by Grace

have played a role as leader of this exodus. Solovyov hailed him as the prophet of the new "universal and social" religion of the future in his *Tri rechi v pamyat' Dostoevskogo*.[20] The Legend, however, caricatures this view. The trinitarian eschatology of the three ages of Montanus is made, not of the progress of spiritual fulfillment which Dostoevsky apparently hoped for and anticipated in numerous places in his writing, but rather of just the opposite: a process of withering and spiritual desiccation climaxing in the secular triumph of the dread spirit of negation and destruction. The eloquence and analytical acumen of the Inquisitor notwithstanding, Christ wins the debate in the Legend, and the reader sees that the intellectual and historical ascendancy of the former entails a tragedy of catastrophic proportions for civilization, mankind, and truth itself. This insight is not communicated discursively but by the immediate impression of the artistic work itself upon the mind as the truth of the "heart" in triumph over the truth of the "head," the conflict between which Dostoevsky rightly viewed as the foundation of the modern existential dilemma, one with which twentieth century man still agonizes and seems to understand little better than did Ivan.

A question of moment for the interpretation of Dostoevsky is reached at this juncture. Is the Legend the vehicle of Dostoevsky's esoteric and true view, one which repudiates through parody and caricature the gnostic, apocalyptical eschatology of the redivinization of history,[21] the spiritual perfection of man in time in a Third Age of the Spirit? While there are undeniable difficulties, the internal evidence of the Legend supports an affirmative answer to this question. Moreover, such an interpretation appears to be reconcilable with the paradox of the dominance of the view of anticipated spiritual fulfillment in time in Dostoevsky's publicist writing. As background the analysis requires clarification of what has been called the "gnostic" viewpoint and its sources in three distinct intellectual currents of Russian thought. These are, first, the pervasive sectarian

---

20 *Ibid.*
21 For the concept of redivinization and the general problem under consideration, see Eric Voegelin, *The New Science of Politics: An Introduction* (Chicago: University of Chicago Press, 1952), 107–89.

movements which gained particular prominence from the middle of the seventeenth century onward and which were especially linked with Western gnosticism by the Bulgarian Bogomils; second, the tradition of Moscow as the continuator of the ecumenical empire of the Third Rome, which had its beginnings at end of the fifteenth century; and, third, revival of the second century Montanist doctrine of the Three Ages by Joachim of Flora in the twelfth century in the West and its complex ramification throughout the later Middle Ages into the modern period.[22] Since the sectarian movements have been of prominent concern throughout this study and the salient aspects of the Third Rome idea are now well known,[23] it is mainly the periodization of history according to the Montanist-Joachitic doctrine that requires brief clarification.

Montanus divided history into the Three Ages of Old Testament Revelation, New Testament Revelation, and the Age of the Church of the Holy Spirit. The Third Age was the culminating one which Montanus and his prophets were themselves to realize: they were *pneumatikoi*, in contradistinction to the old Christians who were called *psychikoi*.[24] Eusebius attributed to Montanus claim to the title of *Paracletos*, because he and his prophetesses Priscilla and Maximilla proclaimed new prophecy which superseded the old revelation of Christ.[25] Joachim of Flora, a leading churchman of the

---

[22] *Ibid.*, 114–15. Dostoevsky reflects a knowledge of the Montanist-Joachitic periodization of history into three stages in the notes; see Dostoevsky, *The Notebooks for "A Raw Youth,"* 172; on gnosticism and sects generally, cf. *ibid.*, 401, 454, 465, 467, 493. Cf. W. Beveridge, "Joachimites," in James Hastings (ed.), *Hastings' Encyclopedia of Religion and Ethics* (12 vols.; New York: Charles Scribner's Sons, 1928) VII, 566–67, hereinafter cited as *Hastings' Encyclopedia;* Hans Kohn, "Dostoevsky and Danielevsky: Nationalist Messianism," in Simmons (ed.), *Continuity and Change,* 504; Karl Löwith, *Meaning in History* (Chicago: University of Chicago Press; Phoenix Books, 1949), chap. 8: "Joachim"; and app. 1: "Modern Transfigurations of Joachism." On Joachism in Russia, see chap. 1, sec. 3, *above;* also, Michael Cherniavsky, *Tsar and People: Studies in Russian Myths* (New Haven: Yale University Press, 1961), 196n.

[23] Cf. Hildegaard Schaeder, *Moskau—Das Dritte Rom: Studien zur Geschichte der politischen Theorien in der slavischen Welt* (1929; repr. 2nd ed.; Darmstadt: Gentner, 1957); Nicholas Zernov, *Moscow the Third Rome* (London: S.P.C.K. Press, 1937); S. V. Utechin, *Russian Political Thought: A Concise History* (New York: Frederick A. Praeger, Inc., 1963), chap. 2; Cherniavsky, *Tsar and People.*

[24] See H. J. Lawler, "Montanism," *Hastings' Encyclopedia,* VIII, 828ff.

[25] Cf. John 14:12–18.

twelfth century, a contemporary of St. Francis of Assisi, influential with Richard of England and Philip of France and, later, with such early leaders of the Reformation as Wycliffe and Hus, revived the Montanist speculation, dividing history into the Age of the Father (ending with Zacharias, father of John the Baptist), the Age of the Son, and the Age of the Holy Spirit which he prophesied would commence in 1260. He was preoccupied with the Third Age of the Eternal Gospel, when men no longer are fettered by the letter but rather live a perfected monasticism of pure contemplation.

> The three ages were characterized as intelligible increases of spiritual fulfillment. The first age unfolded the life of the layman; the second age brought the active contemplative life of the priest; the third age would bring the perfect spiritual life of the monk. From the comparison of structures it appeared that each age opened with a trinity of leading figures, that is, with two precursors, followed by the leader of the age himself. . . . The leader of the first age was Abraham; the leader of the second age was Christ; and Joachim predicted that by 1260 there would appear the *Dux e Babylone*, the leader of the third age. . . . In his trinitarian eschatology Joachim created the aggregate of symbols which govern the self-interpretation of modern political society to this day.

These symbols are four in number: (1) the sequence of Three Historic Ages which climaxes in the third age or realm and can be perceived in the humanistic historiography, in Turgot, Comte, Hegel, and Marx; (2) the Leader, ranging in manifestation from the Franciscan conviction that St. Francis was the *Dux* of the Third Age and Dante's speculations, through the *homines novi* of the later Middle Ages to the supermen of Condorcet, Comte, Marx, Nietzsche, and the "leaders" of the twentieth century; (3) the Prophet, sometimes absorbed into the Leader, through whom the intelligible course of history becomes known—either by direct revelation or by speculative gnosis; in the modern period, with increasing secularization, the prophet is succeeded by the intellectual; and (4) the Brotherhood of Autonomous Persons. With respect to the fourth symbol, Voegelin writes:

> The third age of Joachim, by virtue of its new descent of the spirit, will

transform men into members of the new realm without sacramental mediation of grace. In the third age the church will cease to exist because the charismatic gifts that are necessary for the perfect life will reach men without administration of sacraments. While Joachim himself conceived the new age concretely as an order of monks, the idea of a community of the spiritually perfect who can live together without institutional authority was formulated on principle. The idea was capable of infinite variations. It can be traced in various degrees of purity in medieval and Renaissance sects, as well as in the Puritan churches of the saints; in its secularized form it has become a formidable component in the contemporary democratic creed; and it is the dynamic core in the Marxian mysticism of the realm of freedom and the withering-away of the state.[26]

The political and religious significance of the several forms of gnosticism for Russian thought can scarcely be overstated. While the ancient gnosis as mediated through the sects generally was characterized by the thirst for perfection and radical transformation of evil existence in both personal and cosmic dimensions, the modern gnosis of Joachim as presented in his ideological successors of the nineteenth century (as well as, to at least a degree, the Third Rome symbolism of the court theologians) transformed gnostic doctrine into the speculative reconstruction of the process of history promising transfiguration of the world in time. Gnosis, or a secret knowledge, replaces faith and noetic, or intuitive, reason as the faculty for apprehending ultimate truth and first principles; and the faith symbolisms of Christianity are diverted from their transcendental signification, to be reinterpreted as expressive of the immanent truth of historically unfolding reality, a procedure noticed earlier in the young Marx. A major result of the immanentization of existence is the charging of politics with the same burning ultimacy formerly reserved (in both Christianity and ancient gnosticism) for things transcendent, thereby giving rise to the apocalytpic messianism which was already observed by Tocqueville and which Voegelin and Talmon have shown to be the characteristic mark of modern totalitarian politics and the ideological doctrines animating it. Through the process of Westernization, as this rapidly occurred

---

[26] Voegelin, *The New Science of Politics*, 111, 112–13.

from the time of the French Revolution onward, Russia was penetrated by modern gnosticism in the sense just defined.

The difficulty of the problem before us with respect to Dostoevsky lies in the fact that the Third Rome idea of Russian Orthodoxy in its purely contemplative aspect (as contrasted with the messianic element from which it can be analytically distinguished) entailed a parallel speculation on the progress of history toward spiritual perfection. Nicholas Zernov presents the matter as follows:

> The Russians accepted the challenge of responsibility predicted by [Filofei of Pskov in his letter of 1510 to Basil III, Grand Duke of Moscow, which evokes the Third Rome idea] but their interpretation of the essence of Orthodoxy differed considerably from that of Byzantium. The first Rome bequeathed to Christendom law, order and discipline, and proclaimed the universality of the Church. The old Rome represented the paternal authority of the Father. The second Rome—Constantinople —offered intellectual leadership. It had done much to formulate creeds and combat heresies. Its function was appropriate to the Logos, the second person of the Holy Trinity. The Third Rome, Moscow, expressed the conviction that the entire corporate life of a nation should be inspired by the Holy Spirit. . . . In that art of Christian conduct described by the Russians as *bitovoe blagochestie* (the piety of daily life) the Muscovites were unrivalled. Orthodoxy, etymologically understood as "True Glory" (*Pravoslavie*), permeated their whole culture. The Russians achieved a remarkable spiritual unity. Tsar and boyars, merchants and peasants, all were members of the same Orthodox community, speaking the same language, sharing the same ideal, observing the same pattern of behaviour and completely understanding each other. Their inspiration came from their belief in the Incarnation, confirmed by the drama of the Eucharist, performed on each feast day by the entire nation. The parish church was the Russians' university, their concert hall, their art gallery, and above all the holy place, which reminded them that this world, in spite of its imperfections, was the temple of the Holy Spirit, and that man's vocation was to work for its transfiguration. The bright cupolas of the Russian church adorned with golden crosses, the innumerable icons depicting the triumphant saints, the joy of the Easter celebrations, all these typical manifestations of Russian Christianity eloquently declared the determination of the Russian people to sanctify their national life and uplift it to holiness and brotherly love.

In another passage, the same author writes, "Dostoevsky has been recognized as the foremost Christian thinker of Russia." [27]

If Zernov's authority is accepted, then the question assumes much larger proportions than assessment of the meaning of a chapter in a novel or even of the specific character of the religious experience of a single mystic and artist: the question of Dostoevsky implicitly raises the truly formidable question of the whole of Russian Orthodox Christianity. But it is ambitious enough here to address the smaller issue; and the decision in that respect can be only that, in its spiritual essence, the Christianity of Dostoevsky is unimpeachably pure. Even one who might have been expected to find fault with the contours of his faith, the Jesuit philosopher, Henri de Lubac, arrives at the same judgment: Dostoevsky's "Christianity is genuine; it is . . . the Christianity of the Gospel. . . . He saw the light of Christ." As a prophet, Dostoevsky "gives us a type of truth whose significance is not exhaustible by any of its manifestations in history. . . . To earthly experience he will oppose the experience of eternity. . . . he does not confuse nationalism, even of a mystical and spiritual type, with faith." And, lastly, with respect to Dostoevsky's intent, Lubac writes: "He could not do otherwise than proceed by way of indirect suggestion. For what he had set out to do was to take us as far as the world of the spirit." [28] The difficulty of the overall problem has been well expressed by Walter Nigg: "Dostoevsky certainly makes too little clear that his pathos, with which he awaits salvation through the Russian people, was only separated by a thin line from the narrowest chauvinism." [29] The point for immediate concern is that this thin line does, in fact, *exist* and that in the Legend, more perfectly than anywhere else in his writings, he has traced it in a way which none of his interpreters ever should forget.

The matter can be summarized as follows. Dostoevsky's religious

---

[27] Nicholas Zernov, *Eastern Christendom: A Study of the Origin and Development of the Eastern Orthodox Church* (New York: G. P. Putnam's Sons, 1961), 141, 199.

[28] Lubac, *Drama of Atheist Humanism*, 187, 201, 215, 230, 233.

[29] Walter Nigg, *Religiöse Denker* (Zurich: Büchergilde Gutenberg, 1948), chap. 2, as quoted in Ernst Benz, "Imperialismus der Liebe oder Imperialismus der Macht? Dostojewskij und die russische Politik," *Die Zeitschrift für Religions- und Geistesgeschichte*, V (1953), 37.

consciousness is inextricably bound up with the profoundest stream of Russian Orthodox contemplative experience and thought and, in a unique way, constitutes a sublime expression of this Christian tradition. To impute gnosticism or some other derailment to the central elements of Dostoevsky's mysticism would be by implication to impute it to a main current of contemporary Russian Orthodoxy. These elements come to focus in the person of the Holy Prisoner in the Legend and serve as the background for the monologue of the Inquisitor which, in this way (by relief, as it were), reduces to absurdity by parody and caricature the ambition of the modern gnostic to perfect man and secure unfailing earthly happiness. The Legend is a rare exaltation of man as created with indestructible freedom in the Divine Image. It presents a powerful affirmation of the inviolable ontological structure of the order of being as understood in the Christian tradition. It is at the same time also one of literature's most telling critiques and condemnations of authoritarianism, whose argument cuts equally against the abuse of authority by a Torquemada, a Marat, or a Stalin—or by those who in 1682 burned at the stake the Archpriest Avvakum.

In short, although the relation of the Legend to his exoteric writings on the subject of power remains to be discussed, it is clear that the critique of power and of the propagation of Christian truth through force is too brilliant, exhaustive, and passionate in the Legend for any other expression on the subject of a contradictory kind ever to stand against it and be understood as Dostoevsky's real conviction. The question of indubitably gnostic elements in Dostoevsky is resolved, therefore, by acknowledging the presence, in a variety of complex ways, of these factors especially in the Inquisitor's "synthesis" of anarchism, but denying that they penetrate his thought to the level of esoteric or true meaning and acceptance. This judgment gains substantial support from a consideration of his use of the temptation in the Legend to which attention is now directed.

3. BIBLICAL CONTEXT

The Gospel account of the temptation signals the personal triumph of Christ over the evil operative in the life of man in the world and marks the beginning of the redemption of all mankind from sin through the power and grace of His Messiahship. The experience of this redemptive process is one of the important differences which distinguish Eastern from Western Christianity. The Orthodox experience lies at the foundation of Zosima's "cosmic" or telluric mysticism in which the consubstantiality of all being is predominant. It is reflected in the doctrine of *sobornost'* which symbolizes "salvation as a process of becoming divine, not only for men but for the whole created world." [30] The individual person is seen primarily as member of the community, and the community of Christians forms the "sacred heart" of the entire creation, all of which (both men and nature) undergoes the regenerative process of redemption.

> Spirit and matter are two manifestations of the same reality, and when they are sanctified and made the temple of indwelling grace then the past, present and future join together, and time stops its flow as it merges with the ocean of eternal life and light. . . . the flame-shaped cupolas of the Russian churches with their bright colours proclaim the regenerating power given to the Christian community. They announce the coming transfiguration of the universe, and they preach even now the earth is changed into paradise whenever the Eucharist is celebrated and divine grace received through men's corporate action.

"For the East matter is spirit bearing." There is, through grace, the "gradual redemption of all life on earth," the "transfiguration of the cosmos." The domed, circular church is itself an "image of the cosmos," and stress is laid "on corporate and cosmic aspects of redemption," and "all of men's activities contribute to this transfiguration" including "eating and drinking." [31] Virtually the entire thought of Berdyaev, for example, is an elaboration of this experience of redemption and the role of Christians (the Body of Christ) as part-

---

30 Donald Lowrie as quoted by C. A. Manning in his preface to Solovyov, *Lectures on Godmanhood*, 7. Cf chap. 4, n. 7, *above*.

31 Zernov, *Eastern Christendom*, 261; 250, 276, 279, 297, 299. See also Gregerson, *Transfigured Cosmos*; Nicholas Arseniev, *Russian Piety*, trans. Asheleigh Moorhouse (London: Faith Press; Clayton, Wis.: American Orthodox Press, 1964), 31ff, 46; Ernst Benz, *The Eastern Orthodox Church: Its Thought and Life*, trans. Richard and Clara Winston (Chicago: Aldine Publ. Co. 1963), 209ff.

ners in the redemptive process. Much of Dostoevsky is unintelligible apart from this conception of redemption.

Dostoevsky's use of the temptation does nothing to alter the essential sense of the Gospel account. His technique, rather, is to expand and deepen the biblical meaning of the encounter until the temptation of Christ is not only the true "Hinge of history" [32] but its very epitome as well, the Alpha and Omega of human existence in the eternal present when the God Who became also man rejects the terms of the world and proclaims dominion on His own terms, the new order of being made manifest in the climax of revelation. Dostoevsky has underlined this point by including in the introduction which he prepared for a reading of the Legend the specific information that a Christianity which brings itself into harmony with the goals of the world is bankrupt and has, in effect, succumbed to the Antichrist. The temptations are the summation of the doctrine of the world and, as such, contradict the divinely ordained order of the Kingdom of God. In the Legend the triumphant note of the Gospel account is only signaled by the kiss with which it concludes, and it is otherwise given over to a characterization of the Antichrist as he flaunts his dominion over the world and the generations of men.

The care with which Dostoevsky has portrayed the Grand Inquisitor as the Evil One is noteworthy. In principle virtually everything said in the Old and New Testament about evil, Satan, the Antichrist, and their ilk has been included in the characterization. Dostoevsky ("that explorer of Hell," Vyacheslav Ivanov called him)[33]

---

[32] See G. W. F. Hegel, *Grundlinien der Philosophie des Rechts*, ed. Johannes Hoffmeister (4th ed.; Hamburg: Meiner, 1955), 14. Cf. Karl Jaspers, *Vom Ursprung und Ziel der Geschichte* (Frankfurt: Fischer, 1955), especially 14–32, for the derivative *Achsenzeit* (Axis-time) of world history.

[33] Vyacheslav Ivanov, *Freedom and the Tragic Life: A Study in Dostoevsky*, ed. S. Konovalov, trans. Norman Cameron (New York: Noonday Press, 1957) 122. Cf. the references to hell in the notes: Dostoevsky, *The Notebooks for "The Brothers Karamazov,"* 94–100, 103, 104, 134, 139. In the notes for *Crime and Punishment*, Dostoevsky wrote: " 'We are God's children; we live in hell. There is one, Christ. He took pity on everyone; they laughed at him for this and that, and laugh at him, and "insulted him." He will come. . . . He will spread out his crucified hands, open up his arms, and will say: Come unto me all ye that labor and are heavy laden. You are pigs and beasts. But you suffered. I have seen everything and judged everything. I saw your cowardly vileness, and saw that you suffered more

has contrived in the Legend not only a synthesis of Russian anarchism but an exhaustive analysis of the problem of evil as well. He faithfully reproduces in every detail the Antichrist described by John Damascene, in the following passage which must, therefore, be regarded as the immediate source of the characterization in the novel:

> ... the Devil does not himself become man after the manner of the incarnation of the Lord—God forbid!—but a man is born of fornication and receives into himself the whole operation of Satan, for God permits the Devil to inhabit him, because He foresees the future perversity of his will.
>
> So, he is born of fornication, as we said, and is brought up unnoticed; but of a sudden he rises up, revolts, and rules. During the first part of his reign—or his tyranny, rather—he plays more the part of sanctity; but when he gains complete control, he persecutes the Church of God and reveals all his wickedness. And he shall come "in signs and lying wonders"—sham ones and not real—and he will seduce those whose intention rests on a rotten and unstable foundation and make them abandon the living God, "inasmuch as to scandalize (if possible) even the elect."
>
> ... Then the Lord will come from heaven in the same way that the holy Apostles saw Him going into heaven, perfect God and perfect man, with glory and power; and He shall destroy the man of iniquity, the son of perdition, with the spirit of His mouth.[34]

The celebrated formula of the Inquisitor, "Miracle, Mystery, and Authority" (*Chudo, taina, i avtoritet'*) is quoted from the quintessential characterization of the Antichrist (in II Thess. 2:9) "whose coming (*parousia*) is according to the working of Satan in every power (*dynamei*) and signs (*semeiois*) and wonders (*terasi*) of falsehood." [35] The sentence in which the Inquisitor's formula first occurs reads as follows: "There are three powers, only three powers that can conquer and capture the conscience of these impotent rebels forever, for their own happiness—those forces are miracle, mystery and

---

than those you hurt; and therefore come, and we will fall down . . . all . . . and cry—Lord, may your kingdom come!' " Dostoevsky, *The Notebooks for "Crime and Punishment,"* 85.

34 John of Damascus, *Fount of Knowledge*, bk. 4, chap. 36, p. 400, citing John Chrysostom's Homily 3 on II Thess. 2 and quoting II Thess. 2:9, Matt. 24:24. Cf. *The Notebooks for "The Brothers Karamazov,"* 74.

35 Cf. Acts 2:22 and Matt. 24:24.

authority." The words of the original are as follows: "Est' tri sily, edinstvenniia tri sily na zemle, mogushchie na veki pobedit' i plenit' sovest' etikh slabosil' nykh buntovshchikov, dlia ikh schast'ja—eti sily: chudo, taina i avtoritet." [36] The Russian translation of the New Testament used by Dostoevsky renders the latter portion of II Thessalonians 2:9 in the following language: *so vsiakoiu siloiu, znameniiami i chudesami lozhnymi* ("with every force, or power, and with signs and miracles false") .[37] The sharing of the central words by the two passages can be seen in instances of *sily-siloiu* ("power", "force") and *chudo—chudesami* ("miracle", "miracles"). The word "power" occurs three times in the single sentence in which the Inquisitor first invokes his formula and "miracle" occurs thirteen times in the monologue. A third word, not included in the formula sentence but prominent in the monologue and present in the scriptural passage, is *znamia* which occurs six times in the monologue and has the same root as *znameniiami* (signs).

Taina (mystery) sets the problematic of the Legend considered to be itself apocalypse. The context of Dostoevsky's revelation is, once again, II Thessalonians 2:7–8. "For the mystery of lawlessness and iniquity *(bezzakoniia)* already is at work. . . . And then shall be revealed *(otkroetsia; otkrovenie* = "apocalypse," "revelation") the lawless, iniquitous, impious man *(bezzakonnik)* whom the Lord Jesus *(Gospod' Iisus)* shall at one stroke with the breath of His mouth *(dukhom ust Svoikh)* and appearance of His presence destroy *(istrebit)*." [38] The substance of the Legend as apocalypse is the revelation of the mystery of the *bezzakonie*. The progressive unveiling of the mystery creates the monologue's dramatic power as this climaxes in the confession by which the Inquisitor finally "reveals all his wickedness": "We are not working with You, but with *him*—that is our mystery! (My ne s Toboi, a s *nim*, vot nasha taina!)" [39] Beyond the strict

---

[36] Fyodor M. Dostoevsky, *Polnoe sobranie sochinenii* (12 vols.; 4th ed.; St. Petersburg: Panteleevkh, 1891–92), XII *(Brat'ia Karamazovy)*, 296; Dostoevsky, *Notes From Underground and The Grand Inquisitor*, ed., trans., and with an intro. by Ralph E. Matlaw (New York: E. P. Dutton & Co., 1960), 129–30.
[37] *Gospoda nashego Iisusa Khrista Novii Zaviet na slavjanskom i russkom iazyke* 3. Tisneniem (St. Petersburg: V Tip. Rossiiskago bibleiskago obva, 1822), 705.
[38] *Ibid.*
[39] Dostoevsky, *Polnoe sobranie sochinenii*, XII, 298. English from Dostoevsky, *Notes From Underground*, trans. and ed. by Ralph E. Matlaw, 132.

etymological relationships, the meanings of the key terms obviously evince close relationships: *power* and *force* inform *authority*; *signs* betoken *mystery* and point toward the transformation of the content of the Inquisitor's mystery as used in the Book of Revelation; *miracle* entails both *mystery* and *power* and offers an earnest for *authority*.

The Antichrist of II Thessalonians 2 is drawn from the Belial saga[40] and includes as an element the self-deification of the final enemy of God which characterizes the biblical account from the time of the Book of Daniel and the Maccabeean period. Just as for Ivan "all things are lawful," [41] so also is his Inquisitor clearly the "messenger of lawlessness (*aggelos tes anomias*)," the embodiment of apostasy, as has been seen from the language of the Russian New Testament. In the Pauline construction, which is controlling in the Legend, Belial, the prototype of the man of lawlessness (*paranomos*), is fused with the incarnation of Satan, the devil in human form (the original representation of the pseudomessiah) to form the Antichrist. Paul keeps Satan himself in the background, in keeping with the Jewish tradition. Just "as God's representative is the Lord Jesus Christ, so Satan's active representative is this mysterious figure, whose methods are a caricature of the true messiah's." [42]

The Grand Inquisitor is, then, a millennial figure created upon a biblical foundation. He towers over the earthly drama as the Great Questioner of Cartesian descent, the Antichrist who does not tempt Christ but who stands as the representative of universal mankind enthralled by evil to challenge the omnipotence of the divine Logos of being. In the mouth of the Great Questioner, the temptation ceases to be that and becomes a prophetic analysis of immanentist opportunism and destruction in history. Into him Dostoevsky has woven all of the ancient representations of evil from Ahriman and Prometheus onward. He has brought together a monstrous synthesis in epic proportions of sectarian Christs and gnostic New Men in his chthonic hero. Among much else, the Inquisitor is also one of the "clever people" (*umnye liudi*)[43] whom Dostoevsky often mentioned

---

[40] Cf. II Cor. 6:15.

[41] Dostoevsky, *Polnoe sobranie sochinenii*, XII, 305.

[42] James Moffat, "Introduction," in W. R. Nicoll (ed.), *Expositor's Greek Testament* (5 vols.; Grand Rapids: Eerdmans, n.d.), IV, 17.

[43] Dostoevsky, *Polnoe sobranie sochinenii*, XII, 303.

in correspondence and publicist writings—such persons as Belinsky, Chernyshevsky, Dobroliubov, Herzen, Turgenev, and the phalanx of Bazarovs[44]—those whose agony in existence breeds impatience of Providence: why, indeed, as Belinsky asked, perfection and happiness tomorrow and not today? The Great Questioner, of illustrious lineage, stands as the symbol of perennial arrogance, negation, and lust— and as the emblem of man's earthly destiny. The rebellion is Ivan's, the prophecy, Dostoevsky's.

4. THE FIRST TEMPTATION

Christ replies to the three temptations by scriptural quotation in the Gospel account, although he makes no reply at all in the Legend.[45] The first temptation, that the stones be made into bread, recalls the boast of John the Baptist that God possessed the power to make sons of Abraham from the stones of the desert (Matt. 3:9) and the expression "stones for bread" (Matt. 7:9) is played upon by Dostoevsky both in the Legend and elsewhere. The significance of the first temptation for Dostoevsky is expounded in a letter written in 1876 to one V. A. Alekseev, a reader of *The Diary of a Writer*, who had expressed alarm at an account given there of a suicide:

> . . . in the temptation of the devil are blended three colossal universal ideas and after eighteen centuries the more difficult of these ideas have not and still cannot be settled.
> "Stones and bread" means the present social question of *environment*.

---

44 That is, the "clever ones" are the intelligentsia, that unique growth in nineteenth century Russia. As a Petrashevist, Dostoevsky had been one of these himself but turned against them after his exile. Of the Petrashevsky circle Alexander Herzen wrote: "When the Petrashevsky group were sent to penal servitude for 'trying to uproot all laws, human and divine, and to destroy the foundations of society,' in the words of their sentence, the terms of which were stolen from the inquisitorial notes of Liprandi, they were Nihilists." Herzen, "Bazarov," in *My Past and Thoughts*, trans. Constance Garnett (6 vols.; New York: Alfred A. Knopf, Inc., 1924–28), VI, 209. "It was typical that the most popular leaders of the intelligentsia, such as Nikolay Chernishevsky (1828–89) and Nikolay Dobroliubov (1836–61), were sons of priests, and retained a sense of service to a sacred cause when they embraced positivism and nihilism and dismissed Orthodox Christianity as obsolete." See chap. 1, sec. 1, *above*. Cf. Zernov, *Eastern Christendom*, 197.

45 The replies are from Deuteronomy on each of the three occasions, namely 8:3, 6:6, and 6:13; the second reply is supplemented by an allusion to Exod. 17:1–7.

This is not a prophecy;[46] this has always existed. "Rather than to go to the ruined poor, who from hunger and oppression look more like beasts than like men, rather than go and start preaching to the hungry abstention from sins, humility, sexual chastity, wouldn't it be better to *feed* them first? That would be more humane. Even before You there were preachers; but Thou Son of God, the whole world awaited Thee with impatience; Thy steps are high above all mind and intellect; give them food to *save* them; give them a social structure so that they always have bread and order—and then speak with them of sin. Then if there should be sin, that would be ingratitude, but now—with hunger it is against common sense. It is sinful even to ask them.

"Thou Son of God—everything is possible to Thee. Here is a stone, see, like many others. Thou hast only to command—and the stones change into bread.

"Command then that, henceforth, the earth bring forth without toil, instruct people in such science or instruct them in such an order, that their lives should henceforth be provided for. Is it possible not to believe that the greatest vices and misfortunes of man resulted from hunger, cold, poverty and from the impossible struggle for existence?"

Here is the first idea which was posed by the evil spirit to Christ. It is difficult to correct him. Contemporary *socialism* in Europe, even our own, is completely separated from Christ; it is concerned almost completely about *bread*; it looks to science and declares that the cause of all man's miseries is *poverty* alone, the struggle for existence, the 'environment tangle.'

To this Christ answered: "Man does not live by bread alone"—that is, propounded the axiom of the spiritual origin of man. The idea of the devil could lead only to the man-brute; Christ knew that men do not expect bread alone. If, furthermore, there is no spiritual life, no ideal of Beauty, then man grieves, cheats, loses his mind, declines, or turns to pagan fantasies. But since Christ, in Himself and in His Word, is the ideal of Beauty, He decided: it is better to inspire man's soul with the ideal of Beauty; possessing it in their souls, all men become brothers and then, finally, influencing each other, they will also be prosperous. When you give them bread, from boredom they may grant each other beer, become enemies of one another.

But if you should give both Beauty and Bread simultaneously? Then man would be deprived of toil, *personality, self-sacrifice of his own goods*

---

[46] Already here Dostoevsky analyzes the temptation under both the ontological and the prophetic dimensions of revelation; that is, in terms of both the vertical dimension of being as a revelation of structure, and in terms of eschatology: the unfolding of the world in time as the movement toward an end that is revealed.

for the sake of his fellow-man—in a word, he would be deprived of life, the ideal of life. And consequently it is better to proclaim only the spiritual ideal.

. . . If the matter concerned only the relief of one man's hunger, Christ's, then for whom was intended the saying about the spiritual nature of man in general? And it was not at the proper time; even without the devil's advice He could previously have gotten bread, if He had wanted to. At the proper time: remember the present *theory* of Darwin (and others) about the origin of man from apes. Not entering into any theories, Christ straightforwardly explained that in man, besides the animal nature, there *is* also the spiritual one. Now—assume what you will, man came forth (in the Bible it is not explained how God formed him from clay, which comes from stone), but then God *breathed in him the breath of life* (but it is disgusting that, by sin, man can be turned again into a beast.)[47]

Certain points of this commentary are noteworthy. The Russian editor, A. S. Dolinin, remarks that "already here, in the letter, is noted the proportions of the roles of the devil and Christ: the whole force of logic and persuasion is given to the devil—to 'godless socialism' and not to Christ—but to the Devil Reason." [48] The devil's argument is presented in the letter as eminently reasonable, appealing to common sense, humanitarian sentiment, and the findings of sociology and natural science. While Christ's arguments are in part given in the letter, lacking are the elements of caricature and grotesque parody relied upon in the Legend itself, devices used in this later place in the threefold way of: characterizing the Inquisitor as the representative of Satan (or the Antichrist); as means of ridiculing Christ; and as techniques for displaying the absurdity of the eminently "rational" satanic solution to the fundamental questions of human existence. Implied in the letter and prominent in the Legend is the representation of reason as diabolical. The "rationality" of the satanic argument is undermined not only by suggesting absurd consequences, but also by identifying it point-blank as essentially ir-

---

[47] Fyodor M. Dostoevsky to V. A. Alekseev, June 7, 1876, No. 550, in *Pis'ma*, ed. A. S. Dolinin (4 vols.; Moscow-Leningrad: Akademia, 1928–56), III, 211–12; Cf. David Magarshack, *Dostoevsky* (New York: Harcourt, Brace & World, 1963), 352–53; also Konstantin Mochulsky, *Dostoevsky: His Life and Work*, trans. and with an intro. by Michael A. Minihan (Princeton: Princeton University Press, 1967), 538–39.

[48] Dolinin, Note to No. 550, in Dostoevsky, *Pis'ma*, III, 363.

rational. By spurning the *cognitio fidei* as an indispensable mode of knowing, the rationalist-gnostic loses contact with the ground of truth. The immediate aporia which opens, the substance of the meaning of the first temptation, is that the true nature of man is obscured: "beside the animal nature, there *is* also the spiritual" in man—and precisely this differentiates him from the beasts and makes him what he *is*. Hence Christ's reply: "Man does not live by bread alone, but by every word that proceeds out of the mouth of the Lord does he live" (Deut. 8:3). Without the spiritual bread of Life, the true manna of heaven, man ceases to be himself: to embrace the temptation would entail the destruction of humanity.

Dostoevsky is at pains to emphasize that this is no mere speculation or hypothesis about man, but the revelation by the divine *Logos* of a "secret of nature," an ontological fact which supplies the keystone of Dostoevsky's philosophical anthropology. So far from Dolinin's conclusion that there is "inconsistency" in Dostoevsky and "changeableness' and that "his lip-coolness" in support of his "humble-Christian world-concept . . . puts a deep crack in his world-concept," [49] the "rationality" of the Inquisitor is shown to be just its opposite, his "truth" the substance of error—and hence, the Inquisitor's words about error are applicable to himself. Ratiocination based on fantasy rather than truth can but be irrational because predicated upon unfounded assumptions as premises, the very "Tower of Babel" itself. A "clever" hypothesis can only apparently overcome a contradictory ontological reality: "Jesus speaks not only as authoritative, but as sovereign in the sphere of truth." [50] Faith is the essential requirement, and the absence of faith is the fatal flaw of all those represented in the Great Questioner. At the apocalyptical level of the symbolism, faith on the part of Satan himself—the succumbing to the temptation of which Dostoevsky's "pettifogging devil" speaks to himself cry "Hosannah!"—would be to cause the world to stand still, not simply in that there could be "no events" and existence would stagnate, but in that this is the formula

---

[49] *Ibid.*

[50] Geerhardus Vos, *The Self-Disclosure of Jesus: The Modern Debate About the Messianic Consciousness* (New York: George H. Doran Co., 1926), 61.

for the Apocalypse and the Kingdom of God.[51] The "Hosannah" of
the opening of the Legend may be recalled. As employed there it is
the "Hosannah" of Christ's triumphal entry into Jerusalem on Palm
Sunday, an acknowledgment by the people of His Messiahship, a
shout of joyful recognition mingled with penitence and prayer for
salvation accorded the transfigured Christ. Hence for the Devil to
shout "Hosannah" would be the eschatologically decisive, faithful
confession of a penitent heart.[52] It can scarcely be doubted that, in
the smothering night of rebellion and inordinate pride vividly perceived as a blight sweeping over the face of the earth, Dostoevsky
sought hope beyond the darkness in the glorious dawn that surely
will come.

For Solovyov the significance of the first temptation depends upon
the explanation of philosophical anthropology as incipient Christology: Christ is the God-man, but the first of a divine species Who
prefigures the race of God-men to appear with the culmination of
the redemption of the cosmos. He therefore argues that to Christ, as a

> being subjected to the conditions of material existence is presented the
> temptation to make material welfare the goal, and his divine power the
> means of attaining it: "if thou be the Son of God, command that these
> stones be made bread." Here the divine nature—"if thou be the Son of
> God"—and the manifestations of that nature—the word "command," are
> to serve as means for the satisfaction of a material need. Christ in answer
> to this temptation asserts that the Word of God is not an instrument of
> material life, but itself is the source of the true life for man. . . . Having
> overcome this temptation of the flesh, the Son of Man receives authority
> over all flesh.[53]

---

51 See Dostoevsky's reflections on the paradoxicality of immanentist perfection
in Fyodor Dostoevsky, *Was vermag der Mensch?—Ein Brevier*, ed. Reinhard Lauth
(Munich: Piper, 1949), 247: "To attain such an exalted goal as personal perfection
would be . . . quite meaningless, if after attaining it everything should be ex-
tinguished and disappear, and if after the attained goal there should be no life
for a human being."

52 Matt. 17:1–13; 21:9; Mark 11:10–11; John 12:13; Ps. 118:25–26; Zech. 9:9; cf.
Dmitri Merezhkovsky, *Tolstoy as Man and Artist with an Essay on Dostoevsky*
(New York: G. P. Putnam's Sons, 1902), 293.

53 Solovyov, *Lectures on Godmanhood*, 197. Solovyov's central teaching with
respect to Godmanhood is formulated in the following language: "The due relationship between Divinity and nature in humanity, which was reached by the
person of Jesus Christ as the spiritual center or head of mankind, must be as-

5. THE SECOND TEMPTATION

There is no discursive commentary by Dostoevsky on the meaning of the second temptation. In the Legend it serves in a striking way as the occasion for the repudiation of faith by the Great Questioner and the affirmation of the faith of the unconstrained heart as the inevitable means of salvation by Christ. The Inquisitor in chiding tones reminds the Prisoner: "When the wise and dread spirit set Thee on the pinnacle [*pterugion*] of the temple and said to Thee, 'If Thou wouldst know whether Thou art the Son of God then cast Thyself down, for it is written: the angels shall hold him up lest he fall and bruise himself, and Thou shalt know then whether Thou art the Son of God and shalt prove then how great is Thy faith in Thy Father.' " [54] But to put faith to such a test is to supplant it with doubt, and Jesus rejects this subtle temptation in the Gospel account with the words: "Again it is written, Thou shalt not tempt the Lord thy God." The episode at Massah will not bear repetition.[55] Faith is itself proof—proof in the soul. What need, therefore, for a lesser proof, for proof of a phenomenal and rationalistic kind? The very attempt would be to dissolve the faith bond itself and substitute pride of mind for the mystery of man's blessed participation in divinity. Christ, the symbol of faith, is Himself bound by faith, His power united with the Father is in faith. It cannot be used to test the very reality of which it is a manifestation without simultaneously destroying that reality. All three temptations exemplify rejection of the principle that the end sanctifies the means: on the contrary, the means must be strictly consonant with the end. The truth of revelation must be apprehended in faith; there is no short cut to it. The atonement itself—and hence Christ's whole Messiahship —depends upon faith. The Inquisitor notes that the same "op-

---

similated by all of mankind as His body." Or, again: the "Manifestation and glory of the sons of God . . . is the full realization of the free God-man union in the whole of mankind in all the spheres of its life and activity; all these spheres must be brought into concordant divine-human unity, must become parts of the free theocracy in which the Universal Church will reach the full measure of the stature of Christ." *Ibid.*, 199. See also Matthew Spinka, *Christian Thought from Erasmus to Berdyaev* (Englewood Cliffs: Prentice-Hall, Inc., 1962), 142ff.
54 Cf. Ps. 91:11–12.
55 Cf. Deut. 6:16 and Exod. 17:7.

portunity" to "prove" His divinity was spurned at Golgotha. Salvation is through faith, the faith of which Jesus as the Incarnate *Logos* is embodiment, emblem, and great Exemplar. Precisely here can first be glimpsed the eschatological hardness of Christ as a theme of the Legend. There is no blinking the essentiality of faith to salvation: "I am the way and the truth and the life. No one comes to the Father but through me" (John 14:6).

The rival "ways" represented by the Inquisitor and his Prisoner suggest the classic passage in Matthew: "Enter in through the narrow gate; for wide the gate and broad the way that leads to destruction, and many are they who enter through it: for narrow the gate and straightened the way that leads to life, and few are they who find it" (Matt. 7:13–14). Nor is it altogether inappropriate that the next verse in Matthew reads: "But beware of the false prophets, who come to you in rainment of sheep, but within are rapacious wolves" (Matt. 7:15). Who is the Inquisitor but such a wolf in sheep's clothing? What is his way but the broad road to destruction? The mystery of faith is too demanding. It ill suits those who crave dominion over men and history.

One should not fail to notice the Inquisitor himself to be one of the weak and rebellious men whom he so despises as devoid of manhood. It is *he* who is too weak for faith, is a sheep turned ravening wolf. The loathing disrespect for men as weak and infinitely malleable by nature derives not so much from empirical observation and shrewd insight as from a nauseous self-awareness of personal decrepitude. Like other "realists" he cynically and sneeringly judges by the standard of his own diseased self. He enlists all mankind as accomplices to his sin and as evidence that his twisted soul is a cosmic necessity, the norm of a miserable world. And he will prove he is right, even if he must mutilate the whole of humanity to do it. The self-seeking psychotic will preach a new mystery. Happiness depends upon blind conformity to the new social order in systematic isolation from transcendence, from the silent voices of grace in human existence: the Inquisitor confides that "it's not the free judgment of their hearts, not love that matters, but a mystery which they must follow blindly, even against their conscience." A more massive experience than faith, one which brings the experientially "ultimate" closer to hand and lends itself to manipulation through political and psychological mass management, can better form the lives of men and "save them" from themselves. Thus, while Christ in the wilderness conquered sin of the mind and received authority over the minds of men, the Inquisitor accepts the counsel of the evil spirit and grasps dominion over the world of dead souls.[56]

6. THE THIRD TEMPTATION

The Inquisitor concedes his very slogan "Miracle, Mystery, and Authority" to be a mere propaganda. The apostasy manifested by the coming of the man of lawlessness or sin (*hamartias*; *anomias*), the son of perdition (*ho hyios tes apoleias*), must first occur, according to the biblical account, as a necessary prelude to the second Advent of Christ (II Thess. 2:3). But the mystery (*mysterion*; 2:7) lies precisely in his lawlessness, while his power, signs, and wonders are false or lying (*pseudos*) (2:9). The doctrine of the Inquisitor, therefore, is concentrated in the unsupported assertion of raw power without any true authority and equally independent of either miracle or mystery. His tyranny is founded in the void which opens beneath the feet of Christ in the third temptation, whose substance is defection from being—an illusory nothingness informed only by pretentious will. The real mystery is only partially disclosed in the course of the second temptation; more clearly, it is existential alliance with the spirit of negation and destruction, the rationalistic denial of mystery on principle through paradoxical assertion of a contrary mystery: the self-sufficiency of rebellious human reason.

> And what use is it for me to hide anything from Thee? Don't I know to Whom I am speaking? All that I can say is known to Thee already. And is it for me to conceal from Thee our [real] mystery? . . . Listen then. We are not working with Thee . . . that is our mystery . . . we took from *him* what Thou didst reject with scorn, that last gift *he* offered Thee, showing Thee all the kingdoms of the earth. We took from *him* Rome and the sword of Caesar, and proclaimed ourselves sole rulers of the earth . . . we shall triumph and shall be Caesars, and then we shall plan the universal happiness of man.

---

[56] Cf. Solovyov, *Lectures on Godmanhood*, 197.

The mystery is consciously fraudulent, not at all as it has been represented, and the authority is equally false: while rule is in "Thy
name," the power is that of Satan—that is, it is no more than negation. The miracle of abundant earthly bread and material well-being
is, likewise, a lie and no miracle at all: "Receiving bread from us,
they will see clearly that we take the bread made by their hands from
them, to give it to them without any miracle. *They* will see that
we do not change stones to bread." It is all a deceit in which, however, men fearfully and knowingly participate—a terrible subterfuge,
warned against in the Gospel but in fact incapable of touching Christ
and His Elect.[57]

Dostoevsky's analysis is relentless. All those movements in history
which extravagantly claim divine authority and possession of in-
fallible truth—and which in support of these claims effect the destruction of freedom in the name of freedom, justice in the name of
justice, man in the name of humanitarianism, tradition in the name
of truth—are exhibited as afflicted by hypocrisy and shameless bankruptcy. *"Those who love men in general hate men in particular"* is
the principle axiomatic to Dostoevsky's analysis.[58] The pompous
trappings of vaunting authoritarianism are stripped away to leave
naked the ignoble kernel of the phenomenon: at bottom the rule of
the messianic ideologue is motivated by megalomania's simple lust
for power. The miracle, mystery, and authority of the Inquisitor
may, in accord with his own confession, be translated by socialism,
rationalism, and empire.

The peremptory "Begone Satan!" with which Christ in the Gospel
dismisses the rejected Tempter and his third temptation finds an
exegetical gloss in Christ's words to Pilate after the recurrence of
temptation at Gethsemane and on the eve of His glorification at
Golgotha:

---

[57] *E.g.* Matt. 7:15; cf. John 14:30; 16:11,33; I John 5:18.
[58] Dostoevsky, *The Notebooks for "The Brothers Karamazov,"* 33. In *The Notebooks for "A Raw Youth,"* Dostoevsky wrote: "Atheism—I have felt universal love,
but I don't love Mother" (p. 540), and "I am destined to love *everybody,* and so
no one" (p. 421). This disorder is reflected in both Ivan's humanitarianism and
in Fyodor Pavlovich's libertinism as diverse manifestations of a common libidinous
perversion—Zosima's existential hell, which is the equivalent of Augustine's *amor
sui.*

My kingdom is not of this world [*He Basileia he eme ouk estin ek tou kosmou toutou*]; if my Kingdom were of this world, my attendants would fight that I might not be delivered up to the Jews; but now my kingdom is not from hence. Pilate therefore said to Him, Then a king art thou? Jesus answered, Thou sayest it, for I am a King. I for this have been born, and for this I have come into the world, that I may bear witness to the Truth. Everyone that is of the truth hears my voice. Pilate says to Him, What is truth [*aletheia*]? [59]

This is also the doctrine of the Christ of the Legend. It is the doctrine of the crucifixion and the resurrection. The reconstruction of the meaning of the Legend at this point is confirmed by Dostoevsky's sketches and notes. To the assertion "there is no truth, no God," the author juxtaposes "the clever Pilate who reflected on truth. . . . What is the Truth? It stood before him, Truth itself." Nor does Dostoevsky fail expressly to affirm the metaphysical ground of the Christian theory of being: "What is life?—To define oneself as much as possible, I am, I exist. To be like the Lord Who says I Am Who Is." [60] The Supreme Being revealed from Genesis through Malachi points toward the image of the perfect Man Who stands equally before Pilate and the Inquisitor as the Truth Who Is.

The Kingdom of God cannot be built from the resources of the world—not by socialism, rationalism, and the force of empire, in Dostoevsky's words—but by hope, faith, and love through the redeeming grace of Christ. The miracle, mystery, and authority of the Inquisitor are blatantly and patently false and lead only to the earthly Hell of tyranny and totalitarianism. They gain credence only because they infringe upon the majesty of God: "Jesus the Nazarean, a Man by God sent forth to you by works of power and wonders and signs, which God wrought by Him in your midst" (Acts 2:22). So far from rejecting these forces from the hand of Satan—whose "truth" is *pseudos* and who, hence, has no such genuine power to confer—all that was rejected was the pale shadow and perverted sham of real powers inherent in Jesus as the Son and manifested in

---

59 John 18:36–39.
60 Dostoevsky, *The Notebooks for "The Brothers Karamazov,"* 75, 102, 98; cf. 223; Exod. 3:14; cf. Gen. 1:1, 2:4, 14:18, 15:2, 17:1, 21:33; Exod. 34:6; I Sam. 1:3; Mal. 3:18; and Ps. 2:7; Heb. 1:5.

His ministry. Only in their perversion by the willful abuse and arrogant pretense of spiritually deranged men do these divine powers become destructive of freedom and instruments of existential disorder.

The monologue of the Inquisitor is an apocalypse revealing the secret workings of evil in the world. It is not merely an impeccably constructed Christian meditation but also is an empirically based diagnosis through mythopoetic exemplification of the terminal cancer of the soul in its most overwhelming and hideous historical configuration. But the revelation of rebellion leaves untouched the primordial problem of the world and the ultimate mystery of being. Dostoevsky has left the ontological moorings intact. The Legend may, in this respect, be regarded as a therapeutic reaffirmation of the vertical tension of existence and of the truth of being in itself of intrinsic existential power.

Solovyov's account of the third temptation complements the foregoing interpretation of Dostoevsky's meaning.

The third temptation was the last and strongest one. The enslavement to the flesh and the pride of the mind have been removed: the human will finds itself now on a high moral level, is conscious of being higher than the rest of creation; in the name of this moral height, man can wish for the mastery over the world in order to lead the latter to perfection; but the world lieth in sin and will not voluntarily submit to moral superiority: [it may seem] therefore that the world should be forced into subjection, that it is necessary [for Christ] to use His divine power to force the world into subjection. But such a use of coercion, i.e., of evil, for the attainment of a good would be [equivalent to] a confession that evil is stronger than the good, that the good by itself has no force. It would be *falling down* before that *element of evil* which dominates the world . . . the human will is directly challenged with the fateful question: what does it believe, and what does it wish to serve—the invisible might of God or the force of evil that openly reigns in the world? And the human will of Christ, having overcome the temptation of a plausible desire for power, freely subjected itself to the true good, denying any agreement with the evil which reigns in the world: "Then saith Jesus unto him: Get thee hence, Satan: for it is written, Thou shalt worship the Lord thy God and Him *only* shalt thou serve." Having conquered the sin of the spirit, the Son of Man received supreme authority in the realm of the spirit; refusing to submit to the earthly power for the sake of the dominion over the earth, He acquired for Himself the service of the powers of heaven: "and, behold, angels came and ministered unto Him." [61]

The correlation of the three temptations with subsequent history is made explicit in Solovyov, but it is only the history of the West that manifests this process. The order in which the "aggregate of mankind" in the "objective, historical process" has succumbed to the same three temptations resisted by Christ follows a different sequence from the one given in Matthew: the pride of life comes first, historically, the lust of the flesh last. Roman Catholicism fell victim to the first, Protestantism to the second, and socialism and positivism to the third in the historical sequence.

Solovyov begins by saying: "Historically, the Christian Church has been composed of all people who have accepted Christ; but Christ can be accepted either inwardly or outwardly." He may be accepted through an inner experience which consists of spiritual regeneration, or merely by intellectual acknowledgment and subsequent external conformity to the Commandments. "Such external Christianity contains the danger of falling into the first temptation of the evil beginning. That is to say, the historical appearance of Christianity has divided all mankind into two groups: the Christian Church which possesses the divine truth and represents the will of God upon earth—and the world which remains outside of Christianity . . . [and] lieth in evil." [62] External Christians, not truly regenerated by Christ, may nonetheless be dedicated to propagation of the faith and expansion of the church. Because the world, lying in evil, does not easily submit to the sons of God, they may resolve to subjugate it by force. "Part of the church, led by the Roman hierachy, succumbed to that temptation—and dragged with it the majority of Western humanity in the first great period of its historical life, the Middle Ages." The specific error of this action lies in reliance upon "hidden unbelief" causing the force of evil to be treated as superior to the power of Christ Who appears to require

---

61 Cf. Deut. 6:13; John 14:30. Solovyov, *Lectures on Godmanhood*, 197–98.
62 Solovyov, *Lectures on Godmanhood*, 200–201.

the "alien and even directly opposite means of coercion and deceit";
this is "not to believe in God." The embryonic tendency of early
Catholicism was ultimately manifested in Jesuitism: "that extreme,
purest expression of the Catholic principle—[in which] the moving
force was an outright lust for power, and not the Christian zeal;
nations were being brought into subjection not to Christ, but to
the Church authority; the people were not asked for a real confession of the Christian faith—the acknowledgment of the Pope . . .
and obedience to the Church authorities were sufficient." It may be
remarked that the theme of the succumbing of Roman Catholicism
to the third temptation, so emphasized in the Legend as well as in
this passage from Solovyov, is already fully developed in *The Possessed* (written 1870–72). The following language is there used:

> . . . you [Stavrogin] believed that Roman Catholicism was not Christianity;
> you asserted that Rome proclaimed Christ subject to the third temptation
> of the devil. Announcing to all the world that Christ without an earthly
> kingdom cannot hold his ground upon earth, Catholicism by so doing
> proclaimed Antichrist and ruined the whole Western world. You pointed
> out that if France is in agonies now it's simply the fault of Catholicism,
> for she has rejected the iniquitous God of Rome and has not found a
> new one.[63]

The falsity of such Christianity, Solovyov stated, was early recognized in the West itself and eventuated in the Reformation. "Protestantism rebels against the Catholic way of salvation as an external
act, and demands a personal religious relation of man to God, a
personal faith without any traditional ecclesiastical mediation. But
personal faith, as such, *i.e.*, as a merely subjective fact, does not contain in itself any guarantee of its verity—such faith requires a criterion." At first, the Bible was this criterion. But a book requires understanding which, in turn is based on analysis; hence, reason became
the actual source of religious truth, with the result that Protestantism
succumbed to rationalism, a development which was logically inevitable and occurred historically. What, then, is the substance of ra-

---

[63] Fyodor M. Dostoevsky, *The Possessed,* trans. Constance Garnett (New York:
Random House, Modern Library, 1936), pt. 2, chap. 1, 252.

tionalism? "It consists essentially in the belief that the human mind is not only a law unto itself but gives laws to all that exists, in the practical and social spheres. This principle is expressed in the demand that all life, all political and social relations, be organized and directed exclusively on the foundations worked out by the personal [individual] human mind, regardless of any tradition, of any immediate faith."

This demand informed the Enlightenment and culminated in the French Revolution. It found supreme theoretical expression as the "essence of German philosophy" from Leibniz through Kant to Hegel. "This self-confidence and self-assertion of human reason in life and knowledge is an abnormal phenomenon, it is the pride of mind: in Protestantism, and in rationalism which issues from it, Western humanity fell into the second temptation." The gap between claims and performance soon showed the contradiction inherent in rationalism: "the kingdom of reason proclaimed by the French Revolution ended in a wild chaos of insanity and violence" as passions asserted the reality of the irrational force in human nature. "[The] historical downfall of rationalism was only the expression of its inner, logical contradiction, of the contradiction between the relative nature of reason and its unconditional [absolute] claims . . . the self-elevation of human reason, the pride of the mind, at the end inevitably leads to its downfall and abasement."

Experience showed the falsity of rationalism: human reason was inadequate to master either the passions and lower range of human existence in life or "the facts of the empirical reality" in science. That is, it found itself opposed by what Solovyov terms the "material beginning"; and from this it was concluded "that the material element in life and knowledge—the animal nature of man, the material mechanism of the world"—is essential being or reality. Materialism and empiricism, which found their end forms in economic socialism and positivism, therefore succeeded to the dominion of European politics and thought, and the West thereby succumbed to the third and "last temptation of the evil beginning." While the course of this development still has not been completely run, its falsity and internal contradictoriness are plain. From the material element of discord and chance, the goal of unity and integrity is sought; the attempt is made to organize a just human society and establish a universal science. But the material substratum must be ordered by a formative principle and that this cannot be human reason has been shown. It is, therefore, necessary to have recourse to another and more powerful principle of unity.

> An attempt to actually place the material beginning alone at the foundation of life and knowledge, an attempt to realize, in fact and in full, the lie that man shall live by bread alone, such an attempt would perforce lead to the disintegration of mankind, to the destruction of society and science, to a universal chaos. To what extent Western humanity . . . is destined to experience all those consequences—cannot be said in advance. In any event, having learned by experience the falsehood of the three "broad ways", having experienced the deceitfulness of the three great temptations, Western humanity sooner or later must turn to the truth of Godmanhood.[64]

7. Culture and Crisis

A full statement of Solovyov's analysis has been given because of its interest for the student of the Legend. Serge Bulgakov asserted that "it is obvious that Vladimir Solovyov had a tremendous influence on Dostoevsky." [65] Whatever the precise relationship between the *Lectures on Godmanhood* and the Legend, it is clear that both adopt similar approaches to the temptation and that the former sets forth the subject matter in philosophical language. This is of assistance to a theoretical analysis of the Legend. There is, however, some hazard in relying upon Solovyov in that his presentation involves a "sophiological" metaphysical doctrine and an anthropology not present, and perhaps not even implicit, in Dostoevsky.[66] Solovyov's exposition also shows the influence of the Hegelian dialectic, conceived as determining the dynamic of history in accordance with the superimposed allegory of the temptation, in a way that Dostoevsky's

---

[64] The foregoing is quoted and summarized from Solovyov, *Lectures on Godmanhood*, 197–204.

[65] Sergius Bulgakov, *The Wisdom of God* (London: Williams and Norgate, 1937), 24.

[66] Cf. Reinhard Lauth, *Die Philosophie Dostojewskis in systematischer Darstellung* (Munich: Piper, 1950), 465n.

Legend does not. Finally, a far stronger strain of Western "individual-
ism" (or Christian "personalism") is to be found in Dostoevsky than
in Solovyov, whose mysticism is decidedly pantheistic. The protest
raised in the Legend against authority is the protest of the old
"Underground Man" of the sixties and the affirmation of man's
indestructible freedom,[67] but with a tremendous difference: the
man in the Inquisitor's underground knows, not merely that he *is*,
but that he *is* God's man. There is a more purely religious and poetic
insight in Dostoevsky who, not having been technically trained in
philosophy, is not constrained by the categories of philosophical (or
what is more to the point, theosophical) thought.

The dialectic of history, according to Solovyov, moves forward
from the third crisis in the West toward an ultimate synthesis of
salvation from the East: the goal of history is the free universal
theocracy concretely visualized as an ecumenical empire ruled by
the Russian Tsar and an ecumenical church ruled by the Roman
Pope! In the 1878 lectures, however, Solovyov does no more than
affirm the purity of Russian Orthodox Christianity: "The East did
not fall into the three temptations of the evil beginning—it preserved
the truth of Christ." He then develops an idea also taken up by
Dostoevsky, namely the conception of culture.[68] Russia kept the
truth of Christ in her soul—but she never realized it in external
actuality nor "created a *Christian culture* in the same manner as the
West has created an anti-Christian culture." Moreveor, the Eastern
church "could not have realized the Christian truth." Why not?
What is "a truly Christian culture?" It is the "establishment in the
whole of human society and in all its activities, of such a relationship
among the three elements of the human being as was realized individually in the person of Christ." Now the three elements unified
in man are "the divine, the material, and that which binds both

---

[67] See Robert Louis Jackson, *Dostoevsky's Underground Man in Russian Literature* (The Hague: Mouton, 1958), 13, 54n.
[68] See the letter of Dostoevsky to K. P. Pobedonostsev of May 19, 1879, cited in
chap. 3, n. 4, *above*. This theme is prominent in *The Notebooks for "A Raw
Youth,"* 32, 365, 380, 445, 522, 545ff (education and the nobility); 307, 472, 504,
527, 551 (Slavophilism and the concord of the Russian community); 424ff, 477,
497, 514, 524, 529, 540 (lack of "foundations since Peter the Great," "unfinished
people" and, therefore, "underground men").

together, the properly human . . . and the properly human element
is the mind (*ratio*), *i.e.* the relationship of the two others." The essential relationship for the establishment of a Christian culture requires free coordination of the two lower elements (the rational and
the material) with the divine or Spirit through voluntary subjection
to it not by force but in that it is the good. For such a *free* subjection
of the lower elements to the divine to so occur, naturally and without coercion, it is necessary that each of the three elements of human
nature has maturity and independent standing in its own right.

> Otherwise the truth would not have anything on which it could manifest
> its action, in which it could become actualized. But in the Orthodox
> Church the enormous majority of its members were captivated into obe-
> dience to the truth through an immediate [direct] inclination, not through
> a conscious [reflective] process in their inner lives. The really human ele-
> ment [*i.e.* mind, reason], in consequence, proved in the [Eastern] Christian
> society to be too weak and insufficient for a free and rational carrying
> out of the divine beginning, and the Christian consciousness was not free
> from a certain *dualism* between God and the world. Thus the Christian
> truth, mutilated and finally repudiated by the Western man, remained
> imperfect in the man of the East.

The remedy for the imperfection and disproportion in the East is
to foster full development of the embryonic human element there—
that is, reason and personality. This critical task can be undertaken
at the present stage of history because a full development of reason
and personality has taken place in the West and has been introduced
from there into Russia. The negative immediate results in the West
thus augur well for a future age as the dialectic unfolds itself. In
the Slavic East "all the forces of its spirit [were] attached to the
divine [beginning] and preserved it, working out in itself the con-
servative and ascetic attitude necessary for that [function]." Mean-
while, the whole energy of the West was applied to development of
the human element, necessarily at the expense of the divine truth,
"which was at first mutilated and then altogether repudiated."
Through the approaching dialectical union of the unique forces of
both Russia and Europe the "true society of Godmanhood, created
in the image and likeness of the God-man Himself" as a "free con-

cordance of the divine and human beginnings" can finally be realized. "[The] divine element of Christianity, preserved in the East, can now reach its perfection in mankind, for now it has the material upon which it can act, in which it can manifest its internal force: namely the human element which has been emancipated and developed in the West." [69]

While it can scarcely be said that anything in the Legend reflects this prognosis of Solovyov's, Dostoevsky's concern for the problem of culture and the inadequacy of the indigenous theoretical underpinnings of Russian civilization supplied a significant part of the backdrop to his struggle to prevent Western ideology from taking by storm the increasingly intolerable intellectual vacuum of nineteenth century Russia. Dostoevsky was hardly the ecclesiastical syncretist that Solovyov was even in the eighties. The warning in the Legend is primarily pointed against the evil West, although, like Solovyov, Dostoevsky knew that the destiny of Russia was inevitably bound up with things European, if not necessarily with Europe itself. His urgent problem was to discover how to adapt for Russian use the great achievements of the West without destroying the priceless and the unique in Russian tradition. The absence of a Russian culture was the very core of this problem as he understood it, and he never really solved it to his satisfaction. Nor, it may be added, did Russia; and the old Russia eventually fell before the very forces against which Dostoevsky had so remarkably striven.

With respect to the use of the temptation in the Legend, it may finally be said that misunderstandings of Dostoevsky's intention arise both from inattention to the biblical and specifically Christian setting dominant in the episode and from the vehement acumen with which the Inquisitor puts his case to the silent Prisoner. The torrent of sneering invective and shrewdly insolent innuendo staggers the reader: the forces of darkness seem to have all the good arguments. What, indeed, could Christ have said? Small wonder He remained silent! Even Pobedonostsev wrote Dostoevsky after reading the Legend to

---

[69] Solovyov, *Lectures on Godmanhood*, 194, 204–206; cf. Peter Zouboff's "Introduction," *ibid.*, 39–66. See also Theodore L. Wesseling, "Vladimir Soloviev: An Interpretation (I)," *Eastern Churches Quarterly*, II (1937), 18–23.

inquire nervously, "What answer can be given to all of these atheistic statements?" [70]

The whole devastating refutation of the Inquisitor is present in the Legend itself, but this is hardly ever understood. The Legend, particularly in the central part 5 (fig. 1) which includes the temptation, is a vindication of the Christian faith as powerful as any in literature. But one hears only the Great Questioner. The tragic proportions of this blind spot are sensed in the words of another student of *The Brothers Karamazov*: "Here is a true gift to us, perhaps Dostoevsky's supreme gift. Ivan's picture of himself we immediately recognize as our self-portrait; the God that is dead for him is dead for us; and his Karamazov-God of tension and terror is often the only one we are able to find." [71] It is difficult to imagine a more solemnly eloquent testimonial to the prophetic in Dostoevsky. The twentieth century is so nearly the Age of the Inquisitor that the real meaning of the Legend is unintelligible, unheeded, and almost undiscovered.

---

[70] Quoted by Dolinin (ed.), in Dostoevsky, *Pis'ma*, III, 363. Similarly, Temira Pachmuss is convinced that Christ's silence is an admission that he cannot refute the charges. Pachmuss, *F. M. Dostoevsky: Dualism and Synthesis of the Human Soul* (Carbondale: Southern Illinois University Press, 1963), 123.

[71] William Hamilton, " 'Banished from the Land of Unity': A Study of Dostoevski's Religious Vision through the Eyes of Ivan and Alyosha Karamazov," *Journal of Religion*, XXXIX (1959), 261.

CHAPTER VI

METAPHYSICS OF REBELLION

Dostoevsky's ethics and metaphysics are inseparable from his anthropology of the healthy and of the diseased psyche. The analysis of the typology of human characters, in turn, provides the foundation for his political theory. He retains and even refines Plato's insight that the substance of society is psyche and that a diseased psyche, if socially pervasive, produces a diseased society; this insight is displayed in the whole of Dostoevsky's work, which includes an encyclopedic inventory of psychic, pneumatic, and social disorders. The Legend itself is, in one of its aspects, a myth of paradigmatic disorder. The anthropology of disorder is the dominant stratum in his work, the level of thought which pulls together the great existential issues of ethics, politics, and metaphysics. Dostoevsky's power as a writer and brilliance as a thinker derive not from technical craftsmanship alone but from an experiential virtuosity which convincingly authenticates the full range of human inclination and action.

It has been shown that one can scarcely comprehend Dostoevsky in the Legend without careful attention to the theological setting. An understanding of the nature of evil and its relation to the good greatly depends upon passages in the novel outside the Legend in which the devil appears. The statement in the Legend can be amplified by recalling Ivan's experiences.

Evil in existence, as analyzed in *The Brothers Karamazov*, is carefully concentrated in a specific quarter of the overall problem of theodicy. It is the evil which arises from human action. The mischief in the creation against which Ivan rebels is, therefore, not a rebellion directed toward the besetting evil of a Job nor the ravages of natural calamity and physiological disease. It is rebellion against the suffering generated by the imperfection of man, symbolized by the Fall, and remediable through perfection in grace by Christian accounting. Not a word is said by Ivan against naturalistic, surd evil; only the evil (sin) freely chosen by men through exercise of reason and will is condemned—and the essence of man along with it, because the only conceivable solution of this problem of evil available to the rationalist-gnostic is destruction of the nature and personality of man as the seat of reason and freedom.

The rebellion of Ivan is thus a repudiation of Christ and faith as inefficacious remedies for the exigencies of existence and a repudiation of the order of the Creator, which permits man the luxury of an imperfect nature capable of freely choosing self and lustful malice rather than God and the ethic of Love. Ivan's tentative solution is encompassed in the metaphysical rebellion of the Inquisitor which negates the old order of the creation so as to establish the new order of Reason and Justice. Through "New Men" human reason contrives a systematic control net for society, obliterating freedom and establishing a secular Golden Age.[1]

1. The Devil and Ivan: Active Negation and the New Man

In the chapter entitled "The Devil. Ivan's Nightmare" (bk. 11, chap. 9), Ivan has just returned from his third interview with Smerdyakov, his half-brother. There he learned that it was Smerdyakov and not Dmitri who killed their father Fyodor Pavlovitch. Once again at home he collapses in a delirium brought on by this news and Smerdyakov's justification of it in Ivan's own words, "Everything is lawful." In this state, Ivan is confronted for a second time by the devil.

The devil is a sympathetic figure who explains that he genuinely loves men: indeed, he is perhaps the only person in all creation who

---

[1] On myths of the Golden Age and modern eschatological myth, see Mircea Eliade, *Myth and Reality*, trans. Willard R. Trask (New York: Harper & Row, Publ., 1963), 54ff, 174–84.

loves the truth and genuinely desires good. But although he is basically good hearted and not really inclined to negation, he has been
commanded and predestined from the beginning of creation to go
against his grain and "to deny," to be the critic and the source of
irrationality in history.

He himself was never able to understand this providential decree
which, he says, was issued before the beginning of time. He is not
the Creator. But he is an essential factor in historical life, without
which there would be no events. Without his offices as critic and
denier, life "would be nothing but one 'hosannah.' " But it has been
decreed that this is not enough for life: "the hosannah must be tried
in the crucible of doubt."

This is all comedy and farce from the devil's own viewpoint. The
tragic part is that men take life too seriously. His own uncorrected
demand was simply for annihilation. But constrained as he was to
operate within terms of existence which he did not prescribe and to
abide by a truth beyond comprehension, he serves the truth of his
own nature as best he can. Life thereby receives its characteristic
stamp: *suffering*—"for suffering is life." And he enigmatically asks:
"Without suffering what would be the pleasure of it? It would be
transformed into an endless church service; it would be holy but
tedious."

The devil, curiously like the Inquisitor, twice warns Ivan he is
expecting too much of him; he must moderate his expectations and
not demand "everything great and noble." Then they will get along
better. The reason for this is clear. The devil is, after all, only a
negative force—the "minus" in life, capable only of destruction;
impotent to create anything, he can only erode the ground of existence. His providentially enjoined role is to ruin thousands for the
sake of saving one, and while he is aware that there is a transcendent
truth and that in the end he will be reconciled, he does not know
whether *his* truth or the *other* will "turn out the better" until the
secret of creation finally is revealed.

The devil in this conversation reminds Ivan of his poem, "The
Grand Inquisitor," and of another, called "The Geological Cata-
clysm," in which it seems Ivan decided "last spring" that "there are

new men." Ivan's idea of reordering the world was to destroy everything and start all over again with cannibalism.

But the problem is far simpler in the devil's view: "Stupid fel-
lows! (these new men) they didn't ask my advice!" he says. "I maintain that nothing need be destroyed, that we only need to destroy
the idea of God in man, that's how we have to set to work."

While the devil disapproves of Ivan's method, he otherwise seems
enthusiastic about the project. Once the idea of God is destroyed, the
old concept of the universe and the old morality will, of themselves,
also disappear and clear the way for the brave new world of Ivan's
new men. For he recognizes the order of soul and society to depend,
not upon man's whim, but upon transcendent Being as intellectually
articulated in the "Idea of God." The prospective society would unite
all of mankind for the purpose of taking from life all of the joy and
happiness of this world. The new men would be filled with a titanic
pride that would transform them into the long-awaited man-gods
who could deploy zeal hitherto wasted on dreams of heaven and
immortality infinitely to expand the mastery of nature through science and technology. Waging the intellectual battle totally to sub-
due nature would provide compensatory pleasure in life and reconcile the new men to their scientifically assured ultimate mortality.
They would accept death proudly and serenely, knowing there is
no hereafter. The love of God would be succeeded by an even more
fervid and palpable brotherly love than has heretofore been possible
because, though expectant of no extrinsic rewards, there would be
no waste through dissipating thoughts of eternal love.

A timetable for arriving at this age of the new enlightenment is
not of critical importance because anyone "clever" enough to discern the truth of existence becomes a new man in the very act. As
such, he immediately (even if all alone among the people of the
world) can reorder life according to the new morality and proclaim
himself a man-god. As there is no Being superior to him, he occupies
the first rung in existence: he is God, a law unto himself. "Everything is lawful" means the man-god can act as it is most convenient
to himself and need pay no heed to conventional morality and the
other barriers erected by the slave-man. "There is no law for God.

Where God stands, the place is holy . . . 'all things are lawful' and that's the end of it!"

The Inquisitor and Ivan's new men, whatever their surface distinctions, are patently identical. They are in revolt against God, afflicted with an advanced stage of megalomania which allows them to convince themselves that, although God exists and has created the universe, they know better than does He how existence should be ordered. Radical immanentization of existence is characteristic of each. The most devastating statement of this position appears in the form of Ivan's confession to Alyosha. It constitutes both a trenchant diagnosis of the psychic condition of one who can look with longing toward the reign of the Inquisitor, and Ivan's pneumatological portrait. Alyosha's equally impassioned reply to this impassioned outburst (that Christ has atoned) set the stage for the Legend.[2]

Ivan knows there is suffering where there is no guilt. This he cannot bear. He must have justice "here on earth," so that he can see it for himself. "I want to see with my own eyes the hind lie down with the lion and the victim rise up and embrace his murderer," he says. All the religions of the world are built upon this longing for the eternal harmony in which "everything that lives and has lived cries aloud: 'Thou art just, O Lord, for Thy ways are revealed.' "

But, he asks, if "all must suffer to pay for the eternal harmony, what have [innocent] children to do with it?" For himself, he rejects the whole business. "While there is still time I hasten to protect myself and so I renounce the higher harmony altogether. It's not worth the tears of . . . one tortured child. . . . It's not worth it because those tears are unatoned for. They must be atoned for, or there can be no harmony. But how?"

I accept God and am glad to, and what's more I accept His wisdom, His

---

2 On "pneumatological characterology" in Dostoevsky as a resumption of a kind of analysis done by Plato, Huarte, Bacon and Vico, see Alois Dempf, *Die Drei Laster: Dostojewkis Tiefenpsychologie* (Munich: Karl Alber, 1946), 85–87. For the significance of the content of the chapter entitled "Rebellion" as it stands in juxtaposition to the Legend, see Robert L. Belknap, *The Structure of "The Brothers Karamazov,"* Slavistic Printings and Reprintings, LXXII, ed. C. H. Van Schooneveld (The Hague and Paris: Mouton, 1967), 53, 55–56.

purpose—which is utterly beyond our ken; I believe in the underlying order and the meaning of life; I believe in the eternal harmony in which they say we shall one day be blended. I believe in the Word to which the universe is striving, and which Itself was 'with God,' and which Itself is God and so on. . . . Yet would you believe it, in the final result I don't accept this world of God's, and *although I* know it exists, I don't accept it at all. It's not that I don't accept God, you must understand, it's the world created by Him I don't and cannot accept. [Even though] I believe like a child that suffering will be healed and made up for . . . human contradictions will vanish . . . that in the world's finale, in the moment of eternal harmony, something so precious will come to pass that it will suffice for all hearts . . . comforting all resentments . . . [atoning for] all crimes of humanity . . . that it will [be] possible to forgive [and] justify all that happened with men—but though all that may come to pass, I don't accept it, I won't accept it. . . . That's the root of me, Alyosha; that's my creed. (*The Brothers Karamazov,* I, 240.)

While one is dealing with Dostoevsky in the Legend, he is also dealing with the ostensible composition of his creature Ivan. It is significant to observe, therefore, that Ivan is a man consciously in revolt against God because God's creation outrages his humanitarian sense. Ivan is even more tender and loving toward humanity than the God Who is Love and Truth. He finds that the proffered eternal harmony isn't "worth it." But this is the very spot where doubt plays its role. It would not, it could not, be worth it *if* there were to be no eternal harmony at all, Ivan reasoned. And is it even worth it, considering the absence of scientific information about eternal harmony? There are only the traditional expectations, and aren't these probably only so much mishmash? Ivan's new men boldly acknowledge that death is the end of it. In the Legend the program treats mankind *as if there were* no eternity to be reckoned with. Ivan means the suffering of the hundred thousand to be aggravated by this same doubt which he himself feels—combined with associated doubts, such as a vision of a sentimental Christ deprived of eschatological hardness and capable of being fended off by such injunctions as the old Inquisitor's last words to his departing Prisoner: "Go, and come no more . . . come not at all, never, never." Two thousand years is a long time, Ivan can have thought, introducing the evidence of history once more. If the Judgment cannot be wished away, we humanitarians can at least defend ourselves by having accomplished in the interim worthwhile works which demonstrate a love of mankind *superior even to God's*. But, then, perhaps, the expectation of the Second Coming belongs in limbo with all the other old wives' tales. In any of these cases, by any of these lines of reasoning, Ivan could have arrived at his conclusion that it isn't worth it. Such is the nature of doubt as it operates in the fertile field between belief and disbelief.

The notion of God is retained but becomes anachronistic and functionless—thereby destroyed—in its traditional sense. The bond of faith having given way, God is at best isolated in transcendence, at worst He is proclaimed to be dead. Theology is emptied of meaning to become mere anthropology. The devil has the audacity and candor to propose outright destruction of the idea of God in the minds of men. In the Legend religion has clearly become the opiate of the people—but this is to be dated from the ascendance of the Inquisitor and his kind. The question remains as to the psychic condition of the suffering hundred thousand, those who have knowledge of good and evil. Are they atheists? Is atheism possible among human beings? Can the idea of God be destroyed in the minds of men? Or is this an instance of mass sublimation induced by psychological management, in which the belief in God is retained (because man can but know He exists) but is transmuted and displaced as the ordering force in the soul by a skillfully manipulated immanentist principle? Dostoevsky does not discursively answer this question. There is as evidence of his answer only the action of the Grand Inquisitor, who "holds to his idea" despite a direct confrontation with Christ. Luther's summation is, in principle, definitive: "Der Mensch hat immer Gott oder Abgott." [3]

---

[3] Quoted in Emil Brunner, *Man in Revolt: A Christian Anthropology*, trans. Olive Wyon (Philadelphia: Westminster Press, 1957), 25n; cf. 38. Dostoevsky almost quotes Luther in *The Notebooks for "A Raw Youth"*, ed. and with an intro. by Edward Wasiolek, trans. Victor Terras (Chicago: University of Chicago Press, 1969), 178–79: "Man cannot exist without bowing before something. Without it, no man could stand himself . . . he has been created that way. Let him reject God, and he will bow before an idol made of silver [stone], or of gold, or one that is in his mind. That's the kind of godless people they all . . . are! They are idolaters, that's what they are, and not godless." Cf. *ibid.*, 275–76, 513, 534, 542, 550. "This is enthusiasm. . . . They even reject God religiously." *Ibid.*, 318.

2. REBELLION AS SPIRITUAL DISEASE[4]

Dostoevsky's portrayal of the Inquisitor in the Legend constitutes a complex and almost impenetrably profound anthropology of spiritual disorder. The attempt here will be to articulate only the salient points in the analysis.

(a) Freedom and evil as possibility. The essence of man is his freedom of conscience in the knowledge of good and evil. According to the verdict of free choice, man can either ascend the way of active love through conscience formed by faith in response to revelation and find fulfillment in the perfect freedom and beatitude of Christ as His elect, as the gods grown out of history; or man can rebel against the prompting of conscience as the purveyor of an absurd mystery built upon "all that is exceptional, vague, and enigmatic," and follow "the spirit of the earth" from the uncertainty, confusion, and suffering of faith through the pride of life, the lust of the flesh, and the lust of the eyes to ultimate sin and the rejection of transcendence.

(b) From absolute freedom to absolute tyranny. The absolute freedom of rebellious man, claimed in the name of reason and in light of historical experience, is license which perverts the meaning of freedom on principle, enslaves man to his passions, leads him to the anarchy of passionate self-assertion and gratification ending in cannibalism, fraticidal war, the surfeit of self-indulgence which, exacerbated by blasphemy and faithlessness, makes man the most miserable of creatures. From this *bellum omnium contra omnes*,[5] there emerges a chastened mankind—the new man of socialism—purged of its obstreperous elements and anxious to surrender its freedom in exchange for bread, peace, salved conscience, and the modicum of comfort and self-indulgence which constitutes material happiness. Rebellious man progresses from the tyranny of the libidos to the tyranny of an external power—or, rather, of the *libido dominandi* politically organized.

(c) Beyond good and evil. Out of the *anomia* of shattered spiritual

---

[4] It should be noted that Dostoevsky himself designates rebellion spiritual disease, paralleling thereby the usage of Plato whose term is *nosos*. See, for example, Dostoevsky, *The Diary of a Writer*, trans. Boris Brasol (2 vols.; New York: Charles Scribner's Sons, 1949), II, 959ff; cf. Plato, *Laws*, 888c.

[5] Cf. Thomas Hobbes, *Leviathan*, chap. 13.

and social order emerges the new ethic of absolute submission to absolute power. Everything is lawful for the ruling suffering saviors (man-gods) without qualification and for subject mankind (slave-men) with permission. "Oh," raptures the Inquisitor, "they will thank us for allowing them to sin." The principle of the earth spirit, of sensuous, gluttonous life, the "strength of the Karamazovs—the strength of the Karamazov baseness," provides the positive orienting force in existence. There is no crime, "hence" no sin; no soul, and no immortality, "hence" no God; no reckoning beyond human happiness conceived in tellurian and utilitarian terms.[6]

(d) The ultimate lie. But the escape beyond good and evil is not, in fact, possible. The Inquisitor's ideology is built upon an acknowledged lie, which is even more of a lie than he admits. It is a metaphysical swindle. As Ivan's devil jeers in sublime mockery: "He can't bring himself to swindle without a moral sanction. He is so in love with truth—" (*The Brothers Karamazov*, II, 307). The hundred thousand elite rule with the knowledge of good and evil and know they have rejected Christ and embraced Satan. But to be truly beyond good and evil, neither Satan nor God may exist. This is precisely the rejection demanded by the Euclidian reason of Ivan; but the ontological status of the soul, even in the absence of faith as a controlling center, gives the lie to the "logical" conclusion. "Homeopathic doses [of faith] perhaps are the strongest," the devil tells Ivan (*The Brothers Karamazov*, II, 302); and no man, not even the Inquisitor or Ivan, can escape the gnawing doubt of reason's conclusions which is the sediment of faith in homeopathic doses. The lie of the Grand Inquisitor is, thus, the lie in the soul, a species of Plato's "true lie" (*alethes pseudos*), the arch-lie of human existence. The experiential configuration of rebellion can be stated in terms of Dostoevsky's "three-cornered" theory of consciousness as follows: the will of the "I" is the sum of existentially relevant being *even if* the "Not I" embraces not only the postulated nothingness (absolute evil) but the transcendentally real "Thou" (the Good) as well. Otherwise stated, the crux of the matter is as Alyosha says it is: not reason

---

[6] Cf. Paul Ramsey, "No Morality without Immortality," *Journal of Religion*, XXXVI (1956), 90–108.

and not experience but a faithless, hardened heart and the "lust for power, of filthy earthly gain, of domination" (*The Brothers Kara-mazov*, I, 267). As a type, the man-god is a variety of megalomaniac: a religious fanatic who spiritually is too weak for faith. In the radically closed dream world of the superman, everything prohibited in the real world is permitted, and the lie in the soul can be both believed and disbelieved simultaneously, a disease of the soul first diagnosed by Plato.[7]

3. ETHICAL THEORY

For Dostoevsky the sufferer, the problem of good and evil is neither a dogmatic nor speculative one but is existential. Underlying the agony of Ivan, however, is the anguished ancient query, "si Deus bonus est, unde malum?" There is the impoverishment of the problem of evil previously indicated which leaves surd evil aside in favor of preoccupation with the evil instrumental in man, for it is the mystery of man which is celebrated and which Dostoevsky seeks to penetrate with the resources of his intellect and experience. The alternatives of the Inquisitor's solution of the problem of evil and suffering are the classic possibilities of man as *non posse peccare* or as *posse non peccare*. That these notions can be regarded as not merely expressive of a logical dichotomy but as the ground of the solution to the problem is itself a measure of the rebellion of Ivan and his creatures. The attitude strictly depends upon a denial of the ontological status of God as the Creator and source of order in the creation, and this, in turn, reflects the death of God in the experience of Ivan and of those he represents. The supersession of the old men by new men incapable of evil entails a rationalistic onslaught which presumes to eliminate evil in man by existential fragmentation of the Good, banishment of freedom, and excision of anything historically identifiable as morality; for the entire moral order is dependent upon man's resolute resistance to and abstention from evil in act and thought to the limits of his capability.

---

[7] Cf. Plato, *The Republic*, 382 a–b; 572e–576b. On the "three cornered" theory of consciousness in Dostoevsky, see A. S. Steinberg, *Die Idee der Freiheit: Ein Dostojewski-Buch*, trans. Jacob Klein (Lucerne: Vita Nova, 1936), 150–52.

The presentation in the novel is equivalent to the classical Christian solution of the problem of good and evil. Evil is essentially negation, pure negation and denial, the "minus" in existence. "For evil," wrote John Damascene, "is no more than the privation of good, just as the darkness is the absence of light." Because man cannot bear nothingness, existential evil becomes centered in the Augustinian *amor sui*.[8] But, at bottom, self-love itself is devoid of content; the man turned radically inward upon himself falls into the abyss of his own nothingness. The superman's alternative to this horror is the moral sanction of the Inquisitor: the love of self expanded into an anemic love of mankind which forms as humanitarian pity enforced by a lust for power growing, specifically, from the megalomaniac's jealousy of God. Nietzsche's utterance is prototypical: "If there were a god, I could not endure not being he." [9]

Dostoevsky fought his fight, the "Unseen Warfare" of the soul, in the darkness of the depths of human existence. His study of evil in human nature and society, of sin and the devil, of atheism, nihilism and socialism is an exhaustive report from the wilderness of life,

---

8 John of Damascus, *Writings* [*The Fount of Knowledge*], trans. Frederic H. Chase, Jr. (New York: Fathers of the Church, Inc., 1958), 209; cf. 384–87. The Augustinian analysis of evil is close to that of the Greek theologians; and, in any event, Augustinian theology was familiar to nineteenth century Russians. Thus, George P. Fedotov, in E. J. Simmons (ed.), *Continuity and Change in Russian and Soviet Thought* (Cambridge: Harvard University Press, 1955), 182, wrote that through Tikhon Zadonsky the "fundamental ideas of Saint Augustine now made their first entrance into Orthodox theology." See St. Augustine, *City of God*, bk. 11, chap. 22, where the Manichaean notion of natural evil is disposed of; bk. 12, chaps. 6 and 7 on evil as negation and a defection of the will, hence traceable to a *deficient* cause; also, the *Enchiridion*, chaps. 9–16. Cf. Vladimir Lossky who pronounces evil to be "not a nature *(physis)* but a condition *(exis)*," and who further states: "Evil is nothing other than an attraction of the will towards nothing, a negation of being, of creation, and above all of God, a furious hatred of grace against which the rebellious will puts up an implacable resistance. Even though they have become spirits of darkness, the fallen angels remain creatures of God, and their rejection of the will of God represents a despairing intercourse with the nothingness which they will never find. Their eternal descent towards non-being will have no end." Lossky, *The Mystical Theology of the Eastern Church* (London: James Clarke & Co., 1957), 128–29. Cf. Dionysius the Areopagite, *On the Divine Names and The Mystical Theology*, ed. and trans. C. E. Rolt, Translations of Christian Literature, Series I: Greek Texts (London: S.P.C.K.; New York: Macmillan, 1920), chap. 4, secs. 19–35, pp. 111–30.

9 Friedrich Nietzsche, *Also sprach Zarathustra*, Vol. VI of Nietzsche, *Werke* (24 vols.; Leipzig: Kroener), 124.

from the "Underground" as he called it. And life is Dostoevsky's preoccupation. His mysticism is predominantly telluric, his love Dionysiac. In the depth of life's horrors and despair he sees a light. Doctrinally, again, the answer is classically Christian: Good is God and all that participates in divine being; and God is revealed in Christ who is, ineffably, love, and freedom, and truth—the unique "higher idea." But the problem of good and evil is the real arena of Dostoevsky's striving. Doctrinally, the answer is faith: one maximizes good and minimizes evil through faith. The goal of human endeavor is the eternal harmony, the Kingdom of God—conceived apocalyptically as the climax of history and concretely as personal spiritual beatitude, salvation, and resurrection. The integrity of the human personality is never compromised. But the gulf that separates man from God is the one that divides the finite from the infinite. What, then is the way to God for man? Here is the question. The way is *faith*, and each man must learn for himself what faith is. Here is the stumbling block. The answer is not easy, nor is the way. It is the *Via Crucis*, the agonizing Way of the Cross, the path of suffering. To come to the Light and make it his own, man must freely choose and accept the proffered love of God through faith. The man who balks and rejects is the rebel.

Dostoevsky balked and rebelled; he probed rebellion to its limits and, finding it a dead thing dealing only death and destruction, returned to the Way and only Light he had found in all the vast reaches of existential darkness. His Song of the Way is not one long Hosannah: it is ribald and blasphemous, as filled with curses as with hallelujahs. But one hears in its dominant resolution the authentic Hymn of Hope of a courageous and authentic man who knew all of life and avoided none of it.

4. METAPHYSICAL REBELLION

Satan is death and thirst for self-destruction, whose ideal is "peace in nothingness, in eternal death," Dostoevsky wrote in the notes for *A Raw Youth*. "But Satan knows God; how then, can he deny Him?" [10] Ivan's affirmation of the "I" is done by means of alliance

---

[10] Dostoevsky, *The Notebooks for "A Raw Youth"*, 59.

with the traditional Satan. And while his Inquisitor says as much, when Alyosha informs Ivan that this is rebellion, the latter replies as though the thought had not occurred to him. " 'Rebellion? I am sorry you call it that,' said Ivan earnestly."

This exchange points to the crux of the problem of Ivan's metaphysical rebellion. He is a positive figure, striving to articulate in thought and deed an affirmative solution to the crushing misery of faithless existence. Not only power of intellect, but nobility of thought and character dignify Ivan. In the first instance he is not impressed by doctrine (which he fully comprehends) but by reality—by the atrocity, brutality and suffering infesting Holy Russia, by the beneficence, beauty, and fruitful love which he finds in the world of nature: "the little sticky leaves, and the precious tombs, and the blue sky, and the woman" he loves. The supernatural Christian God of power and compassion is dead for him, or at best so layered over with spiritually deadening self-esteem that He provides no balm to a tormented and sensitive soul. But, somehow, nature—even divine nature—does not really suffice. There remains before him only the superb image of Christ, the God-man (*Bogochelovek*) whose mercies and understanding reach the infinitude of divine Love. How, indeed, can He endure the sufferings of the innocent children, the agony of existence where there is no retribution to pay because there is no guilt? And with the icon of the humane Christ who is eternally just and infinitely love before him, Ivan turns in love to his fellow men to found a social order in which man and nature can blend in happy harmony to live life purged of pain and fear. Ivan's are humanitarian motives. Out of love he calculates what it is that men hunger after, what it is that can bring happiness and peace to human lives, what in the equation of existence needs substitution in order for love to reign and barbarous abuse be banished.

One answer is contained in the ideology of the Inquisitor, and its apology is the monologue. But the monologue is also a second confession of an ardent heart. Ivan is a believer. He believes in Christ. He believes that Christ revealed a truth that has been perverted by the Orthodox Church. For Christ was the first man to become God and to perfect within Himself all that man had from the beginning attributed to the God in the Heavens. The mystery of the Incarnation is nothing else except Man *is* God, and the God of the Heavens exists only in human consciousness. In this way Ivan is led to utter what Dostoevsky regarded as the Roman Catholic principle—which, however, is a gloss on Feuerbach.

"We love God because he first loved us." What, then, is it that I love in God? Love: love to man. But when I love and worship the love with which God loves man, do I not love man; is not my love of God, though indirectly, love of man? If God loves man, is not man, then, the very substance of God? That which I love, is it not my inmost being? Have I a heart when I do not love? No! love only is the heart of man. But what is love without the thing loved? Thus what I love is my heart, the substance of my being, my nature. . . . Thus if God loves man, man is the heart of God—the welfare of man his deepest anxiety. If man, then, is the object of God, is not man, in God, an object to himself? Is not the content of the divine nature the human nature? If God is love, is not the essential content of this love man? Is not the love of God to man— the basis and central point of religion—the love of man to himself made an object, contemplated as the highest objective truth, as the highest being to man? [11]

So the essence of Christianity can be summarized: *"Man has his highest being, his God, in himself*; not in himself as an individual, but in his essential nature, his species. . . . Homo homini deus est."* This kind of Jesus atheism, as it may be called, is the core of Ivan's religiousness. It lies, moreover, at the heart of contemporary "radical theology." [12]

Actuated by this conviction, the Christ of the Legend is the triumphant figure of the Palm Sunday entry into Jerusalem, not the Christ of the Passion, nor the Resurrected Christ, nor the eternal

---

[11] Ludwig Feuerbach, *The Essence of Christianity*, trans. George Eliot (New York: Harper & Row, Torchbooks, 1957), pt. 1, chap. 4, "The Mystery of the Incarnation; or, God as Love, as a Being of the Heart," 57–58. Cf. Fyodor M. Dostoevsky, *The Notebooks for "The Brothers Karamazov,"* ed. and trans. Edward Wasiolek (Chicago: University of Chicago Press, 1971), 80–81.

[12] Feuerbach, *The Essence of Christianity*, app., sec. 1, p. 281. See Thomas J. J. Altizer, *The Gospel of Christian Atheism* (Philadelphia: Westminster Press, 1966) which is essentially an elaboration of Ivan's doctrine in its religious dimension. The volume may be read as a commentary on the Legend from this viewpoint.

Word whose place is at the right hand of the Father. He is the humanist's Christ whose revelation is of the God in man. It is because of the conflicting Christologies of the brothers that Ivan can earnestly recount the Legend to Alyosha (in fear and trembling to be sure) and not be in the absurd position of simply refuting his own timorous belief through caricature. He has, indeed, brought his confession to Christ Himself. Feuerbach, too, commended prayer.

Yet Ivan is not oblivious of the difficulties of his good and true solution to the problem of the human condition. He knows that this is the rational reading of Christianity, one wholly in keeping with demands of the scientific mind. He knows that it embraces genuine ethical merit and that it is motivated by love. Yet he is agonized by doubts. Surgically to excise supernaturalism from Christianity ends the duality in man and permits the embrace of Sodom and the Madonna at once, thereby fulfilling a thirst of the human heart. The latent rites of Mother Moist Earth can be revived to the satisfaction of the people who, in truth, want earthly bread above all. On this principle Eden is restored, Paradise regained, and the Dionysian orgy at Mokroe (Moisture) of Mitia and Grushenka augurs well for the hopes in man's new estate; except that the orgy, like Ivan's nature worship, somehow does not work out. Ivan knows this is the acknowledged province of sin and Satan in the traditional Christian view. He discerns that it is not enough simply to proclaim the man-god (*chelovekobog*). To secure his blessings to the land, not only must man be substituted in the existential equation for God, but necessity must be substituted for freedom as well. The prime difficulty under the old dispensation, the Inquisitor makes clear, was that freedom of choice was bequeathed man; and if left to himself without direction, man destroys himself. Hence new men must be fashioned through conditioning within the framework of a police state: in the act this involves the destruction of human reason as well as the breaking of the will of man, for these are the constituents of freedom; that is, it involves obliteration of the very being of man: "Since man was made both rational and free, he received the power to be unceasingly united to God by his own choice." [13] Heavy as the

---

[13] John of Damascus, *Fount of Knowledge*, 354.

burden is, the Inquisitor willingly shoulders it. Ivan becomes reconciled to Feuerbach's insight that "God" is not found in every man
singly but only in the species collectively as its essential nature. So
individuals must be segregated as in all gnostic communities into the
believers and the perfect, into the slave-men and the essentially representative man-gods. Still this is not the end of the troubles. For the
goal of the Inquisitor's society is happiness and justice. It is not
governed by truth. But men thirst for truth; and, as Marx observed,
to believe in divine origins and destiny is natural to men. Hence
they must be allowed not only physical indulgence but also the
intellectual and spiritual indulgence of efficacious lies: they must be
taught that theirs is the way to eternal salvation, that whatever is
allowed them is good, and that there is no evil except disobedience
to the man-gods' decrees. The final substitution in the existential
equation, therefore, is lie for truth. In this way the primordial Eden
is restored as a mock paradise in which the commandments of
Yahweh are supplanted by the decrees of the Inquisitor, where no
tree of the knowledge of good and evil can grow, and those who trans-
gress are burned at the stake to the greater glory of the man-god.
The Final Age of total freedom and unlimited pride is revealed.
The suffering and murder against which Ivan had recoiled in God's
world have ended by becoming institutionalized instruments of total
control in the church become the state in a perfect city. The moral
and intellectual bankruptcy of the "solution" is clear to him even
before the murder of Fyodor Pavlovich. Still, despite reason, he
"believes" and perseveres.[14]

---

[14] Cf. Albert Camus, *The Rebel: An Essay on Man in Revolt*, trans. Anthony
Bower (New York: Random House, Inc., Vintage Books, 1956), 282. The church
becoming the state and the "Kingdom of this world' is an explicit theme sketched
in Dostoevsky's notes to the novel; cf. *The Notebooks for "The Brothers Karamazov*," 41–42, 263. The suggestion of this development was not only the "Catholic
Idea" which Dostoevsky nourished, but the specific developments of the seventies
(while he was living abroad in Germany) of the proclamation of papal infallibility
and the beginning of the Bismarckian *Kulturkampf* which was understood as the
struggle between two civilizations or cultures not radically unlike the struggle
depicted in the Legend. The refusal of Peter the Great to appoint a patriarch
in 1700 and the creation of the Holy Synod in 1721 permanently to supplant the
patriarchate, thereby firmly establishing the principle of caesaropapism and political domination of the Russian Church, was viewed by the Old Believers and

The more general range of the problem of metaphysical rebellion, beyond Ivan's perspective, can now be circumscribed.

The doctrine of the Inquisitor is an onslaught against Being as nonreality whose effect is the denial of the contingence or dependence of the creation. Elaborated as a theoretical construction, it forms a closed ideological system which purposely distorts and obscures reality rather than illumines it. The result parallels the Marxian intention, not to interpret the world (as philosophers have done), but to change it. Man's restorative recourse to transcendent Being is, therefore, in principle severed; and, in practice, the disoriented isolation of man in existence is secured through enforced state monopoly of metaphysical and religious symbols whose meaning is perverted. Man, society, and history are experientially absorbed as reflective consciousness into the processes of nature which constitute the substance of being.

Denied participation in Being through this radical reduction, the destruction of man follows as a matter of course from the destruction of the order of being. As an experiential alternative, the consubstantiality of man with the life-force immanent to nature is sub-

---

sectarians as a further evidence of the reign of the Antichrist and is at least a supporting idea in the Inquisitor's doctrine, as Vasili Rozanov already argued in 1891. Cf. Thomas G. Masaryk, *The Spirit of Russia: Studies in History, Literature and Philosophy*, Vols. I and II, trans. Eden and Cedar Paul (2nd ed.; New York: Macmillan Co., 1955); Vol. III, ed. George Gibian, trans. Robert Bass (New York: Barnes and Noble, Inc., 1967), III, 43–46, 128–29. It is interesting that in 1877 Dostoevsky, faced in the *Diary* with choosing between Bismarck and the pope, comes down with enthusiasm on the side of the former: "On foot and barefooted, the Pope will go to the beggars, and he will tell them that everything the socialists teach and strive for is contained in the Gospel; that so far the time had not been ripe for them to learn about this; but that now the time has come, and that he, the Pope, surrenders Christ to them and believes in the ant-hill.

"Roman Catholicism does not need Christ. (This is all too clear.) What it strives for is universal sovereignty. It will say: 'What you need is a united front against the enemy. Unite, then, under my power, since I alone—among all powers and potentates of the world—am *universal*; and let us go together!' Probably Prince Bismarck foreshadows this picture, because he alone among all diplomats was so quick-sighted as to prefigure the viability of the Roman idea and that energy with which it is determined to defend itself regardless, by any means. It is inspired with a devilish desire to live, and it is difficult to kill it—it is a snake! This is what Prince Bismarck alone—the principal enemy of the papacy and the Roman idea—realizes to the fullest extent." Dostoevsky, *Diary*, II, 738; cf. the May–June, 1877, issue, chap. 3, *passim; ibid.*, 727–45.

stituted as the new ordering center. The affirmation of the biological as the essence of being is accompanied by the formation of the order of society as a confessional state. Destruction of the human personality is effected by compelling individuals to subsist only at the level of the controlled common consciousness. Privacy, private property, life of the family, and any competition of a plurality of independent ordering sources are eliminated to the end that spiritual integrity is impossible and actualization of the range of personal existence blocked.[15] The reverse conversion of the soul toward self as the only ordering center and the understanding of self as a mere configuration of the communal life-force supply the instrumentality for absorption of the psyche into the somatic subsistence of man and provide the means of nailing the soul to the passions. Inasmuch as corporeal destruction of men is not feasible short of total annihilation, the communalization of existence is correlated with the absolute atomization of society into two-dimensional individuals utterly dependent upon the regime.[16] Personality and humanity are thereby relinquished to the ruler,[17] who alone remains intact in the exercise of reason and freedom. The split between truth and justice which underlay Ivan's initial rebellion now becomes intelligible as the identification of justice with the pride of life[18] of the self-serving megalomaniac, hence, with the existential lie par excellence. The rejection of suffering in the creation and its replacement by suffering at the hands of the man-god are thereby shown to be, in fact, the repudiation of the salvation and the promise of the Kingdom of God which is only attainable through suffering.[19] The cumulative outcome of the substitutions made in the equation of being by the

---

15 Cf. Aristotle, *Nicomachean Ethics*, bk. 2, especially 1262b10–23, 1263a21–1264-a11; see Eric Voegelin, *Plato and Aristotle* (Baton Rouge: Louisiana State University Press, 1957), Vol. III of Voegelin, *Order and History* (3 vols. to date; Baton Rouge: Louisiana State University Press, 1956—), 320ff.

16 Cf. Hannah Arendt, *Origins of Totalitarianism* (New York: Harcourt, Brace, 1951), 316–17.

17 Cf. Thomas Hobbes, *Leviathan*, chaps. 16, 17.

18 In the Russian religious horizon, Ivan's insistence upon "justice" is both a suggestion of his Western orientation and a sign that he is infected by the supreme sin, *pride*. The view is suggested in a sentence by Pseudo-Chrysostom, commenting on the parable of the Pharisee and the Publican: "Justice falls by arrogance; sin is destroyed by humility." Quoted in George P. Fedotov, *The Russian Religious Mind* (New York: Harper & Row, Publ., Torchbooks, 1960), 220.

19 See Matt. 24:8, John 16:21.

system—of lie for truth, man for God, necessity for freedom—is the metamorphosis of man and society into the purely necessitous, instinctive subsistence of a colony of insects. Radically separated from God and from his own humanity, man and humanistic love subsist in the image of the spider: the most rapacious, cannibalistic expression of instinctive life.

The dominant symbolism of the Legend as an apocalypse of evil emerges in the eschatological myth of New Jerusalem become New Sodom (Rev. 11:8) where, at the hands of an apostate Elijah-John the Baptist,[20] Christ is crucified without cease. The substitution of massive Dionysian somatic frenzy for participation through faith in transcendence, identification of the bad *eros* with the good *eros* and *agape*, and confusion of demonic passions with the Holy Spirit result in equation of the sacred in its enthusiastic manifestation with the scabrous sadism of the voluptuary.[21] Within the prison walls of the Inquisitor's de Sade fortress the inmates perform as holy rituals the vilest deeds of perversion, torture, and murder to the satisfaction of masters whose every whim is a decree and whose especial delight is their knowledge that the flowers of evil of the city's liturgy outrage holiness.[22] The Inquisitor's vaunted control over procreation among his slave-men is the means of withholding or dispensing the grace of immortality in his dark realm, and the theme of suffering is

20 See Rev. 11:3. On the identification of John the Baptist with Elijah, see Mark 9:13, 2–8; cf. Mark 1:2–5; II Kings 1:8; Zech. 13:4; Mal. 4:5; but, also, John 1:19–34. Since the archetype of the man-god is a blend of the ancient gnostic pneumatic and the modern gnostic or Joachitic spiritual man, it is of pertinence that Joachim's text for the beginning date of the Third Age of the Spirit as A.D. 1260 is precisely that which supplied Dostoevsky with his myth of the New Sodom, Rev. 11:3: " 'And I will permit my two witnesses [Moses and Elijah], clothed in sackcloth, to prophesy for 1260 days.' "

21 On the good *eros* and the bad, see Plato, *Republic*, 573b, d; cf. *Gorgias*, 481d–e. On the understanding of *agape* in Eastern mysticism, as contrasted with that of the West expressed in Peter Lombard and Thomas, see Lossky, *The Mystical Theology*, 213–14. Cf. Ronald A. Knox, *Enthusiasm: A Chapter in the History of Religion* (New York: Oxford University Press, 1961), especially chap. 13, 578ff.

22 The "Marquis de Sade" is mentioned in the description of Karmazov voluptuousness in the notes for bk. 5; see Dostoevsky, *The Notebooks for "The Brothers Karamazov,"* 73. Satanism, sadism, the scabrous and grotesque are obviously interests of Dostoevsky in this novel (as well as elsewhere) and are implicit in the doctrine of the Inquisitor, despite his own wizened ascetic air. The gross blasphemy of the Legend is itself sadistic. For the compatibility of the monastic atmosphere of the Legend and debauchery as well as torture and murder, Dostoevsky might have chosen from a great variety of models. Ivan the Terrible

linked with the perversion of sexuality as an ingredient of the dis-figurement of nature: "For the invisible things of him from the crea-tion of the world are clearly seen, being understood by the things that are made, *even* his eternal power and Godhead; so that they are without excuse" (Rom. 1:20). The "all is lawful" of Ivan must, then, also be translated by Montigny's "tout est bien, tout est de Dieu." [23]

---

supplied one such example. George Vernadsky describes Ivan with his private household, the *oprichnina:* "When [Ivan] created the oprichnina, his dreaded political police, its headquarters assumed all the aspects of a monastery, with himself as abbot. . . . prayer alternated with wild orgies, and the oprichniki . . . wore black garments and were called 'brethren.' " Vernadsky, *A History of Russia* (4th ed.; New Haven: Yale University Press, 1954), 98, 103.

The works of de Sade himself, of course, supply countless examples, such as the spectacle of the monks in the Convent Sainte Marie des Bois: "To lend keener edge to the orgies, Florette was made to appear toward night in the same robes of the [miraculous] Virgin which had won so much homage [during the day]. The costume greatly excited the monks, and they subjected Florette, dressed as she was, to all their wildest whims. 'It's really too bad that this poor girl has to suffer so for the failings of the Virgin,' the Superior said, in one of his quieter moods. Then they stretched her flat on a large table. They lit wax candles. They took the image of the Savior and placing it near her loins, desecrated upon her the most solemn of mysteries. Unable to bear such a sight, Justine fainted. When she was seen in this state [Dom] Severino [the Superior] said she was next to serve at altar, in order to make herself more familiar with this ceremony. They put her in Florette's place, and she was made to absorb within her the holy wafer. The sacrifice was then consummated, and, blaspheming, Severino defiled both Justine and the sacred symbol at one and the same time." Marquis de Sade, *Justine, or the Misfortunes of Virtue* (New York: Castle Books, 1964), chap. 12, p. 68. Mario Praz wrote: "Sadism . . . as Huysmans himself also remarks, is a 'bastard of Catholicism,' and presupposes a religion to be violated. . . . Sadism and Catholicism, in French Decadent literature, become the two poles between which the souls of neurotic and sensual writers oscillate, and which can definitely be traced back to that *'épicurien à l'imagination catholique'*—Chateaubriand." Praz, *The Romantic Agony,* trans. Angus Davidson (2nd ed.; London: Oxford University Press, 1951), 306–307; for sadism in Dostoevsky, cf. *ibid.,* 336–37, 401–402. Praz also observes (p. 401) that *sodom* does not necessarily connote an un-natural act in Russian usage but *confusion.* It has the biblical meaning here. On Dostoevsky's relationship to Chateaubriand, see Robert Louis Jackson, *Dostoevsky's Quest for Form: A Study Of His Philosophy Of Art* (New Haven: Yale Univer-sity Press, 1966), 202–203.

23 On immortality through the procreation of children, see Plato, *Symposium,* 207–208. In the Legend this notion is combined with the notion of gaining im-mortality through "fame"—by being preserved in the memory of mankind—as a product of humanistic historiography as this developed in the West in course of secularization. Cf. Jacob Burckhardt, *Civilization of the Renaissance in Italy,* trans. S. G. C. Middlemore (New York: Oxford University Press, n. d.), pt. 2, pp. 76ff. Darles de Montigny, *Thérèse philosophe* (1748), which inspired the "Divine Marquis" himself, was to have been used by Dostoevsky in an important way in the projected *Life of a Great Sinner.* Cf. Praz, *The Romantic Agony,* 166n16.

Sadistic delight in blasphemy is a determinant of the imagery of the Legend. Ivan's humanistic Christ is a sadistic caricature. The identification of the Antichrist with the surrogate Elijah, John the Baptist—"who is almost the personification of the witness of the Old Testament" and is linked in the most intricate way with Christ's whole messianic mission—is sadistically blasphemous.[24] So also is the substitution of New Sodom for New Jerusalem, the vision of the Kingdom of God; and no better is the description of man's pilgrimage through history as destined to climax, not in the epiphany of the God-man transformed through the beatific vision, but in the theophany of the man-god, denizen of a secular hell suspended above the void.

The inversion of being is thereby achieved in the searing apocalypse of the eschatological city of the man-god.[25] The experiential ground of existence is torn and mutilated beyond all recognition. The Light of revelation is obscured and transformed to become the mysteriously compelling glow of the base ardor of distended demonic pride, a metastatic deformity grown in the will of the divine image which it first corrupts, then disfigures, and finally consumes.

---

[24] C. K. Barrett, "John," in Matthew Black and H. H. Rowley (eds.), *Peake's Commentary on the Bible* (London: Thomas Nelson & Sons, 1962), 738–39.

[25] For the inversion of existence and its philosophy, see Callicles in Plato, *Gorgias*, 481c *et seq*. The similarity of Callicles' "*philosophy*" and that of de Sade is little short of amazing.

CHAPTER VII

PHILOSOPHICAL ANTHROPOLOGY

1. Personal Freedom and Human Nature

The marvelous effectiveness of the Legend largely derives from its being the meeting of the God-man and the man-god. A harrowing adventure in human freedom, the mode of the *poema* is mythic. It is set at the experiential juncture of time and eternity—death. The devout old man of ninety speaks *sub specie mortis*, looking upon life in retrospect and forward into the void. Indeed, at one level, the Inquisitor *is* death, destruction, and negation itself. But the tragic pathos of the confrontation derives from his being a man and not an impersonal cosmic force.

From the perspective of Dostoevsky, man, created in the image and likeness of God, is destined to become the God-man—by grace perfected through faith in Christ after death in the culmination of the process of *theosis* begun in the here and now. It is a dynamic conception of man linked with the complex of philosophical and theological problems encompassed by cosmology, ecclesiology, and Christology. Existence is essentially the process of redemption or salvation in which man and all the creation are saved from the evil introduced into created being by the will of man. The goal of this process is deification or union with God, so that anthropology has as its outcome Christlike perfection: in the person of Christ the uncreated divine nature assumed the form of the created human nature; in the human person the created nature of man takes on the uncreated divine nature of God and man is transformed into a created god. This process is intertwined with the dynamism of the cosmos, a notion profoundly meditated by Solovyov and Fyodorov. In the mainstream of Russian Orthodox thought the cosmos is conceived as originating in the creative will of God and as having as its vocation and end participation in the fullness of divine life. With the establishment of the "second church" (after the "first church" of paradise) in the wake of Golgotha and Pentecost, the contingent and created universe bore within it a new body of uncreated plenitude which it cannot contain—the church considered to be the body of Christ.[1] The plenitude of grace and divine energies within the church serves to transform men through the Holy Spirit. Outside the church these same energies have wrought the created universe and serve as external causes, the constant willing of God which preserves it from destruction. The transformation of the cosmos calls for its entry into the church—necessitates that it too become the body of Christ and at the culmination of the ages become the Kingdom of God as the fulfillment of its vocation.

In this redemptive drama the role of man is of central importance, because the estrangement of created from uncreated being is the result only of the evil freely willed by man. "Sin is the invention of the created will," St. Gregory of Nyssa stated. While full elaboration of this doctrine need not be undertaken here, it may be remarked that this view explains Dostoevsky's exclusive interest (previously noticed) in the evil done through the human will. The source of evil, however, is not alone the human will: it includes also the demonic will of the fallen angels whose creation antedates that of man. But evil is only given effect as negation and the tendency to destroy through the person of man as he chooses to defect from the will of God. Suffering, destruction, disease, and death itself are, therefore, ultimately traceable to the freely sinful human will as a condition that is, strictly speaking, *un*natural. For by nature all that *is* is good, as coming from the hand of God. Even the demons are

---

[1] Vladimir Lossky, *The Mystical Theology of the Eastern Church* (London: James Clarke & Co., 1957), 121ff. The account of Orthodox anthropology is generally indebted to *ibid.*, chaps. 5 and 6.

not devoid of goodness: inasmuch as they *are* (rather than are *not*), they partake of Being and goodness.[2]

Man is situated at the intersection of created and uncreated being, himself a personal being who participates in both the intelligible and sensible spheres of reality, an epitome of all the realms of being. The cardinal distinction of all Christian anthropology is that between nature and person. By his nature man is a microcosm, as Plato and Aristotle knew, a summation of the whole range of being and a participant in it. In his person, however, man bears the seal of God as if imprinted upon his nature, by which means he participates in divine Being. Each man in a unique way is a whole unto himself, graced with the image of God and the uncreated in a manner that is ultimately an ineffable mystery. There is one human nature manifested in a multiplicity of human persons or hypostases. The person is the indefinable and unique something that is dearest and most particularly manifested in each man as making him himself. The nature is understandable in itself as the complex of characteristics shared in common by each man with all other men that make them generically *man*. Nature and grace are not juxtaposed. Grace is in human nature as the condition of its being and of its inclination to the Creator through the decision of the person. The primary qualities of person are uniqueness, wholeness, and the faculty of the choosing will manifested in freedom. This faculty may be regarded as the "formal" image of God, the condition for fulfillment as the perfect image in union with God, and the essence of personality. The person in its wholeness together with the nature is the image of God in man, the foundation of the indestructible dignity of each man, and that which puts men into relationship with God in the personal experiential confrontation that is the touchstone of Christian mysticism.[3]

The nature of man is, however, inseparable from person. It is divided by the Greek Fathers into either the dichotomy of body and

---

2 *Ibid.*, 111ff, 130ff, 135. See John of Damascus, *Writings* [*Fount of Knowledge*], trans. Frederic H. Chase, Jr. (New York: Fathers of the Church, Inc., 1958), 234–37, 384–89.

3 Lossky, *The Mystical Theology*, 119–20, 125.

soul or, alternatively, the trichotomy of body, soul, and spirit (*soma, psyche, pneuma* or *nous*). The classifications differ only terminologically and are in effect the same.[4] Through the person the nature is brought into relationship with God, a relationship that is unique in each person. By his nature man acts, wills, knows. The freedom of man is specifically the freedom of the person vis-à-vis the nature to choose among the actions, natural willings, and knowledge available in the potential of one's nature as a man. Hence the orientation of the man in being is his free affair. He can orient himself toward God and heighten the bond of participation toward personal union with Him in the attitude of mutual love and awareness that tends to perfect his mutilated nature; or he can orient his person toward the nothingness of the individual self and further the "laceration" (as Dostoevsky calls it) that is sinful defection from the will of God.

Precisely here the distinction between individual and person is to be observed, for the two are not the same; indeed, in a sense they are antithetical. The individual is the prideful assertion of the uniqueness and independence of the self called *samost'* in Russian ("egoism") that moves a man away from God to claim the fullness of human nature as his own. It is this specific act which comprises the Inquisitor's rebellion and necessarily implies the denial of human nature to the slave-men of his city. This tendency in men is induced by the unnatural fragmentation of the common nature into a multiplicity of physical embodiments. Thus it is rooted in man's bisexuality and perpetuation of the present fallen state by procreation. In accord with this view, the first man (whose nature was whole) is distinguished from the second (called "Adam") whose companion, Eve, was created out of his nature by God in a prevision of sin known by the anticipatory faculty in divine omniscience. Individuation as expressed in the somatic aspect of man's being, while not evil as coming from the hand of God, is refractory to the good and the mark of human imperfection. The individual is a confused intermixture of person with nature done in the name of freedom by affirmation of the self through the expression of pride. The result of such an assertion actually, however, is the loss of true personal

---

4 *Ibid.*, 127.

freedom and an isolation from God that brings suffering and death. The whole of Christian monasticism is rooted in the need to break the "individual," in the sense just defined, in order to free the "person" from natural necessity: that is, asceticism is "a free renunciation of one's own will, of the mere simulacrum of individual liberty, in order to recover the true liberty, that of the person which is the image of God in each one." [5]

The image of God in man, then, is not a part of man, but "the person which includes the nature in itself." The original unity or wholeness of nature is reestablished through free choice of the person who attunes himself to the will of God, forsaking the individual will, by participation in the mystical body of Christ that is the church. The church as the body of Christ is the common nature of man. The Christological ecclesiology of the Pauline epistles complements the cosmological doctrine of the church. It is, finally, to be said that insistence upon the indestructibility of the human person prevents derailment of the Eastern conception of mystical union by falling into pantheism: even in perfect deification the integrity of the human person remains intact. Equally, it is also true that no degree of sin, degradation, or evil can eradicate the divine image in man.[6]

The freedom and Promethean pride of man is such, however, that he can spurn faith and his destiny and proclaim himself transfigured through his own grace into the man-god. The Inquisitor is man devoid of faith and, hence, of hope. He loves no one—neither himself, nor his fellow men, nor God. Like Ivan himself, he has rejected the creation. But at the root of this rejection lies not pity for the innocent who suffer, but the rebellious assertion that man has not been created by God and, therefore, he is no dependent being but lord and master of time and the world. Indeed, this is all that truly *is*. For the arrogance of the Inquisitor reflects the conviction that not God has created man, but man God. The shadowy figure of the Holy Prisoner is, like Ivan's devil, only a hallucination. In this aspect, as has been seen, the Legend is a study in Feuerbachian theology.

---

5 *Ibid.*, 122.
6 *Ibid.*, 121. See Rom. 12:4–5; I Cor. 12:12–27; Eph. 1:23; 2:16; 3:06; 4:12,16; 5:23,30; Col. 1:18; 2:19; 3:15; also Heb. 13.

But Dostoevsky goes beyond this. He shows that the rebellion of man, made in the name of man, ends not only by destroying God but by destroying man as well. Like Marx, the Inquisitor would also doubtless refer to the peasants as "troglodytes." [7] Obsessed with power, the man-god loathes not only God in His transcendence but the image of God in existence; for, by Dostoevsky's accounting, the essence of man is his free participation with God in the process of creative redemption. The man-god must eradicate this freedom if he is to attain dominion over society and reduce man to the merely human. Man in his personal freedom can challenge authority monopolized in society, just as the man-god has challenged God's authority in being. But with his person obliterated and deprived of freedom, man effectively ceases to be human and becomes little more than a species—a herd of cattle, even an insect. The dehumanization of man is the first task of the humanist. Dostoevsky called it the creation of the "Ant-heap," the building of the "Tower of Babel." Starting from unlimited freedom, the man-god arrives at unlimited despotism.

At the most profound level, the Legend is an allegory of the cosmic drama of the creation as this is played out in the history of mankind and in the microcosm of the human soul. At the center of the drama lies the irony of human freedom; the fact of freedom in the person of man at once marks man as God's own and permits him to rebel and assert that he is himself God. "Man was created a rebel," the Grand Inquisitor reminds his Prisoner. This statement points beyond the allusion to Prometheus to the Beginning itself. The estrangement of man from God in the Fall was the primordial act of rebellion by the creature against the Creator—and, likewise, the primordial act of human freedom. By it man became "like one of us, knowing good and evil," and the Elohim tremble lest man should next eat of the tree of life and challenge the Lord God Himself. By his free act man renounced his dependence and lost the understanding of his creaturely relationship. He asserted for all time his independence and autonomy of will and knowledge. Yet

---

[7] Cf. Evgueny Lampert, *Studies in Rebellion* (New York: Frederick A. Praeger, Inc., 1957), 142.

withheld from him is the fruit of the tree of life; so man must face death, and human life becomes thereby a quest for immortality.[8] The Legend is "permeated with burning and fire" [9] as the symbolism of the "flaming sword which turned every way, to guard the way to the tree of life." Seen in this way, Dostoevsky's assertion that immortality and God are one and the same idea becomes fully intelligible.[10] The man-god is the primordial rebel who seeks to breach the gates by will and knowledge and, unaided, possess himself of immortality, regain the Paradise he has lost, and establish dominion over the creation in which the Lord God himself would then be Prisoner.

But the man-god's freedom in the search for immortality has derailed because it is infused by prideful rebellion. In the enormity of this pride and in knowledge of good and evil, he turns his back upon the way of salvation through grace. A desiccated and diseased soul and the bitterness of defeat are written in the withered face and menacing mien of the ancient cardinal. His rejection of Christ also finds place in the searing symbolism of burning and fire: the pride of the Inquisitor kindles the flames of hell in his own soul. As the conscious accomplice of Satan—"that wise and dread spirit, the spirit of self-destruction and non-existence"—he lives the last acrid years of life himself in hell, sating his pride as tyrant of an earthly hell of his own making, and glimpsing through the suffering of his own wretched soul the smoldering eternal torment. Yet, there is comfort: through his grace, mankind is with him. Over and over again in the notes, Dostoevsky asks himself what is hell; by the words of Zosima in the novel he defined it existentially: hell is "suffering of the inability to love." [11] The vagaries of rebellion and evil are

---

8 Gen. 3. Cf. Gerhard von Rad, *Genesis: A Commentary*, trans. J. H. Marks (London: S. C. M. Press, 1961), 32.

9 Ralph E. Matlaw, *The Brothers Karamazov: Novelistic Technique* (The Hague: Mouton, 1957), 32.

10 Gen. 3:24. See Dostoevsky to N. L. Osmidov, February 18, 1878, in E. C. Mayne (trans.), *Letters of Fyodor M. Dostoevsky to His Family and Friends* (New York: Horizon Press, 1961), 234.

11 Fyodor M. Dostoevsky, *The Brothers Karamazov* trans. Constance Garnett (2 vols.; London: J. M. Dent & Sons, Ltd., 1927), I, 334; cf. Dostoevsky, *The Notebooks for "The Brothers Karamazov,"* ed. and trans. Edward Wasiolek (Chicago: University of Chicago Press, 1971), 94–100, 103–104, 134, 139.

legion, but that which freedom seeks as its own is salvation through Christ Who is Love revealed.[12]

The figure of Christ transforms the Legend from a mocking, blasphemous tirade—of keen interest to the political theorist, of course—into a sublime drama of altogether unaccountable power. Dostoevsky means the Legend to be an encounter with the ineffable numen, the divine *Logos* Himself, and T. E. Lawrence has called it, "the fifth Gospel." [13] The Christ of the Legend appears as the holy *sudarium*, the archetypal Christ-icon of Eastern Christendom.[14] The

---

[12] Vyacheslav Ivanov, *Freedom and the Tragic Life: A Study in Dostoevsky*, ed. S. Konovalov, trans. Norman Cameron (New York: Noonday Press, 1957), 140ff.

[13] Quoted in Robert Payne, *Dostoevsky: A Human Portrait* (New York: Alfred A. Knopf, Inc., 1961), 363. The Inquisitor's argument has been examined from the viewpoint of political theory by Neal Riemer, "Some Reflections on the Grand Inquisitor and Modern Democratic Theory," *Ethics*, LXVII (1957), 249–56; cf. Alois Dempf, *Die drei Laster: Dostojewskis Tiefenpsychologie* (Munich: Karl Alber, 1949), 56–79; also, Nicolas Zernov, *Three Russian Prophets: Khomyakov, Dostoevsky, Solovyov* (2nd ed.; London: S. C. M. Press, 1944), 108.

[14] The *sudarium* (handkerchief used in Roman times) with the imprint of Jesus' face seems to have been the first form of icon. The dogmatic fixation of the Christ icon was drawn from an "apocryphal document of the early church, the so-called Epistle of Lentulus." Ernst Benz, *The Eastern Orthodox Church*, trans. Richard and Clara Winston (Chicago: Aldine Publ. Co., 1963), 12. The letter is dated as "hardly . . . earlier than the thirteenth century" by M. R. James, *The Apocryphal New Testament* (Oxford: Clarendon Press, 1924), 477. However this may be, Lentulus' portrait of Christ expresses the iconographic model for His representation. The writer was supposed to have been Pilate's superior. It reads as follows: "There hath appeared in these times, and still is, a man of great power named Jesus Christ, who is called by the Gentiles (peoples) the prophet of truth, whom his disciples call the Son of God: raising the dead and healing diseases, a man of stature middling tall, and comely, having a reverend countenance, which they that look upon may love and fear; having hair of the hue of an unripe hazel-nut and smooth almost down to his ears, but from the ears curling locks somewhat darker and more shining, waving over (from) his shoulders; having a parting at the middle of the head according to the fashion of the Nazareans; a brow smooth and very calm, with a face without wrinkle or any blemish, which a moderate colour (red) makes beautiful; with the nose and mouth no fault at all can be found; having a full beard of the colour of his hair, not long, but a little forked at the chin; having an expression simple and mature, the eyes grey, glancing (?) (various) and clear; in rebuke terrible, in admonition kind and lovable, cheerful yet keeping gravity; sometimes he hath wept, but never laughed; in stature of body tall and straight, with hands and arms fair to look upon; in talk grave, reserved and modest [so that he was rightly called by the prophet] fairer than the children of men." Ps. 45:2. Quoted from James, *The Apocryphal New Testament*, 477–78; cf. Benz, *The Eastern Orthodox Church*, 12–13: "The Byzantine Christ-type is modeled after this description."

killing of Christ by Ivan through humanistic perversion must inevitably fail. For the verbal icon set before the faithful in Dostoevsky's poem in flaming hues of gold and red is evocative of the eternal Son who is altogether beyond the malice of men. The two-dimensional Christ of the Legend is a window into eternity through which streams the healing energies of grace that quicken in the breast of the pious the heart-knowledge of the ineffable splendor of the Holy Trinity revealed through Him. This experiential argument *ex silentio* is incontrovertible and, in its way, utterly convincing. The effort to divinize the world and oneself becomes an absurd pretense. In the Light of transcendence the meanness, shabbiness, and fraudulence of the Inquisitor and his enterprise are perceived with an unblinking clarity that volumes of analysis could not equal.

In the drama of rebellion, the rebel is confronted with the truth of being. That he can withstand this confrontation and hold to his idea nonetheless is consistent with Ivan's previous declaration that he would reject the universal harmony, bought through the suffering of the innocent, "even if" he were wrong. So awesome is human freedom! And, indeed, he *knows* he is wrong. Yet he persists and even renews his efforts to achieve the impossible—the attempt to transfigure himself and existence by iron determination of will. The metastasis of the will finds expression in the dark apocalypse of metaphysical rebellion. Its modality as sin is metastatic faith, symptomized in Ivan's declaration that he must see with his "own eyes the hind lie down with the lion." [15] It rests on the insistent decree that man and being *are* transformed—by arbitrary definition—despite the apprehended constancy of God and the unimpaired reality of the *conditio humana*. The more rationally evident it becomes that the program is mistaken, the more irrationally furious becomes the effort to effectuate it.

2. TIME AND ETERNITY

The dominant tone of the "Legend," however, is not the measured

---

[15] For the concept *metastatic faith,* see Eric Voegelin, *Israel and Revelation* (Baton Rouge: Louisiana State University Press, 1956), Vol. I of Voegelin, *Order and History* (3 vols. to date; Baton Rouge: Louisiana State University Press, 1956—), 452ff. *The Brothers Karamazov,* I, 249; cf. Isa. 11:6–9; 65:25.

PHILOSOPHICAL ANTHROPOLOGY

grandeur of the Beginning but the exaltation of the End. The prophecy of the Grand Inquisitor is the apocalypse of the end of history, and Dostoevsky's notes for the Legend include the spectacle of the earth vomiting forth the great swarm of locusts which heralds the Last Judgment.[16]

Rebellious man perseveres to the End. The apocalyptical arrogance of the Grand Inquisitor represents man, unable to breach the gates to Paradise, rendering mankind captive. God is left in the isolation of His transcendence. The creation comes under the dominion of the man-god. Existence becomes the very definition of Hell, and the notes juxtapose the questions: "What is *hell*? What is life?" Not merely men as individuals, but mankind itself stands estranged from the creator by dupe and design. The spirit of the earth has triumphed in the hearts of men. The Grand Inquisitor, at the head of rebellious mankind, challenges Christ to render His Judgment against the hundreds of millions who have known no sin (because he has corrected the creation)—*if He dares*! In the notes, the last word of the Grand Inquisitor reads: "And if there is a single sinner, it is You yourself!" [17] The reign of the Antichrist thereby reaches its climax.

The familiar conception underlying this rebellion is the gnostic cosmology which conceives the creation to be the work of Satan.[18] On this alternative, the Creator-God of Genesis (Ivan's "Old God" of the notes) can be identified with him, and Jesus can be regarded as his emissary—hence, the "seductive" ambiguity of the Legend. The roles of God and Satan are reversed from the traditional ones. As the survey of revolutionary forces in nineteenth century Russia has indicated, the attitude was commonplace in Dostoevsky's horizon. Camus saw the point clearly and wrote that

---

16 Rev. 9:3. See W. Komarovich, *Die Urgestalt der Brüder Karamasoff* (Munich: Piper, 1928), 515; Dostoevsky *The Notebooks for "The Brothers Karamazov,"* 79.

17 Komarovich, *Die Urgestalt der Brüder Karamasoff*, 515, 539; cf. *The Notebooks for "The Brothers Karamazov,"* 78, 79, 98.

18 See Paul Miliukov, *Outlines of Russian Culture*, trans. Valentine Ughet and Eleanor Davis (3 vols.; Philadelphia: University of Pennsylvania Press, 1943), II, 3–5. Also, F. J. Powicke, "Bogomils", in James Hastings (ed.), *Hastings' Encyclopedia of Religion and Ethics* (12 vols.; New York: Charles Scribner's Sons, 1928), II, 784 and the literature cited in chap. 1, sec. 3, *above*.

revolution is the incarnation of good. This struggle, which surpasses politics, is the struggle of Luciferian principles against the divine principle. Bakunin explicitly reintroduces into rebellious action one of the themes of romantic rebellion. Proudhon had already decreed that God is Evil and exclaimed: "Come, Satan, victim of the calumnies of kings and of the petty-minded." Bakunin also gives a glimpse of the broader implications of an apparently political rebellion: "Evil is satanic rebellion against divine authority, a rebellion in which we see, nevertheless, the fruitful seed of every form of human emancipation." Like the Fraticelli of fourteenth-century Bohemia [sic], revolutionary socialists today [!] use this phrase as a password: "In the name of him to whom a great wrong has been done." [19]

The shifting back and forth between the conventional and the revolutionary categories does not veil the central point: the "divine" is the hideous and wicked that destroys the god in man, the "evil" and "satanic" is this god and the matrix of revolutionary morality and immortality.[20] This is the Inquisitor's confession. The pattern seems to be confirmed also by Ivan's curious affirmation that he accepts God but rejects his creation.

The affirmation, however, clearly has more than one possible meaning: (a) rejection of Christ as the Son of God and the sole means of salvation, and affirmation of a satanic viewpoint equivalent to the traditional doctrine of the Antichrist (Rev. 13); (b) rejection of Christ as a devil and emissary of the evil Creator God, a gnostic view which looks to the true hidden God of absolute transcendence; (c) rejection of the present world system as the domain of fallen man and Satan, the "Beast of the earth," as articulated in the Inquisitor's discourse, and affirmation of the good Old God of the first creation, prior to the Fall, perhaps after the longing of Rousseau and Schiller. All three possibilities, and any combination of them, imply revolu-

---

[19] Albert Camus, *The Rebel*, trans. Anthony Bower (New York: Random House, Vintage Books, 1958), 157–58. On the "Old God" and Christ's "seductiveness" (an appellative of the Antichrist in the New Testament), see *The Notebooks for "The Brothers Karamazov,"* 76, 84; cf. Rev. 13, 17.

[20] See Robert J. Lifton's study of Maoist thought as the psychology of immanentizing transcendental symbolisms, *Revolutionary Immortality: Mao Tse-tung and the Chinese Cultural Revolution* (New York: Random House, Vintage Books, 1968).

tionary destruction of the present world as an absolute good, the essential prelude to the true, final harmony. The Inquisitor consistently argues in terms of "A"—the acceptance of the world system rejected by Christ in the temptation. Ivan's position is more obscure; and he seems to offer the Legend as a kind of trial balloon (as the notes say), a possible way out of the misery of existence which is conceivably superior to the way offered by Christian faith. He is engaging in the pastime of intellectuals—that is, speculating; he believes in *something*—he must believe in something: justice, goodness, and reason in the abstract—but beyond that confusion and uncertainty reign. Is Christianity the way to these? Or is Satanism and destruction of the great world conspiracy the way? Or is there yet another way, one in which natural and material existence can be transformed (perhaps through science?) into the means of escaping human misery and attaining bliss, at least for a time?

The discussion does not exhaust the alternatives: after all, John of Damascus had tabulated 103 heresies already in the eighth century! Not only is "everything permitted" but anything is possible. If, however, one considers Ivan as representative of the ideologies Dostoevsky most sought to combat (the Roman idea as Satanism, socialism, and atheism), then at least his major inclinations can be identified with the rejection of eternity and immortality and acceptance of the modern gnostic reduction of being to historical existence. On this reading, the split between transcendent and immanent being is absolute. Truth is treacherously hidden. God, in his transcendence is *deus absconditus*, if he exists at all: the creation is in any case evil, and the Christian revelation does not reveal the *agnostos theos* to whom alone veneration is due. This true god can be identified with the enemy of Yahweh, Satan, by the gnostic paraclete. The Unknown God of the Christian contemplative is absorbed into the Unknown God declared by the gnostic pneumatic. The way to salvation lies through a gnosis, a secret wisdom gained by the privileged few. This alone enables man to overcome the world and save himself. For man bears the light of the "true god" that the world powers term "Satan." The connection between gnosticism and nihilism, here depicited by Dostoevsky, is confirmed by modern scholarship.[21] The general configuration entails the anarchistic rejection of all authority, the destruction of the powers which order social and individual existence, and the reorganization of the world in accordance with the secret "truth" gained through the gnostic illumination. The decisive points of connection between ancient and modern gnosticism are, therefore, two: the established world order is evil and its total destruction is justified; this is a recondite truth that will appear an absurdity to conventionally oriented men: it is a secret knowledge or wisdom (gnosis) possessed only by a small elite charged with the mission of saving mankind from the evil world (perhaps but in the atheistic forms not necessarily attributed to the Creator-God) and the reigning world powers—the "Establishment" in the parlance of the 1970s. The varieties are infinite and Dostoevsky was well acquainted with them, whether in the guise of political and social revolutionists, or as the populist Chaikovskists with their Joachite God-men, or as the *Raskol'* and the Russian sectarian movements such as the Khlysty and Skoptsy.[22] The idea that the Roman Catholic

---

[21] See, in particular, Hans Jonas, "Gnosticism and Modern Nihilism," in Jonas, *The Gnostic Religion: The Message of the Alien God and the Beginnings of Christianity* (2nd ed.; rev.; Boston: Beacon Press, 1963), 320ff; cf. 46, 64, where the parallel between Heidegger and the gnostic speculation is discussed. On the "Unknown God," see *ibid.*, 288 and *passim*. On nihilism as the fruit of all major philosophical movements of the modern period, see Stanley Rosen, *Nihilism: A Philosophical Essay* (New Haven: Yale University Press, 1969). The question of the "Demiurge" in Dostoevsky is treated in Melvin Rader, "Dostoevsky and the Demiurge," *Sewanee Review*, XXXIX (1931), 282–92. See also Ramiro de Maeztu, "Dostoevsky the Manichaean," *New Age*, XXXII (1918), 449–51, 497. The political connections of "modern" gnosticism are made in Eric Voegelin, *The New Science of Politics: An Introduction* (Chicago: University of Chicago Press, 1952), 110ff. See, also, Lampert, *Studies in Rebellion*, 137ff, 155ff; Nicholas Berdyaev, *The Russian Idea* (New York: Macmillan Co., 1948), 148–55 and *passim*; J. L. Talmon, *Political Messianism: The Romantic Phase* (New York: Frederick A. Praeger, Inc., 1960), especially pts. 1 and 2.

[22] See Dostoevsky to Apollon N. Maikov, December 11, 1868, in Mayne (trans.) *Letters of Dostoevsky*, 158; also Dostoevsky to Maikov, March 25, 1870, in *ibid.*, 190. The Khlysty, Stundists, and sectarians generally were frequently discussed or alluded to in the *Diary*. On the Chaikovskists and their Joachism, see Franco Venturi, *Roots of Revolution: A History of Populist and Socialist Movements in Nineteenth Century Russia*, trans. Francis Haskell (New York: Grossett & Dunlap, Inc., 1966), chap. 18, and Michael Cherniavsky, *Tsar and People; Studies in Russian Myths* (New Haven: Yale University Press, 1961), 196n.

church would become the vehicle for this massive and disciplined gnostic rebellion is perhaps drawn from Comte, where the notion is well developed, rather than solely from Dostoevsky's well-known aversion to Catholicism.[23] The notions that Catholicism was heresy and that the pope was the Antichrist, of course, go back into the middle of the first millennium of the Christian Era. They were given great currency by the Franciscans (in the wake of Joachim's speculation) in the thirteenth century and were common accusations during the Reformation in the West. The idea was as old as the Schism in the East and gained momentum in Russia with the proclamation of Moscow the Third Rome early in the sixteenth century.[24]

The welter of ambivalence that has been noticed more than once during this study is both a source of artistic greatness in the Legend as well as of inevitable confusion in its interpretation: no neat analysis can possibly do justice to the work because an almost terrifying technique of ambiguity has purposely been employed in its creation. This is neither to alibi in desperation nor to imply that the author did not know what he was doing. On the contrary. There is no little merit in A. S. Steinberg's argument that Dostoevsky's novels are, in fact, "artistic laboratories" in which the author experiments with the entire gamut of theoretically possible "ways and means at the disposal of modern man in his struggle for the survival of human freedom," the whole being completely controlled by the "symphonic dialectic" of the writer as artist-scientist. And Robert L. Belknap has demonstrated, in a way surpassed by no other reader of *The Brothers Karamazov*, both the extraordinary complexity of the novel so that the "elements in the world described [there] are interrelated with a degree of complication comparable to that in the reader's own world"; and the precision of Dostoevsky's craftsmanship in unifying a thousand-page novel around a four-level scaffolding of inherent, historical, sequential, and narrative structures. Ambiguity and ambivalence are inevitably present in a portrayal of the whole net

---

23 Cf. Auguste Comte, *Cours de philosophie positive* (6 vols.; Paris: Bachelier, 1841), V, 434. See chap. 6, n. 14, *above*.

24 See Norman Cohn, *Pursuit of the Millennium* (Fairlawn, N. J.: Essential Books, 1957), illustration of the pope as Antichrist dated 1545, opposite p. 16. Cf. the discussion, *ibid.*, 102ff, and see the index under *Antichrist*.

of possibilities, the potentialities of individual psychic and historical states, and, finally, of actions which are not simply described
but analyzed in terms of conflicting motivations—as Belknap himself
finally admits.[25] If any feeling for the marvelous richness of the
work, on the one hand, and for the great authoritativeness of the
writer's convictions, on the other hand, is to be attained and made
intelligible, then it is both valid and vital to ferret out conflicting
components and to distill a coherent meaning from the Legend.

The Legend in its entirety has been considered by some to be an
anarchistic manifesto.[26] Any discussion of this aspect of the work
must be cautious so as not to misunderstand Dostoevsky. Insofar as
Dostoevsky is directly concerned here about problems of social order,
he is concerned because of man's relation to the order of transcendent
Being. With respect to any authoritarian apparatus—sacerdotal or
political or totalitarian—which intervenes between man and the
divine, Dostoevsky affirms the inviolability of human freedom and
the autonomy of the individual person under God. To authoritar-
ians, this may well be anarchism. But that Dostoevsky was either a
political anarchist or an "embattled reactionary ideologue" is not
to be proved from the Legend because the questions themselves are
inapposite.[27] The overall issue is, however, a real one, the solution
of which turns on the obscure problem of differentiation in Dostoevsky's thought.

The Legend resolves the central paradox of existence in such a
way that Ivan and Alyosha (not to mention scores of interpreters
over the last ninety years) can draw diametrically opposed conclusions from it.

Ivan, its ostensible author, intended it to be an incontrovertible

---

25 A. Steinberg, *Dostoevsky* (New York: Hillary House, Publ., 1968), 98–99; cf.
56–60, 100–118; and see the same author's *Die Idee der Freiheit: Ein Dostojewski-
Buch,* trans. Jacob Klein (Lucerne: Vita Nova, 1936), 63, where he speaks of the
"net of ontological possibilities" in *The Brothers Karamazov.* Robert L. Belknap,
The Structure of "The Brothers Karamazov," Slavistic Printings and Reprintings,
LXXII, ed. C. H. Van Schooneveld (The Hague and Paris: Mouton, 1967), 66, 22,
110–12.
26 Cf. Nicholas Berdyaev, *Dostoevsky,* trans. Donald Attwater (New York: World
Publ. Co., Meridian Books, 1957), *passim.*
27 Philip Rahv, "The Legend of the Grand Inquisitor," *Partisan Review,* XXI
(1954), 250.

indictment of the human condition, of Christianity as the foundation of the social and spiritual order, and to be a refutation of the claims of Christ sufficient to make Him superfluous.[28] He is irrelevant to man and life as they truly are and only exacerbates human misery. The power of this attack has been observed. There is an element of playful suspense in Ivan and his "poem," however, which also is noteworthy. Ivan never utters on his own authority his most famous slogan, "All things are lawful"; it always occurs as a quotation expressing his idea but drawn from another source. The ultimate source has been shown to be the Bible, but the slogan draws together meaning from a wide variety of other sources as well. The sudden smile which plays across his face after the Inquisitor's *"Dixi,"* explained as the indication of incipient epilepsy, also suggests aesthetic distance. Further, there is the denial, in the face of Alyosha's outburst, of the seriousness of the Legend: "Why, it's all nonsense, Alyosha. It's only a senseless poem of a senseless student." In the interview with the devil, Ivan is ashamed of the Legend and forbids him to speak of it. In the notes to the Legend, a suspension of judgment, an ambiguous wandering between doubt and faith is indicated, rather than the rabid atheism of Ivan's double, the Inquisitor himself. It is all only a trial balloon, Ivan says there twice.[29] While the Legend expresses the "furnace of doubt," the most powerful argument Dostoevsky could conceive for the thoroughgoing atheist, his hero has been kept back a little distance from the plunge into the

---

28 Neither in the Legend nor elsewhere does Dostoevsky debate the question *whether* Christianity is the foundation of the social and political order. That is taken as self-evident, or "axiomatic" as he would say, and from age eighteen onward he was profoundly convinced that Christianity was "the foundation." The shorthand expression, "the foundation," runs through his publicist writings like a thread. Cf. letter to his brother, Michael, January 1, 1840, in Mayne (trans.,) *Letters of Dostoevsky*, 13. Dostoevsky's fullest statement of his views on this subject is to be found in the penultimate issue of the *Diary* (August, 1880, iii); Dostoevsky, *The Diary of A Writer*, trans. Boris Brasol (2 vols.; New York: Charles Scribner's Sons, 1949), II, 981ff. Cf. Dostoevsky, *The Notebooks for "A Raw Youth"*, ed. and with an intro. by Edward Wasiolek, trans. Victor Terras (Chicago: University of Chicago Press, 1969), 307, 424ff, 472, 477, 497, 504, 514, 524, 529, 540; Dostoevsky, *The Notebooks for "The Brothers Karamazov,"* 184–95, 212, 255.

29 See Komarovich, *Die Urgestalt der Brüder Karamasoff*, 538; cf. *The Notebooks for "The Brothers Karamazov"*, 75, 77.

abyss. The Legend is a mythic projection of a tendency in the soul of its supposed author and no more, the outpouring of a "noble passion" by Ivan who stands between the twin abysses of the Karamazov character: abasement and high triumph, judgment and mercy, the demonic and the angelic.[30] This is a devastating characterization of the tragedy of the modern intellectual. The incomprehending yet guilty horror in Ivan that his egregious verbal and metaphysical diarrhea induced the actual murder of his father by the half-witted literalist Smerdyakov, finds striking parallel in the German "idealist" whose support of Hitler in the thirties turns into the sickening lamentation, "Wir haben es nicht so gemeint!" amidst the stench of Buchenwald and Dachau in the forties. Everything was said in fun, for the best; it's all only a game, a line in the cosmic vaudeville. Who would think such things could be taken seriously? Ivan is drunkenly playing at the game of existence; he intends only the best.

There is also in this attitude of Ivan toward the Legend the suggestion of a parallel attitude on the part of the Christ toward the creation: perhaps it won't work out, perhaps man *is* too weak, it is all a cosmic experiment, just another "trial balloon—a trial soap bubble, and nothing else"; or, alternatively in the notes: "LET THEM SUFFER, SINCE HE ATE *THE APPLE*." In the passage as published Ivan explains (in the Second Interlude) that the Inquisitor in his old age had concluded that men were "weak rebels, incomplete, experimental creatures created in jest." Playful ambivalence also explains the "blasphemy" uttered in the Legend by the victims in the Inquisitor's world: "Bathed in their foolish tears, they will recognize at last that He who created them rebels must have meant to mock them." [31] D. H. Lawrence seized upon this element in delight to explain the meaning of the kiss which the Holy Prisoner placed on the lips of the Inquisitor: "Jesus kisses the

---

30 Cf. *The Notebooks for "The Brothers Karamazov,"* 222–25, 254–57.
31 Quoted from Matlaw's translation in Fyodor M. Dostoevsky, *Notes From Underground and the Grand Inquisitor*, ed., trans., and with an intro. by Ralph E. Matlaw (New York: E. P. Dutton & Co., 1960), 131; *The Notebooks for "The Brothers Karamazov,"* 77.

Inquisitor: Thank you, you are right, wise old man. Let them be glad they've found the truth again." [32]

The ambivalent juxtaposition of naïve play and wrenching agony in Ivan both intensifies the bewilderingly tragic pathos of the Legend and supplies the key to his symbolic function in the novel. Representative of the intelligentsia of the age, he is the wanderer (skitalets) of whom Dostoevsky spoke so profoundly in the Pushkin Speech and in his reply to the criticisms of A. D. Gradovsky. On the part of Dostoevsky this is, itself, a clever play with symbols. The new man of Russia has been subtly identified with the sectarians, the Khlysty, and the extremists of the Raskol' called the Stranniki or "Wanderers." The juxtaposition of play and agony in Ivan thereby dissolves into the verbally ecstatic poetry of the Legend, showing the kinship of the Russian intelligentsia with the rigorously ascetic sectarians who induce the wandering soul of Christ into themselves through their ecstatic song and whirling dance. Ivan's psychic convulsiveness displays his affinity with the sectarian seeker after God.[33] The gnostic connection is underscored but hope is also affirmed.

---

[32] D. H. Lawrence, "The Grand Inquisitor," in Selected Literary Criticism, ed. A. Beal (New York: Viking Press, Inc., 1956), 241. On D. H. Lawrence and the Legend, see Edward Wasiolek, Dostoevsky: The Major Fiction (Cambridge: M.I.T. Press, 1964), 164–65. The "play" element here is of significance for the understanding of the Legend as myth. See J. Huizinga, Homo Ludens (Boston: Beacon Press, 1955). Cf. Plato in the Laws, 887c, where God is praised by stories told "both in jest and earnest, like charms."

[33] The theme is developed on another level in books 8 and 9 of the novel, in the relationship of Grushenka to Alyosha and to Dmitri; cf., also, Dostoevsky, The Notebooks for "The Brothers Karamazov," 109–60. See the Diary for August, 1880, passim. Also see the chapters in The Possessed of that title (pt. 3, chaps. 5 and 7). Dostoevsky makes the implicit connection express by characterizing the "new Russian" of "the future" as a peasant sectarian of the time of Tsar Paul I. The reference is to Konrad Selivanov, "Christ Peter III" of the castrati Skoptsy. See Dostoevsky to Apollon P. Maikov, March 25, 1870, in Mayne (trans.), Letters of Dostoevsky, 191. The "Wanderers" of the Schismatics are the Stranniki or Beguni (fugitives) for whom the state and church are in Antichrist's power and the Orthodox Church is Satan's prophet. They were particularly characterized by their fierce denunciations of the tsar and tsardom and for their attacks on the Orthodox priests as the lying prophets of Antichrist. The Bogomil-Manichaean duality is pronounced with the Beguni and even more so with the Khlysty and Skoptsy. See A. von Stromberg, "Russian Sects," in Hastings' Encyclopedia, XI, 338. Also see Frederick C. Conybeare, Russian Dissenters, Harvard Theological Studies, X (New York: Russell and Russell, Publ., 1962), 159–60. For the sources of the Russian sectarian movements see the detailed study by Karl Grass, Die

The wanderer is a symbol of search for truth, of seeking man open
to divine truth. Ivan and the intelligentsia, like the religious sectarians, are potential believers, as is every man. The sanctity of human endeavor and the pull of the divine which it reflects has been
recognized from the time of Plato onward and is a major theme in
Pascal whom Dostoevsky already knew at age seventeen. Dostoevsky
made this erotic seeking the mainspring of his character's motivations, and in so doing he affirmed the Christian anthropology that
sees in every passion the secret search for God, a vindication that man
is the divine image. It is this affirmation that gives a touch of the
sublime even to such figures as Fyodor Pavlovich or Smerdyakov. As
the matter is phrased by Etienne Gilson:

> . . . human love, in spite of all its ignorance, blindness and even downright
> error, is never anything but a finite participation in God's own love for
> Himself. Man's misery lies in the fact that he can so easily deceive him-

---

russischen Sekten (1907–14; 2 vols.; repr. ed.; Leipzig: Zentral-Antiquariat, 1966),
especially I, 172–75, 261–64, 301–360; 588–648. The Bogomil relationship is discussed in ibid., 626ff, and the gnostic character of the movements (particularly of
the Khlysty) at ibid., 636–48. Grass strongly affirms the asceticism of the Khlysty
(ibid., 313–60) and argues for their ecstatic rather than mystical character, finding
mysticism to be foreign to Russian religiousness generally and introduced there
largely from Western sources (cf. ibid., II, 222–69). Conybeare questions the
gnostic connection of the Khlysty (Conybeare, Russian Dissenters, 357). In the
language of the Russian hesychasts, wandering as a spiritual phenomenon is
prelest' (Gr. plane), the manifestation of the attitude of samost' or egoistic
forgetfulness of God in orientation toward the individual self: it is "the corruption of human nature through the acceptance by man of mirages mistaken for
truth; we are all in prelest.' " E. Kadloubovsky quoted in Jon Gregerson, The
Transfigured Cosmos: Four Essays in Eastern Orthodox Christianity (New York:
Frederick Ungar Publ. Co., 1960), 58. Within the hesychastic discipline, the condition of prelest' and forgetfulness is overcome through the remembrance (anamnesis)
of the Sacred Name in the "Jesus Prayer," so that the adept becomes the God-
centered or theocentric man. Cf. ibid., 58–74. In this aspect, the Legend can
be seen to be a meditative recollection of the name of Jesus in this mystical tradition. The outcome of this meditative process is the movement in the soul from
wandering and evil to the apprehension of Christ as the Divine Light. The explanation of the Tabor transfiguration (cf. Matt. 17:2; Mark 9:2) is that no
change occurred in Christ, only in the disciples' awareness of Him. This is also
the outcome of the spiritual pilgrimage from prelest' to the vision of Light. Ibid.,
65. A similar meditative dynamic lies at the core of the Legend. Cf. the wandering
symbolism in Dostoevsky, The Notes for "A Raw Youth," 513, 523, 533, 538, 541,
552–53. For yet another view of the wanderer symbolism, see Dmitri Chizhevsky,
"Comenius' Labyrinth of the World," in Horace G. Lunt, et al. (eds.), Harvard
Slavic Studies (4 vols.; Cambridge: Harvard University Press, (1953–57), I.

self as to the true object, and suffer accordingly, without even suspecting that he does so; but even in the midst of the lowest pleasures, the most abandoned voluptuary is still seeking God; nay more, as far as regards what is positive in his acts, that is to say in all that makes them an analogue of the true Love, it is God Himself Who, in him and for him, seeks Himself. . . . no Christian philosopher can ever forget that all human love is a love of God unaware of itself. . . . To will any object is to will an image of God, that is, to will God; to love oneself, then, will be to love an analogue of God, and that is to love God.[34]

Gilson's reliance on the doctrine of the Thomistic *analogia entis* does not affect the essential conformity of his understanding of the problem with Dostoevsky's view of it. The very impulse to love is itself divine and is a reaching out for God; but the immediate object of love determines the consequences of the act for the man. These consequences range from sin and perdition to beatitude and mystical union. But, indeed, nothing is essentially evil; and all that *is* bears something of divinity in it. Thus, St. Gregory Nyssa suggests that the soul of man is like a mirror, either reflecting God or receiving into itself "the image of formless matter, where the passions overthrow the original hierarchy of human being." [35] In the search of the wanderer, Dostoevsky sees goodness; in the failure to apprehend the true object of that search he sees destruction in existence and damnation in eternity.

Alyosha, on the other hand, sees the Legend to be a hymn of praise to the humiliated Savior Who suffered in silence before His accusers and Pontius Pilate and Who suffers throughout time in silence before those who rebel and blaspheme. The intent of Dostoevsky here is marvelously intricate and subtle. At the center, however, is Russia's "Word"—the long awaited revelation "to the world

---

34 Etienne Gilson, *The Spirit of Mediaeval Philosophy*, trans. A. H. C. Downes (New York: Charles Scribner's Sons, 1940), 274, 278, 286. To expound the differences between the Orthodox and Thomistic analyses of this problem lies beyond the scope of the present purposes. Cf. Lossky, *The Mystical Theology*, 210–20. On Dostoevsky's early knowledge of Pascal, see Dempf, *Die drei Laster*, 11, 77. Steinberg notes the argument that the mystic and philosopher Vladimir Solovyov is the prototype of Ivan; see A. Steinberg, *Dostoevsky* (New York: Hillary House, Publ., 1968) 109–10.

35 Lossky, *The Mystical Theology*, 132.

[of] her own Russian Christ, whom as yet the peoples know not, and who is rooted in our native Orthodox faith." [36] In the Legend Dostoevsky has undertaken to utter that "Word." Revealed in the Christ of the Legend is the Russian Christ as meditated by contemplatives from the time of Boris and Gleb. It is the kenotic Christ of self-humiliation, suffering, love, humility, and voluntary sacrificial death; it is the Christ of the hesychasts, of the *Philokalia* and the *Unseen Warfare*, whose life is the transfiguration wrought through mystical silence in constant prayer. At a slightly different level, the Christ of the Legend is Russia herself, the "God-bearing people," the true "Holy Russia" of Dostoevsky's meditations, whose faith is perfected through centuries of suffering in silence and humility and who now must face the last great antagonists, Leviathan and the Antichrist himself.[37] And at yet another level, the Christ of the Legend is the church, the body united with the Head in a prefiguration of eternity. For the Inquisitor holds the church in bondage, and because it is Christ's body, what else can explain the strange Visitor's appearance but the desire that an account of clerical stewardship be given? The Christ treasured in every faithful heart here confronts the earthly Vicar in love but no less also in judgment.

The picture of Christ, thus, weaves together the principal elements of Russian devotion. Beside the hideous chastity of the Inquisitor in his titanic pride, the ascetic purity of Christ confirms the vanity of the world and the senselessness of power. The rankling invective of the Titan meets only the meditative silence of the God-man, a silence reflecting the principle basic to Orthodoxy that the church as Christ is unalterable, its traditions and forms all being vehicles of saving grace. This is the point of the Inquisitor's derision at Christ's silence, for nothing can be added to perfection, as the Old Believers long argued. The lacerations of prideful abuse are patiently suffered as in the Gospels, and this same humility is the central virtue of Russian Christianity. The letter of the monk James

---

[36] Dostoevsky to N. N. Strakhov, March 18, 1869, in Mayne (trans.), *Letters of Dostoevsky*, 175.

[37] Cf. George P. Fedotov, in E. J. Simmons (ed.). *Continuity and Change in Russian and Soviet Thought* (Cambridge: Harvard University Press, 1955), for this account of the Russian Christ. Also, Zernov, *Three Russian Prophets.*

in the Kievan period expresses the attitude communicated by Christ in the Legend. "The Almighty, borne by Cherubim, is now led in bonds by soldiers; sitting at the right hand of the Father, He stands in the tribunal before the archpriest and Pilate. . . . The face, shining more brightly than the sun, is beaten and spit upon by the ungodly."[38] The highest expression of the Russian religious soul is the "following" of Christ (the Eastern church does not like to speak of "imitating" Christ) by sharing his passion. This kenotic ideal is the expression of *agape*, the simple caritative (not mystical) love immediately evident in the biblical Christ. This element balances the other major tendency of Russian religious life, asceticism, which is combat with the demons that infest the world and man's nature, the mystical quest for purity and spiritual freedom. The kenosis of Christ is expressed by the prayer of St. Boris before His icon on the morning of the day when his brother, Sviatopolk, killed him: "O Lord Jesus Christ, who has appeared on the earth in this image, who deigned to be nailed to the cross and accepted the passion for our sins! Vouchsafe me also to accept the passion." The same prayer is repeated by Dostoevsky before the icon of the Legend. This is the expression of humility, of contrition, the melted heart, the gift to pardon even the murderer through tears shed in a consciousness of common guilt. The doctrine of kenoticism is dominant in Dostoevsky's "word." It is that every disciple of Christ must suffer in this world, and that all innocent and voluntary suffering in the world is done in the name and for the sake of Christ. The words of Prince Vladimir Monomach (d. 1125), one of the great figures of Russian lay religion, almost seem an exegesis of the Legend's Christ: "Our Lord is not man, but God of the universe, who works in a twinkling of an eye everything He wishes and lo, He suffered insults and spitting and blows and was given to death, being Himself Master of life and death, and we—what are we?"[39] The great marvel to the Russian mind is that the heavenly Sovereign became man and endured humiliation. The

---

[38] Quoted from George P. Fedotov, *The Russian Religious Mind* (New York: Harper & Row, Publ., Torchbooks, 1960), 231. On kenosis, see also Gregerson, *The Transfigured Cosmos*, 29ff, 77ff; Lossky, *The Mystical Theology*, 144ff.
[39] Fedotov, *The Russian Religious Mind*, 99, 259; cf. 102, 157.

Christ-centered Christianity of Dostoevsky focuses precisely upon this miracle—and leaves to Ivan preoccupation with the humanity of Christ which he perverts.

The underlying secret of the Legend is that Christ *is* Truth. There is no "other" Truth that can oppose Him: the gnostic delusion lies precisely here, and Alyosha is no gnostic even if Ivan may be.[40] The metaphysical rebellion of the man-god is a grotesque variation on the theme of the central constitutive fact of the *conditio humana*: the Fall of man. And it was to redeem fallen man that Christ, the Incarnate Word, entered history. Without the Fall and the fact of sin there would be no need for Christ or for redemption. The Inquisitor's attempt to abolish sin (like all of that kind) is a covert existential weapon for the abolition of Christ. But however rebellious and deluded man may become, no amount of empirical defection from the order of being can touch the truth of being itself.[41]

It is this ontological perspective which makes so meaningful the kiss of Jesus. To the man of faith—to Alyosha for whom faith is existentially real—it is *en philemati agapes*[42] of the Sovereign God-man who is Love, who taught men to love their enemies and who prayed from the Cross for the forgiveness of His murderers "for they know not what they do." The kiss is that prayer again. "Oh, the crucifixion; that is a terrible argument!" the Inquisitor is made to exclaim in the notes.[43] Yet it is the irreducible paradox and infuriating dysteleology of the crucifixion which, nonetheless, remains the final historical argument of the Legend. Inexplicable as is the mystery of the crucifixion and the atonement, so also inexplicable is

---

40 As previously remarked, this point is expressly stated in the notes; Dostoevsky, *The Notebooks for "The Brothers Karamazov,"* 102. Dmitri Merezhkowsky has made much of the "two truths"; see, Merezhkowsky, *Tolstoy as Man and Artist with an Essay on Dostoevsky* (New York: G. P. Putnam's Sons, 1902), 289ff.

41 Cf. Dostoevsky, *The Notebooks for "The Brothers Karamazov,"* 98, 223; also Voegelin, *Order and History,* I, 464–65.

42 For the *philema agapes,* see I Pet. 5:14 and the comments in George A. Buttrick (ed.), *Interpreter's Bible,* (12 vols.; New York and Nashville: Abington-Cokesbury, 1952–57), XII, 159. Also see A. E. Crawley, "Kissing," in *Hastings' Encyclopedia of Religion and Ethics,* VII, 742ff. For the Pauline *philema hagion* (Holy Kiss), see Rom. 16:16, I Thess. 5:26, I Cor. 16:20, II Cor. 13:12; also, by implication, Phil. 4:21. See also Luke 7:45,48.

43 See Komarovich, *Die Urgestalt der Brüder Karamasoff,* 545; *The Notebooks for "The Brothers Karamazov,"* 75.

the mystery of suffering and of human rebellion. But that these things serve the inscrutable purpose of divine Providence is not in the faithful heart—neither of a Job nor of a Dostoevsky—to deny. In a Russian folk legend, Christ kisses Judas after the betrayal: both the betrayer-rebel and the Savior have essential roles to play.[44]

3. THE LAST JUDGMENT

The transhistorical aspect of the Legend is, however, not to be forgotten. The eschatological hardness of Christ also finds expression in the kiss as the wrath of God. Here is no sentimental, simpering Christ as some have supposed. For the Love of the Savior in no way impairs His sovereign authority in being: beyond the grave, at the end of time, men shall be judged with a Judgment that is not their own. The kiss in this sense is the seal of impending certain destruction set upon the lips of the prophet of Satan by the righteous God. It is the Kiss of Death, not of course, in the Rabbinical tradition of the *bi-neshikah*, but in the meaning of the *pneuma tou stomatos autou* of the New Testament prophecy of the End. "Then will be revealed the lawless one whom the Lord will consume with the breath of His mouth and annul by the appearing of his coming." [45] For the Russian evocation of Christ is always simultaneously in the guise of Pantocrator—Judge of Creation—and of slave in the kenotic attitude. The twin poles of this religious attitude are love and fear, for both of these experiences belong to the human confrontation with the biblical God. Behind Dostoevsky's imagery in the Legend is the vision of the Resurrection and the echo of the words of Gennadius:

---

44 Cf. Eric Voegelin, "Bakunin's Confession," *Journal of Politics*, VIII (1946), 30. The action of Christ in the Legend is also to be explained by the experience of *umilenie*, which is a distinctive manifestation of Russian religiousness. The term designates a sudden softening of the heart or a flood of deep emotion and compassion in the heart. "It is a sudden and unexpected impulse which takes hold of a man, a feeling of inexplicable tenderness which seizes the hardest of hearts. . . . it is the thrill of love and forgiveness, the tears of repentance and joy, and the gift of self offered in joy." Nicolas Arseniev, *Russian Piety*, trans. Asheleigh Moorhouse (London: Faith Press; Clayton, Wisc.: American Orthodox Press, 1964), 75–76; cf. 81, 132.

45 II Thess. 2:8. This is the only place in the New Testament where it is said that Christ destroys Satan with the "Breath of His mouth." Cf. Isa. 11:4 and Job 4:8–9. This action is included in John Damascene's characterization of the Antichrist; cf. chap. 5, sec. 3, *above*.

"Remember the Judgment; expect to answer and receive retribution according to thy deeds; and believe that it will be so." [46] The spectacle of the Resurrection icon brings forward the specifically Eastern conception of the meaning of salvation. It is that Christ directly fights against and destroys the demonic powers of creation and descends into hell itself to free the damned. [47] This "harrowing of hell" is drawn from a sermon attributed to St. John Chrysostom and forms the culmination of the matins for Easter Sunday:

> Let all partake of the banquet of faith. Let all partake of the riches of goodness.
> Let none lament his poverty; for the Kingdom is manifested for all.
> Let none bewail his transgressions; for pardon has dawned from the tomb.
> Let none fear death; for the death of the Savior has set us free.
> He has quenched death, who was subdued by it.
> He has despoiled Hades, who descended into Hades.
> Hades was embittered when it tasted of His flesh, and Isaiah, anticipating this, cried out saying: Hades was embittered when it met Thee face to face below. It was embittered, for it was rendered void. It was embittered, for it was mocked. It was embittered, for it was slain. It was embittered, for it was despoiled. It was embittered, for it was fettered.
> It received a body, and it encountered God. It received earth, and came face to face with Heaven. It received that which it saw, and fell whence it saw not.
> O Death, where is thy sting? O Hades, where is thy victory?
> Christ is risen and thou are cast down.
> Christ is risen and demons have fallen.
> Christ is risen and the angels rejoice.
> Christ is risen and life is made free.
> Christ is risen and there is none dead in the tomb. For Christ is raised from the dead, and become the first fruits of them that slept. To Him be glory and dominion from all ages to all ages. Amen. [48]

---

[46] Fedotov, *The Russian Religious Mind*, 206.

[47] *Ibid.*, 76–79.

[48] Quoted from Lossky, *The Mystical Theology*, 248–49. The original source of the "harrowing of hell" is the "Gospel of Nicodemus" (also known as the "Acts of Pilate"), pt. 2: "The Descent into Hell." Cf. Rev. 19:20; 20:10. Two Latin versions and a Greek version are translated in James, *The Apocryphal New Testament*, 117–46. The descent by Christ into hell to destroy it and bind Satan is preceded by that of the Forerunner, John the Baptist, who again witnesses to

At the *parousia* the vain pretense of the Antichrist will be played out—*if*, indeed, there be an End! The kiss that burns on the lips of the Inquisitor, the shudder that shakes his frame are consequences of the encounter with infinite Love Who is also the Omnipotent Sovereign. He has met both the grace of salvation and the inexorable power of doom to the iniquitous in that most intimate expression of the truth in Christ. Hence the final words of the faithless and rebellious who can resist such encounter can only be, "Go and come no more . . . come not at all, never, never." And he clings to his idea.

The Grand Inquisitor spoke *sub specie mortis*, but Dostoevsky has spoken *sub specie aeternitatis*. His Legend points toward the eternal destiny of man. Through parody and caricature he constructs a devastating refutation of the inflated and spiritually diseased supermen of all the ages of history. His concern is with the spiritual crisis of our time and its dangers for men. In a uniquely powerful way, the life of man in society is shown not merely to be life in the world but a participation also in the beyond. Mankind is again warned that a diseased social order can destroy the specifically human in the men who are its citizens; and in the wake of this, the wholesale slaughter of man by man in the name of humanity and truth becomes inevitable. The admonition is one to ponder well.

But the Legend is not only an admonition. It is also a spiritual poem of great power and beauty, an affirmation of faith wrung from the suffering soul of the great contemplative Fyodor M. Dostoevsky. It presents a searching mythopoetic analysis of the pitfalls open to all who wander in the wasteland of existence and utters a cry of anguish and compassion for the souls of fellow men whose pride prefigures their destruction. Dostoevsky writes out of love, a love of men won through God's love experienced in himself. His inspiration is the great spiritual figures of the Russian and Greek tradition, but most of all it is the biblical Christ Himself. Dostoevsky

---

His coming. Cf. James, *The Apocryphal New Testament*, Greek II (XVIII), 2, p. 125. Seen in this setting, Christ's kiss is the paschal kiss symbolic of the resurrection and victory over death and poses the issue for Ivan and Inquisitor whether they shall be among those released from hell or be among the eternally bound or destroyed. Cf. Nicolas Arseniev, *Russian Piety*, 53, 131; Tikhon Zadonsky and the paschal kiss are discussed on the latter page.

knows the terms of existence, and he has felt the succour of grace. His poem of the Inquisitor is a gift of tears of compassion shed by a pure heart who prays to God for the forgiveness of his sins and for the salvation of his fellow man, and who is himself wrapped in the Light of union with God—the Light that graces only the great mystic soul.

The Legend is, thus, many things at once: an analysis, a blasphemy, a warning, a curse, a prayer, a confession, a plea, a thanksgiving, a benediction. But above all it is an iconographic vision of God's grace infusing man's existence in this world to bind every wound, heal every heart, and fulfill every man whose soul opens to Him. We hear only the Inquisitor's words, but we see only Christ's face. And it reveals the constancy of love and the undeserved blessing that passes understanding. The symbolism finds completion in the departure of the Prisoner whose Light recedes into the Divine Darkness of the Unknown God of the contemplative. But more immediately He returns whence He has come: *temnie stogna grada*—to the trusting hearts of men whose existence is blighted by the tyranny of the proud but whose spirits are blessed by an eternal Presence.

PART THREE

CONCLUSION

CHAPTER VIII

THE RANGE OF POLITICS

1. THE TRANSCENDENT AND THE IMMANENT

The issue of immanentization in Dostoevsky may now be given specific consideration. It has been alluded to in a number of places in the literature but seems not yet to have been seriously investigated. V. V. Zenkovsky discussed the matter by speaking of Dostoevsky's "Christian naturalism":

> It is a doctrine which places all of its hopes in that Christian illumination of man which entered the world through the Incarnation and found its highest expression in the Transfiguration of the Savior. This is a *Christianity without Golgotha*, a Christianity of Bethlehem and Tabor. It is a specific combination of *Rousseauism* and *Schillerism*, refracted through the prism of Christianity, as faith in "nature" and an acknowledgment of the natural nobility—even though it may be concealed under outer crusts —and hidden "sanctity" of the human soul; or, as Dostoevsky expressed it in an article on George Sand, a recognition of the "perfection of the human soul." [1]

---

[1] V. V. Zenkovsky, *A History of Russian Philosophy*, trans. George L. Kline (2 vols.; New York: Columbia University Press, 1953), I, 412–13. Cf. also J. Middleton Murry, *Fyodor Dostoevsky: A Critical Study* (London: Martin Secker, 1916), 258–59, for the designation of Alyosha as the incarnation of Dostoevsky's gnostic vision: "This Alyosha, the resolute champion, is not a Christian. He has passed beyond the Christian revelation. . . . He may not believe in God, he may know himself for a sensualist, yet he is not confounded, for his knowledge of the great Oneness needs no belief in God for its support, and the beast which he knows within him

The article on George Sand surely is of pertinence in considering im-manentism in Dostoevsky, although the rationalist-naturalism charge cannot be proved from it. In the first place, to have regard for the divine in the human person is not necessarily to ignore Golgotha nor to slight the idea of evil in man, as this study has amply shown.[2] In the second place, Dostoevsky consistently derided the rationalist no-tion of the perfection of man through a system or through a naturalis-tic evolutionary process; and Rousseauism-Schillerism, while at-tractive, is reflected as the specific debility of Dmitri's immaturity and incompleteness in *The Brothers Karamazov*.[3] The real contours of his consciousness have been explored in foregoing chapters. That he looks forward to the perfection of man as the outcome of history is, of course, true; but as the result of the supernatural transfigura-tion of man through grace. It is in terms of an apocalyptical eschatology and a mundane Kingdom of God that the problem of immanentism of Dostoevsky is rightly to be seen. The foreshortening of the End, the preachment of a universal theocracy, Russia as the soteriological vessel, the Great Russians as the chosen people of the New Jerusalem, cosmic religiousness, and even the apophatic mysti-cism of divine illumination in the hesychastic tradition with its roots in the Neo-Platonic writers of Alexandria—these are the principal ele-ments contributing to whatever immanentism there is in Dostoevsky's work.

Schilleresque romanticism surely is of importance, but Nikolai F. Fyodorov and Vladimir S. Solovyov are the dominant influences

---

is no more a beast. He has transcended these sublunary things. Their names are but earthly and blunted symbols for the reality which he bears within him. He is fair and comely; his outward bears the impress of his inward harmony; his body and his spirit together are modulated by the sweet music of other worlds. He is the man who is the promise of all humanity, for whom the old problems are solved by his very being and are not."

2 See the discussion of Dostoevsky's relation to the Kantian "radical evil" in Reinhard Lauth, *Die Philosophie Dostojewskis in systematischer Darstellung* (Munich: Piper, 1950), 519.

3 On Dmitri's incompleteness, see Robert L. Belknap, *The Structure of the Brothers Karamazov*, Slavistic Printings and Reprintings, LXXII, ed. C. H. Van Schooneveld (The Hague and Paris: Mouton, 1967), 72–73. The Rousseauism-Schillerism in Mitia is explicit in the notes; see Dostoevsky, *The Notebooks for "The Brothers Karamazov"*, ed. and trans. Edward Wasiolek (Chicago: Univer-sity of Chicago Press, 1971), 41, 138, 187, 202, 257, 260.

in shaping this gnostic utopian eschatology as it develops to a crescendo in the late seventies. The impact of Fyodorov's strange ideas on Dostoevsky probably cannot be assessed with any great degree of precision, but they are of influence in the thought of the author's last years and form a meaningful thread in *The Brothers Karamazov*. Fyodorov was perhaps unknown by name to Dostoevsky, although Edward Wasiolek states that the author "knew" him. He was the anonymous source of a manuscript (perhaps since lost) received toward the end of 1877 which set forth an activist program of cosmic redemption through brotherly love. It evidently outlined the need for a universal effort by all men to achieve immortality and, through human love radiating from the nuclei of families, to foster resurrection of the dead as well as perpetual life for the living; "this, rather than procreation, being, in his opinion, humanity's supreme task," as Yarmolinsky says. Dostoevsky showed the manuscript to Solovyov and both were enthusiastic at least about the creative role of men in the redemptive process; and Dostoevsky subsequently wrote one of his correspondents that he and Solovyov anticipated the real, physical resurrection of mankind at the end of history. References to Fyodorov's notions in the notes to the novel before us suggest they are probably of significance for the theme of familial love and its violation which is basic to the plot. There is a sense in which Dostoevsky could have pitted the Fyodorov idea that the *"resurrection of our ancestors* depends on us" against the apocalyptical eschatology of both conventional Christianity and the gnostic-socialist movements alike as a kind of evolutionary alternative climax of the drama of redemption. The idea itself revives the ancient Russian ancestor cult discussed in chapter 1 and now decked out in the garb of Orthodox cosmic redemptionism. It is compatible with Dostoevsky's telluric mysticism, populism, and Slavophile propensities, and reinforces the intimacy of the connection between the achievement of salvation and the life of love, for (to quote the notes again), "The family [is] the practical basis of love"; and he was particularly impressed by the biblical story of Joseph and his brothers. Fyodorov's key doctrine is this: "One must live not for oneself (egoism) and not for the others (altruism), but with everyone and for everyone; this is the union of the living (sons) for the resurrection of the dead (fathers)." The resurrection he planned is designated by himself to be immanent, the realization of the Kingdom of God in this world, and he condemned the aspiration toward transcendental perfection beyond history. Fyodorov himself regarded this to be a "Christian" alternative to both socialism and positivism, one which recognizes the moral dimension of man's conquest of nature through science and projects its mystical consequences in ways which amalgamate science fiction with magic and theosophy and lie clearly beyond the pale of any orthodox Christianity, as N. O. Lossky notes. This teaching appears likely to have reinforced Dostoevsky's aversion to any apocalyptical denouement to the unfolding of history because, as with Augustine before him, such expectations—equally rampant in fifth century Rome and nineteenth century Russia and Europe—contradict the essential rationality of the Christian view of man and reality. But this cannot be definitely proved.[4]

---

4 Wasiolek quoted from *The Notebooks for "The Brothers Karamazov,"* 26n; Dostoevsky from *ibid.* 32, 101; cf. 30, 40–41, 97–98, 255; Avrahm Yarmolinsky, *Dostoevsky: His Life and Art* (2nd ed.; New York: Grove Press, Inc., 1957), 348; Nicolai F. Fyodorov quoted from N. O. Lossky, *The History of Russian Philosophy* (London: Allen & Unwin, 1952), 78; cf. also W. Komarovich, *Die Urgestalt der Brüder Karamasoff: Dostojewskis Quellen, Entwürfe und Fragmente* (Munich: Piper, 1928), viii–ix, 539, and *passim.* For the free universal theocracy in Dostoevsky, see the first hints in Dostoevsky to Apollon P. Maikov, January 18, 1856, and the later full statement in the letter by Dostoevsky to N. N. Strakhov, March 18/30, 1869, in E. C. Mayne (trans.), *Letters of Fyodor M. Dostoevsky to His Family and Friends* (New York: Horizon Press, 1961), 83ff, 174–75, respectively. See in Dostoevsky, *The Diary of a Writer,* trans. Boris Brasol (2 vols.; New York: Charles Scribner's Sons, 1949), particularly the following: I, 315; II, 624; II, 979–80; II, 1029–36. Moscow the Third Rome is related to this idea in Dostoevsky. See Moscow as Third Rome as the *Katechon* (II Thess. 2:6) in the discussion by A. von Stromberg, "Russian Sects," in James Hastings (ed.), *Hastings' Encyclopedia of Religion and Ethics,* (12 vols.; New York: Charles Scribner's Sons, 1928) XI, 333–34. The best study of political messianism in Dostoevsky is Avrahm Yarmolinsky, "Dostoevsky: A Study in His Ideology," (Ph.D. dissertation, Columbia University, 1921). Insofar as there *is* in Dostoevsky—whether at the exoteric or the esoteric level—the anticipation that the secular state can be transformed by divine grace into an ecumenical church, the ultimate source of the idea is Joachim of Flora's symbols of the Third Age of the Spirit and the brotherhood of autonomous persons. Cf. Eric Voegelin, *The New Science of Politics: An Introduction* (Chicago: University of Chicago Press, 1952), chap. 4; Voegelin, *Israel and Revelation* (Baton Rouge: Louisiana State University Press, 1956), Vol. I of Voegelin, *Order and History* (3 vols. to date; Baton Rouge: Louisiana State University Press, 1956–), 450ff and the discussion of metastatic faith. The theme of the church as state is explicit in *The Notebooks*

The subtlety of the question of immanentization is well illustrated by what Dostoevsky wrote in the *Diary* on the occasion of the death 'of George Sand in the June number for 1876.[5] He is writing here in the same immediate period of the article about the suicide Pisareva and of the important letter to V. A. Alekseev quoted earlier. The article began with a discussion of the *élan vital* (*zhivaia zhizn'*)—that is, the meaning of life, and Dostoevsky's use of the expression "that these stones be made bread." [6] He condemned as piteous but characteristic of the times Pisareva's implicit "conviction" that "if everyone were provided for, everybody would be happy; there would be no poor and no crimes. There are no crimes at all. Crime is a pathological condition resulting from poverty and unhappy environment, *etc., etc.*" That this socialistic assumption dehumanizes or beastializes man is implied in the repetition of the suicide's words "howl," and "howling." These are used instead of "weep" and "weeping": animals howl but humans weep—and the socialist solution reduces man to the level of a herd of cattle.[7]

In the article on George Sand, it is remarked that her novels had "slipped through" the censorship at a time when almost everything from France but fiction was excluded. This admittance of French fiction had been a dreadful oversight. But, then, all of Belinsky also had "slipped through." In the central passage of the article, Dostoevsky attempts to say the "last word" about the person to whom he attributed the fundamental impetus in Russia toward social revolutionism.

The main thing is that the reader managed to extract even from novels everything against which he was being guarded. At least, in the middle forties, the rank and file Russian reader knew . . . that George Sand was

for "*The Brothers Karamazov*," 41–42, 263. Already in *The Notebooks for "The Idiot*", ed. and with an intro. by Edward Wasiolek, trans. Katherine Strelsky (Chicago: University of Chicago Press, 1967), Dostoevsky is meditating the resurrection of the dead; he wrote (p. 218): "*Reform and resurrect mankind.*"

5 Dostoevsky, *Diary*, I, 341–50.

6 *Ibid.*, I, 337. Brasol in the *Diary*, I, 342, translated *zhivia zhizn'* with the French *élan vital*, which is identified with Henri Bergson. Cf. Fyodor M. Dostoevsky, *Polnoe sobranie sochinenii*, (12 vols.; St. Petersburg: Panteleevkh, 1891–92), X, 191, 195.

7 See Dostoevsky, *Diary*, I, 336.

one of the most brilliant, stern and just representatives of that category
of the contemporaneous Western new men who, when they appeared,
started with a direct negation of those "positive" acquisitions which
brought to a close the activities of the bloody French—more correctly,
European—revolution of the end of the past century. . . . It was precisely
at that epoch that suddenly a new word had been uttered and new hopes
had arisen: men came who boldly proclaimed . . . that the renovation of
humanity must be radical and social. . . . I do not wish to speak here
either for or against [this] movement: I merely meant to indicate George
Sand's true place in it. Her place must be sought at its very inception. . . .

George Sand was not a thinker but she was one of the most clairvoyant
foreseers (if this flourishing term be permitted) of a happy future awaiting
mankind, in the realization of whose ideals she had confidently and mag-
nanimously believed all her life—this because she herself was able to conceive this ideal in her soul. The preservation of this faith to the end is
usually the lot of all lofty souls, of all genuine friends of humanity. George
Sand died a *déiste*, with a staunch belief in God and in her immortal life.
But this does not fully cover the ground: in addition she was, perhaps,
the most Christian among all persons of her age—French writers—even
though she did not confess Christ (as does a Roman Catholic). Of course,
being a French woman, in accord with the conceptions of her compatriots,
George Sand would not consciously adhere to the idea "that in the whole
universe there is no name other than His through which one may be
saved"—the fundamental idea of Orthodoxy—yet, despite this seeming
and formal contradiction, George Sand, I repeat, was perhaps, without
knowing it herself, one of the staunchest confessors of Christ. She based
her socialism, her convictions, her hopes and her ideals upon the moral
feeling of man, upon the spiritual thirst of mankind and its longing for
perfection and purity, and not upon "ant-necessity." All her life she believed absolutely in human personality (to the point of its immortality),
elevating and broadening this concept in each one of her works; and
thereby she concurred in thought and feeling with one of the basic ideas
of Christianity, *i.e.*, the recognition of human personality and its freedom
(consequently, also of its responsibility). Hence, the recognition of duty
and the austere moral quests, and the complete acknowledgment of man's
responsibility. And, perhaps, in the France of her time there was no thinker and no writer who understood as clearly as she that "man shall not live
by bread alone." As to the pride of her quests and of her protest—I repeat
—this pride never precluded mercy, forgiveness of offense, or even bound-
less patience based upon compassion for the offender himself. . . . It
seems that she was partly inclined to value the aristocracy of her extraction
(on her mother's side she descended from the Royal House of Saxony),

but, of course, it may be positively asserted that if she did value aristocracy in people, she must have based it on the perfection of the human
soul: she could not help but love the great, she could not reconcile herself
with the base or cede an idea—and in this particular sense she may have
been excessively haughty.[8]

The same tension is to be observed here as in the Legend. The conceptions of Orthodoxy are juxtaposed to the rationalist-humanitarian
"Rousseauism" of George Sand. The Unknown God of George Sand
was incipiently the God of Christ.[9] She, too, had her faith and something of the Truth, albeit but a spark of the great flame. The attitude Dostoevsky expressed toward the various sectarian movements
—from Stundist to Khlysty—is, in a way, paralleled in this estimate
of George Sand. The wandering search (*prelest'*) of the hungry soul
for the Bread of Life is admiringly recognized, even through a mist
of blasphemy and perversion or through the wild enthusiasm of the
"whirling and prophesying" Christs, God Sabaoths, and Mothers of
God in the convulsive ecstasy of the *radenie*. Recognition of spiritual
longing in the soul of the Russian people—both peasantry and intelligentsia—was the root of Dostoevsky's most profound insights and
the basis of his mystical attachment to the Russian *pochva* and the
narod. He saw intrinsic merit in the religious pathos of the people
despite its primitiveness and fanaticism, and he knew that this was
indispensable to the viable Christian community which he sought
to foster. He saw here, and in the monastic communities where the
faith had been preserved, the only possible sources for the revitaliza-
tion of Orthodoxy. And, in addition to this, he was profoundly convinced that "Russia and Orthodoxy were one and the same idea"
and that this had been so since at least the sixteenth century when
the theocratic doctrine of Moscow the Third Rome was received.
"One has to know Russia," he wrote, "read the Bible!" [10] In the
confused crisis of nineteenth century Russia Dostoevsky sought to
revive the Christian spirit as the timeless answer to the most urgent

---

8 *Ibid.*, I, 346ff, 349–50.
9 Cf. Acts 17:23 for the *Agnostos Theos* which Dostoevsky here, like Paul in
Athens, declares, as it were, before the memory of George Sand.
10 Dostoevsky, *The Notebooks for "The Brothers Karamazov,"* 95.

contemporary needs. To heal the ever-widening breach in Russian society, a breach whose beginnings he dated from Nikon and Peter the Great, he hoped to galvanize the sentiment of the people. He perceived the truth later noticed by Ernst Troeltsch: "There can . . . be no doubt about the actual fact: the sects, with their greater independence of the world, and their continual emphasis upon the original ideals of Christianity, often represent in a very direct and characteristic way the essential fundamental ideas of Christianity." [11]

The sects exhibited a pure spiritual vitality all too rare in the established church. To cleanse the church from within he sought spiritual alliance with the Old Believers and sectarians as true representatives of the popular religious mind; and it is not, therefore, surprising that the monks of Optino-Pustyn rejected the portrait of Zosima and condemned his orthodoxy, just as Father Ferapont had done in the novel. Without agreeing with his settled conviction that Dostoevsky was a religious skeptic and atheist, one can say Masaryk has sensitively analyzed some of the tensions within Dostoevsky's thought:

> Dostoevsky . . . oscillates between mysticism and rationalism because he attempts to understand the problem of religion mystically and then again rationally. He tries, in every possible way, to justify the teachings and rules of the church in which he was raised and which he loves. He vacillates, while always hoping to remain within the mainstream of the folk religion, and thus to reconcile in his religious philosophy the idea of the Russian Church and his own religious ideals. Dostoevsky draws too directly on the scriptures, he does not give enough weight to the tradition of the church. . . . Mystics were often no less dangerous than rationalists, and the churches have always kept a sharp eye on them.[12]

Not only was Dostoevsky concerned with the fragmentation of the Russian community spiritually and the atrophy of the church

---

[11] Ernst Troeltsch, *Social Teaching of the Christian Churches*, trans. Olive Wyon (2 vols.; London: Allen & Unwin, 1931), I, 334.

[12] Thomas G. Masaryk, *The Spirit of Russia: Studies in History, Literature and Philosophy*, Vols. I and II, trans. Eden and Cedar Paul (2nd ed.; New York: Macmillan Co., 1955); Vol. III, ed. George Gibian, trans. Robert Bass (New York: Barnes & Noble, Inc., 1967), 54–55; for Masaryk's final appraisal of Dostoevsky's religion see also *ibid.*, III, 49, 63, 86, 94, 145.

into a mere institution among others, an arm of the tsarist bureau-cracy. He was broadly concerned also with the cultural, intellectual, and spiritual split between the people and the intelligentsia, on one hand, and the intelligentsia and the court circles of the tsardom, on the other hand. His expressions on the subject of culture (and the absence of it in Russia) were essentially accurate and entirely per-tinent to the situation he sought to remedy. Masaryk may again be quoted:

> The Russians took over Byzantine theology, but did not acquire Hellen-ism, or acquired so much only as was implicit in the theology. When we compare Russia with the West we may say that the former knew nothing of Aristotle or of the *corpus juris*; Greek never played in Russia the part that Latin played in the West; there was no humanist movement, no Renaissance, no independent growth of the sciences and of modern philosophy, and above all no Reformation (or Counter Reformation).[13]

Whether there was any philosophy at all in Russia before the mid-nineteenth century is at most questionable, and such as could be found there subsequently was without epistemological foundations and "so mythical and objectivist that even the opponents of ecclesiasti-cal religion [were] nothing but objectivists." The beginning of in-dependent Russian philosophy came only with I. Kireevsky and Khomyakov. "The sum total of knowledge was theology and the-osophy." [14] Moreover, there was no "real and full-fledged scientific investigation in Russia" before the nineteenth century, and even in the field of theology there was "a complete absence of rational scientif-ic thought." The primary explanation of this tragic cultural void was not any religious animosity against learning—learning, wisdom,

---

13 *Ibid.*, II, 490; cf. Francis Dvornik, *The Slavs: Their Early History and Civili-zation,* Survey of Slavic Civilizations, II (Boston: American Academy of Arts and Sciences, 1956), chap. 4, and 248–49. A more positive view (which, however, does not contradict the assessment outlined here) is presented by Thornton Anderson, *Russian Political Thought: An Introduction* (Ithaca: Cornell University Press, 1967), pt. 1.

14 Evgueny Lampert, *Studies in Rebellion* (New York: Frederick A. Praeger, Inc., 1957), 2; Nicholas Berdyaev, *The Russian Idea* (New York: Macmillan Co., 1948), 19, 159; Masaryk, *The Spirit of Russia,* II, 478; I, 41; Cf. Lossky, *The History of Russian Philosophy,* chap. 1.

and scholarship always were praised, even if only rarely practiced. Rather a decisive factor was that the liturgical language was Old Slavonic, a language descended by way of Bulgaria from a Macedonian dialect, one with no great literature of its own. Linguistic isolation from the Mediterranean and European culture worlds of Greek and Latin imposed a stunting handicap on the Russian mind that was never overcome.[15]

The deficiencies were not compensated by the wealth of meditative literature nor by the flowering of historiography. And even the excellence of Russia's histories carried with it the limitations of the cultural horizon. Sacred and profane were indistinguishable, nature and history interpenetrated. The distinctiveness of the two realms so sharply contrasted in the Western mind on the basis of the monumental work of Augustine (who drew his inspiration not only from the Bible, earlier Christian writers, and the Neo-Platonists, but also from the Manichaeans) found little place in early Russian historiography. Instead, there was a pronounced tendency toward naturalistic monism which situated God immanent to history as the key power of social dynamics and infused the entire historical process with eschatological meaning.[16] To the Russian, matter was (and remained) spirit bearing. In this setting the great political myths of the Pious Tsar, Holy Russia, the Land and the People, and the image of Moscow the Third Rome struck root and flourished.[17]

The cultural vacuum was filled only after Peter the Great, and then in such a way as to split Russian society as the rush of Europeanization collided with the civilization's established but critically deficient tradition. Dostoevsky both understood this complex of problems and indicated the nature of the necessary solution to them.

---

15 George P. Fedotov, *The Russian Religious Mind* (New York: Harper & Row, Publ., Torchbooks, 1960), 380; cf. Dvornik, *The Slavs*, 166.

16 Fedotov, *The Russian Religious Mind*, 357; cf. 383–86.

17 See Michael Cherniavsky, *Tsar and People: Studies in Russian Myths* (New Haven: Yale University Press, 1961); also Hans Rogger, "The Russian National Character: Some Eighteenth-Century Views," in Hugh McLean, *et al.* (eds.), *Russian Thought and Politics*, Harvard Slavic Studies (4 vols.; Cambridge: Harvard University Press, 1953–57), IV, 17–34; also articles by Richard Pipes, Marc Raeff, N. V. Riasanovsky, Martin E. Malia, Frederick C. Barghoorn, Ralph E. Matlaw, Robert E. MacMaster, George Fischer, and Robert V. Daniels in *ibid.*

He knew that Russia must both modernize economically and develop "culturally" along Christian lines. But the degree to which he was himself imbedded in the traditional Russian viewpoint makes a clear judgment of the question of immanentism in his thought difficult. A satisfactory answer is possible only if one rejects a monistic interpretation of his work and, instead, distinguishes esoteric and exoteric levels. A single principle cannot explain Dostoevsky, any more than it can satisfactorily explain human existence. And the thinker and artist himself knew this truth.

2. Esoteric and Exoteric Politics

By means of the persuasive power of his political thought, Dostoevsky sought to mend the splintered and disintegrating Russian community. The core of this attempt lay in the reiterated and systematic evocation of the *homonoia* of Orthodox Christianity. Both his great art and his sometimes banal publicist writings contributed in their various ways to the effort. He purposely employed his genius and great prestige in the final years, not merely to prop up a tottering and corrupt social order, but to launch a broadly based renaissance of Russian civilization. He sought to stimulate the rebuilding of Russia on the basis of traditional foundations. The effort appears clearly conceived and rationally executed in the chosen modes of action. He understood the political realities of his (even our) age as has hardly anyone else. He was equally a great patriot of his country and a genius of the pen and of the spirit. He was not above playing on the sentiments, prejudices, and presumptuous hopes of Russians great and small. As often as not his publicist arguments are brazenly *tu quoque* and *argumentum ad populum*: if one enlists the *demos* he must be prepared, on occasion, to play the demagogue.

This political effort, prosecuted by all the means at his disposal, constituted a virtual preoccupation and something more than a mere background to his art, especially from the time of the Nechaev affair (1869). In the winter of 1871 he met for dinner each Wednesday at the house of Prince V. P. Meschersky with a circle including among its members the old fellow-Petrashevist, Danilevsky, and Maikov, Strakhov, M. I. Vladislav, V. V. Grigoriev, T. I. Filippov, and K. P.

Pobedonostsev. The friendship with Pobedonostsev warmed from 1873 onward, and their Saturday evenings together became habitual.[18] In his exoteric writing Dostoevsky intentionally manipulated the symbols evocative of national consciousness as the principal means of achieving his broad political objectives. He knew Russian history and, indeed, studied it all of his life. Karamzin's *History of the Russian State* (in twelve volumes) occupied a place of honor second only to the Bible in his father's house. He was acquainted with it before he could read for himself. "I grew up on Karamzin," he wrote Strakhov in 1870. In the *Diary* he once affirmed that by the age of ten he "already knew almost all the principal episodes of Russian history from Karamzin." This *History* was the "table-book" (especially volumes eleven and twelve), which he read when there was nothing new to read.[19] Following his father's practice, he read Karamzin to his own children during their early childhood. He greeted Danilevsky's nationalistic *Russia and Europe* as an incarnation of his own vision of Russian history.

The exoteric element in Dostoevsky's writing, of course, is not limited to *Grazhdanin* and *Dnevnik* in the seventies. It is to be found in the novels and short stories as well—anywhere, in fact, that the symbols of the tradition and destiny of Russia appear at the level of the "political" narrowly defined. He consciously undertook the task, knowing well the loneliness of the quest and the odds against pragmatic success. Only the Pushkin Speech in June, 1880, which blended exoteric and esoteric politics with personal charisma for one splendid moment, proved for all to see that what Dostoevsky sought to achieve was in fact a real possibility. But the moment passed. If his Herculean efforts ultimately failed, they at least made an impress whose practical effects lasted into the nineties. He understood and exhaustively characterized the nature and varieties of the

---

[18] See Anna Gregorievna Dostoevsky's "Reminiscences of 1871" in Fyodor M. Dostoevsky, *Dostoevsky: Letters and Reminiscences*, trans. S. S. Koteliansky and J. M. Murry (New York: Alfred A. Knopf, Inc., 1923), 144, 239; cf. Masaryk, *The Spirit of Russia*, III, 140–54.

[19] Dostoevsky, *Stavrogin's Confession*, trans. S. S. Koteliansky and Virginia Woolf (Richmond: Hogarth Press, 1922), 159; also Richard Pipes, "Karamzin's Conception of Monarchy," in McLean *et al.*, (eds.), *Russian Thought and Politics*, 35–58.

enemy within and without Russia in the seventies and supplied a rational analysis for solution of the deepening crisis in Russian society. That this attempt failed is not attributable to Dostoevsky's poor judgment, nor because he was "a reactionary revolutionary," nor because of historical inevitability,[20] but primarily because of the political ineptitude and massive inertia of the successors of Alexander II.

3. The Tension of Existence: Institutions and Order

Students of Dostoevsky have characterized his work in many ways, and this is true particularly with regard to the assessment of the relationship between his "religion" and his "politics." Robert Payne has found Dostoevsky closer to Aeschylus than to any one else: "they [*i.e.* Dostoevsky and Aeschylus] possessed the faculty of seeing the chosen creations of their imagination simultaneously *sub specie aeternitatis* and *sub specie temporis,* in the light of religion and in the light of politics." [21] Fedor Stepun has suggested that the history of the church is Dostoevsky's "System"; it "is in fact a kind of 'meta-history', into which are gathered all historical empires—that means all cultural, political, and economic history." Dostoevsky understood the "religious undertone of the atheistic-nihilistic theme of the Russian popular revolution [and the] demonic instrumentation of this theme as a fall through sin of the Russian-Christian Idea." [22] Certainly this may be considered one of the cutting edges of the Legend. The savage caricature of institutionalized Christianity given there cannot be read as only an attack on Roman Catholicism; it is equally a pitiless condemnation of the caesaropapism of Russian Orthodoxy and of the church hierarchy for succumbing to Satan's temptations and perversely accepting earthly dominion at the expense of spiritual bread.

Exoteric and esoteric levels of meaning have been distinguished

---

20 Irving Howe, "Dostoevsky: The Politics of Salvation," *Kenyon Review,* XVII (1955), 49.

21 Robert Payne, *Dostoevsky: A Human Portrait* (New York: Alfred A. Knopf, Inc., 1961), 398.

22 Fedor Stepun, *Dostojewskij und Tolstoj: Christentum und soziale Revolution: Drei Essays* (Munich: Hanser, 1961), 21–22, 48.

here, and the former is in all respects compatible with political and religious conventions of the court of Tsar Alexander II. The latter is the quintessential Dostoevsky who strove to conform himself with the Truth of Being as it was given him to understand it. Dostoevsky never really confused these two spheres; there is, indeed, a clear (if thin) line drawn between them, even when both strands are found together in a single work. The attempt has here been made briefly to suggest some of the motivations which forced the political messianism of Moscow the Third Rome into such prominence in his work. Dostoevsky the patriot sought the preservation of his beloved Russia and used the arsenal at hand to this end. But Dostoevsky the mystic, prophet, philosopher, and artist was bound to no such institutional or national conformity. A Roman Catholic writer has made the point indirectly in complaining bitterly about the cavalier disregard shown the church and the sacramental bond with Christ. Dom Theodore L. Wesseling wrote of Dostoevsky that, "though perfectly conscious of the existence of the Orthodox Church, in [his] relations with Christ there is but his self and Christ: the Church— we are not afraid to say—is flatly ignored. . . . when we see a man writing about Christ and at the same time ridiculing away the Church his "beloved" Christ died for, the very Bride and Child of the Christ's Blood and Cross, then we wonder." [23] It has been noticed that such observations have factual merit. One of Dostoevsky's purposes was to chasten the church. But Wesseling's interpretation of the Legend and, hence, also of the author's faith is fundamentally mistaken, for in a decisive sense the Christ Who appears there *is* the Church itself.

Dostoevsky's great art emerges out of personal spiritual encounter with the transcendent *Realissimum*. The emphasis upon the freedom, rationality, and inherent worth of every man, the inviolability of every human person as a unique bearer of the divine image, arises from a range of experience that is inevitably shattering to institutions and inimical to conventions pretentiously claiming plenary

---

[23] Theodore L. Wesseling, "Vladimir Soloviev: An Interpretation (IV)," *Eastern Churches Quarterly*, II (1937), 195. The cited passage continues: "We are sick of the religious jelly of humanitarian Christianity. We are sick of those sweet philanthropic Christs of artistic emotionalism and *blasé* bourgeois psychology." Cf. Masaryk, *The Spirit of Russia*, III, 54–55.

authority over men. It is, therefore, inconceivable that he should seriously have expected Russia to gain world dominion and establish the Third Rome as the providential climax of secular history. He knew there would always be a "Rome," for indeed men must be governed; and he also knew, unless great precautions were taken, this political dominion could totally absorb the life and spiritual freedom of the human being, thereby essentially maiming him. As powerful as are the elements of apocalyptical eschatology in the work of Dostoevsky, they remained symbolic of hope in the universal redemption of man through grace, emblematic of the open horizon evoked by his philosophy of man and history, the axiological component of his faith; but they did not form the goal of a concrete program of pragmatic political activism. This is not to say Dostoevsky failed to covet political power and even imperial success for Russia, nor is it to say he did not cherish dreams of grandeur for the Russian Empire. But the use of power and coercion, while understood to be proper to the political sphere, was unthinkable to Dostoevsky as an instrument for achieving the Millennium. If the Legend of the Grand Inquisitor means anything at all, it must at least mean that.

What, then, of the free universal theocracy? The question is more delicate, but the foregoing analysis suffices. Dostoevsky always expressed himself with a certain caution on the subject as may, for example, be seen from a careful reading of the Pushkin Speech itself. The burden of what is said amounts to an exhortation to spiritual perfection quite in keeping with both the New Testament and Christian doctrine.[24] The eschatological element is introduced and given pronounced emphasis, but never is it suggested that the free universal theocracy can be achieved either without providential intervention or at any particular time. The tone is expectant, to be sure, even fervid. But even so it is the muted tone of *it may be* that at the End the final Word will be said in Russia. This is a far cry from a declaration that the end of history is at hand or from proposal of a program for achieving that end such as either Fyodorov's or Marx's. It is, moreover, in keeping with the biblical account of the Kingdom of God which can come when and where God wills it and

---

[24] Cf. Matt. 5:48; Eph. 4:12–16.

is a symbol of hope to the Christian regardless of the dogmatically precise or biblically imprecise terms in which the hope finds expression. While Dostoevsky expresses eschatological hope for the coming of the Kingdom of God and gives that expression a sense of urgency, he does not venture to prophesy nor does he propose any program of action beyond exhortation to Christian piety. The transfiguration of the world is an essential part of his expectation, and there is little indication he supposed this could come otherwise than through divine grace as this works through the agency of human participation.

It may, therefore, be concluded that Dostoevsky's thought is free of immanentism even in the decisive area of eschatological expectation. The experience of the consubstantiality of being and of the sacredness of the creation and man's oneness with it is powerfully evident in his work. But the immanent and transcendent spheres are ultimately differentiated and plainly distinguished; and, despite his cosmic mysticism, Dostoevsky does not seem to have relied in any way upon the sophiological doctrine. Reinhard Lauth summarized Dostoevsky's view of history with the words: "Die Geschichte offenbart eine sich verschärfende Trennung, eine Bewegung zu kontraren Polen. *Augustins* Geschichtsbild ist das richtige." [25] This is to say too much. But the sacred and the profane *are* distinguished by Dostoevsky, even as he meditatively strives within the arena of his own soul to hasten the transfiguration of the cosmos through a redemptive irruption of divine grace. That the distinction is no more acute than it is is a tribute to the Christian correctness of the author: in the Christian horizon, contrary to some evident misconceptions, there is no such reality as the *utterly* profane. A dualism of that extremity becomes precisely Manichaean and broadly gnostic.

The similarity between Dostoevsky and Kierkegaard often has been observed. Geoffrey Clive wrote: "Like Kierkegaard he [Dostoevsky] preferred to speak Christianly and honestly. . . . The similar-

---

25 Lauth, *Die Philosophie Dostojewskis*, 519. See the discussion in Zenkovsky, *History of Russian Philosophy*, II, 840ff. Also Wesseling, "Vladimir Soloviev (IV)," 121ff. See the discussion of transcendentalism and immanentism in Dostoevsky's Legend by Antanas Maceina, *Der Grossinquisitor: Geschichts-philosophische Deutung der Legende Dostojewskijs* (Heidelberg: F. H. Kerle, 1952), 79–80.

ity in language as well as in content of Dostoevsky's and Kierkegaard's account of introspective despair almost defies belief." [26] The similarity between these two thinkers is also striking in another way: just as Kierkegaard set out to save Christendom from the Christians, so Dostoevsky aspired to save Orthodoxy from the Orthodox. If Christianity were to remain the foundation of modern Russian society, Orthodoxy must be reborn through infusion of the Holy Spirit.

The means of achieving this is through the experience of single persons. The novel, like the dialogue of Plato, is an exoteric mode of communication: it speaks its truths to everyman. The most effective means of communicating the sense of the fundamental experiences to everyman and evoking them in his life is through myth. This is an essential reason for Dostoevsky's use of it. Lauth observed that it was Dostoevsky rather than Sorel who discovered political myth, as well as the superman, and that he, uninfluenced by Kierkegaard, was both victim of and victor over existential dread.[27] That the Inquisitor himself created a "political myth" as a device for control of his slave-men is clear enough, and this was a brilliant anticipation of subsequent totalitarian praxis. That Ivan contrived a myth of the power of evil and its diverse configurations also is evident. That Dostoevsky, in the same piece of writing, created a third level of myth is an artistic miracle. And to complement each level of myth there is a corresponding experience, on each occasion a vision or revelation —an apocalypse—of the nature and destiny of man. For what Lauth did not mention was that Dostoevsky was also the discoverer of political apocalypse as a mode of apprehending existentially decisive experiences in the modern age of ideology. It was the great discovery of Dostoevsky that, not science, but a derailed religious enthusiasm lies beneath the façade of the modern mass movements. But he simultaneously showed apocalypse in the ancient sense not to be dead: he performed the revelation of the Russian Christ of his meditations with a power that is breathtaking. Myth is a central attribute of Dostoevsky's art, and especially prominent is the mythic presentation of

---

26 Geoffrey Clive, "Sickness Unto Death in the Underground: A Study of Nihilism," *Harvard Theological Review*, LI (1958), 142, 156.
27 See Lauth, *Die Philosophie Dostojewskis*, 45.

rationalism and the city as evil.[28] This point is borne out by analysis of the Legend: the corrosive intellect of the rationalist-gnostic created New Sodom as an abomination of desolation standing in the holy place. Nature and passion, on the other hand, are redemptive; and it is no accident that *The Brothers Karamazov* is not set in the city, but in *Skotoprigon'evsk* (Stockyard, Cattle Jump), and one important episode occurs at Mokroe (Moisture, Humidity). The telluric mysticism of *The Brothers Karamazov* invokes the mythic consciousness in a rich variety of ways, but especially through the use of personal and place names connoting veneration of the life-giving sun and fruitful earth (see chap. 1, sec. 3). *Mokroe* is etymologically related to *Mokosh* (*Moksha*) which designated "Mother Moist Earth," and which like her Scythian predecessor, Api-Anahita, the "Great Goddess," was the protector of semen, childbearing, and sheep breeding. *Volos,* one of the designations of the sun, was the god of cattle breeding. The Slavic word *mir* (the peasant community) is connected with the Iranian *Mithra,* the Middle Persian form of which is *Mihr.* In Persian mythology, which partly lies behind the old Kievan pantheon, Mithra and Anahita were worshiped as a pair, and the former was both "Lord of Wide Pastures" and "Lord of Battles." Both fire and sun were symbolized by the cow in Rusian mythology. The Dmitri-Grushenka (*Grusha* = "onion") conjunction at Mokroe doubly invokes the cosmic-telluric symbolism of fruitfulness, suffering, and cathartic passion, as this is reinforced by the legend of the onion and the theme of dancing which forms the bridge to the folk-religiousness of the sectarians. This realism of the common order is contrasted with the higher realism of the preceding books 5 and 6 in the novel as the two levels of reality—the earthly and the transcendental—which supply the boundaries of the two conflicting laws governing action in the novel, the law of nature and the law of God; the whole, then, is embraced and tends toward synthesis in Karamazovism in which every action is passionate and every passion fraught with redemptive possibility—from lecherous to romantic to mystical love. By showing

---

28 See Donald Fanger, *Dostoevsky and Romantic Realism: A Study of Dostoevsky in Relation to Balzac, Dickens, and Gogol* (Cambridge: Harvard University Press, 1965), 131, 227, 231–32, 258–60.

the human implication of the love experience at all levels and the suffering it always entails, Dostoevsky communicates the mystical insight of the organic oneness of mankind and the whole creation, sustains his teaching of universal guilt and responsibility, and credibly dignifies man's existence (even Karamazov existence) with the prospective fulfillment promised in the epigraph of the novel: "Verily, verily, I say unto you, except a grain of wheat fall into the ground and die, it abideth alone: but if it die, it bringeth forth much fruit" (John 12:24).[29] The whole novel, then, is about redemption and is mythic, the climax of its mythopoesis being the Legend with its articulation of Dostoevsky's great apocalypse.

The author began his mature work with *Notes From Underground*, a defiant assertion of the ineradicable worth of every single human being.

> This reaffirmation of the intrinsic worth of the individual is one of the major links between Dostoevsky and Kierkegaard: both, in essence, stand with what Hegel termed the "Unhappy Consciousness." The Underground Man's attack against "twice two is four" ("Twice two is four is no longer life, gentlemen, but the beginning of death") is an attack against a rationalistic metaphysics which seeks the salvation of the individual through his subordination to and integration with, an all-embracive social or world order.[30]

The Legend of the Grand Inquisitor is this argument carried to its ontological conclusion. The sheer rejection in the *Notes* of rationalism by a man because he refuses to become a mere cipher in a homogeneous system is succeeded in the Legend by the affirmation of the worth of the human person because of his participation in transcendent Being. No mundane system ever can touch the onto-

---

29 Belknap, *Structure of "The Brothers Karamazov,"* 26–34, 47–50, 66–67, 74, 87, 96; Edward Wasiolek, *The Explicator*, XVI (October, 1957), Item 7; Charles E. Passage, *Dostoevsky the Adapter: A Study in Dostoevsky's Use of the Tales of Hoffmann* (Chapel Hill: University of North Carolina Press, 1954), 195; George Vernadsky, *The Origins of Russia* (Oxford: Clarendon Press, 1959), 36, 116, 122–23, 127; *The Notebooks for "The Brothers Karamazov,"* 109–14, 118, 124, 143, 151–52, 155; cf. 33, 39, 202, 235.

30 Robert Louis Jackson, *Dostoevsky's Underground Man in Russian Literature* (The Hague: Mouton, 1958), *ad init.*

logical foundations of human nature as imprinted with the seal of the image of God. The defiance of the *Notes* persists in the Legend but now augmented by a note of triumph. It is because man is what he *is* that freedom can be affirmed and the program of the Inquisitor ultimately be dismissed as the nightmare of a madman.

CHAPTER IX

CONCLUSION: DOSTOEVSKY'S POLITICAL THEORY

The results of this study can now be brought together in the following considerations.

The Legend of the Grand Inquisitor articulates an apocalyptical vision of the present age considered as the penultimate phase of history in the Christian tradition: the reign of the Antichrist. In taking biblical apocalypse as its form, it employs a conception of history as a present under God which moves from genesis through the Incarnation irreversibly toward the *parousia* and the Kingdom of God, an extension of time suspended in the Sabbath of eternity made meaningful through the self-disclosure of the divine *Realissimum* Who is the sovereign Lord of being.

The political theory of the piece finds its axis in the tension of man's attunement to the revealed order of being and his defection from it into radical immanence through conscious rebellion. As a diagnosis of the experiential origins and theoretical structure of spiritual rebellion understood to be the anthropological ground of totalitarianism, Dostoevsky's substantive analysis is without peer in the literature. Erected upon a broad empirical base which includes dominant intellectual currents, vestiges of the ancient cosmic religiousness, spiritual and theological tendencies, conspiratorial and revolutionary movements, and a grasp of the long-range factors determining the movement of history in the modern period, the "synthesis of anarchism" uttered by the Inquisitor is a theoretical masterpiece. Its merit lies not only in that it comprehends in principle all of the forms of ideological terror known to this day, or even in that it shows their common root in spiritual disease and analyzes the pathology in detail—unique though these achievements are. Rather, its overriding merit lies in the philosophical acumen and artistic genius of Dostoevsky's refutation within the Legend itself of the Inquisitor's premises and conclusions on both the intellectual and existential levels. It thereby becomes a reaffirmation of the truth of being of singular cogency and evocative power.

The foregoing chapters dwelt at length on these aspects of the Legend, and only a terse summary is necessary here.

The argument at the intellectual level shows the ideology of the Inquisitor, for all his eloquence, to be a *reductio ad absurdum* because: he knows his own doctrine to be vitiated by lies; he despises the mankind he gratuitously presumes to save; his therapy for the ills of existence can only take effect on condition that man cease to be man and become a domestic animal or an insect. In other words, it is salvation which assures brute existence as its highest reward and supreme enticement and becomes a possibility only through destruction of the *differentia specifica* comprising the human essence, the result yielded being the absurdity that to be saved man must be destroyed *qua* man.

The argument at the existential-metaphysical level confutes the ideology by affirming the following propositions. Man—and this means all men individually—knows himself to be man through immediate experience and differentiates himself from brute animals, hence, no social order representative of only the brutish in man can suffice him as human—that is, man as he is and as he knows himself to be. Man—and, again, this means all men individually—knows God *to be* and himself *not* to be God. His proper place in the hierarchy of being lies somewhere in the range between the perfectly divine and the perfectly brute, both elements he experiences to be present in his nature. Hence, no political order predicated upon the pretended divinity of the ruler, or which fails to acknowledge the participation by all men in the divine as the constitutive element of personal human nature, can suffice man as he knows himself to be. Man, historically and ontogenetically, knows himself to epitomize in his composite nature all the realms of being in the sense of his reciprocal participation in reality from the level of the grossly physical to the level of the divine. The differentiation of the range of experience in the modes of the noetic and the pneumatic—given expression in myth, philosophy, and revelation—enables man: to discover the *locus* of the divine to be beyond the cosmos; to apply to the whole of experienced reality the indices immanent and transcendent; to find in the nonexistent reality of transcendence beyond the world the Is of being, the absolute ground of existence, the Creator of the world, and the source of the order of being, as well as both the origin and destiny of man; and to symbolize himself as the image or representative of God in existence and as His instrument in the unfolding drama of world history. Hence, any concrete political order—whatever the details of institutional configuration, the varieties of traditions and other historical accidents incorporated into it—must as a minimum requirement reflect with greater or lesser adequacy the nature of man and the ontologically grounded order of being as these have been differentiated and become known in history, if it is to be satisfactory as a shelter for human existence. To do less than this and radically to immanentize politics through the apotheosis of biology, sex, race, nationality, power, economics, or in any way otherwise to hypostatize an element of reality is a theoretical derailment (*parekbasis*)[1] which perverts the political on principle by destroying the experientially differentiated tension of being and, therewith, the specifically human in history.

As political apocalypse the Legend is to be understood as authentically prophetic and eschatological in a twofold sense.[2]

Dostoevsky knows that, even if it means the destruction of civilization together with the idea of God in man and the suffering and even slaughter of hundreds of millions of persons, the Inquisitor and his

---

1 Cf. Aristotle, *Politics* 1307a7.
2 Cf. chap. 4, sec. 4, *above*, where the Legend as apocalypse is discussed.

successors can persist in rebellion and achieve rulership over the world. Indeed, the Legend in its predictive aspect is unequivocal in this regard: what the Inquisitor has said will come to pass, and the dominion of the man-god will encompass the peoples of the earth and his reign will extend to the end of time. This element of the Legend can in no way be softened. It is present in all its harshness in the text, a cry of anguish from the depths of the soul. Dostoevsky understood as have few other men the maniacal qualities of the new men who emerged onto the stage of history in the nineteenth century as carriers of the modern gnostic ideology. The demonic blight he saw them bringing across the face of history appeared to him to be so profound and pervasive as to smother mankind itself for all foreseeable time. He points to no easy way out of this night of agony but, like Zosima, only bows to the earth in reverence before coming generations as to those destined terribly to suffer. Thus the Legend is a prophetic preview of the history of our times; and despite past horrors the indication is faint enough that the worst has as yet passed. It is a great irony that few today understand the logic and tendencies of the age so well as did Dostoevsky a century ago.

It is, therefore, of more than perfunctory importance to recapitulate his analysis. The messianic ideologies which he lumps together under the rubric "socialism" pretend to be scientific but are, in fact, political religions which have absorbed and perverted Christian faith symbols to preach a secular doctrine of universal salvation. In lieu of rational analysis of reality, they rest upon a secret wisdom or gnosis drawn from an apocalyptical metastatic faith experience. Through this experience new "truth" is gained and proclaimed. All mankind must accept it and it is to be extracted as a confession from them. The core of modern gnostic ideology is the expectation of a radical change in the nature of man, the conditions of existence, and the structure of being. Ideology is, thus, with certain modern refinements, roughly equivalent to Plato's *doxa* (uncritical opinion) and is unlike *episteme* (scientific knowledge) in two decisive respects. First, it systematically fosters scotosis or intellectual and spiritual blindness to the end that reality is purposely obscured rather than illuminated. Second, it serves as a Pascalian *divertissement* by diabolically absorbing the energies of man and thwarting rational concern for existential problems of critical importance to rational existence through attunement to the order of being.[3] This disruption of man's participation in being is abetted by dogmatic assertions which posit both the irrationality, irrelevance, inaccessibility, or nonexistence of the transcendent ground of Being *and* the self-contained existence of man and nature as sole or controlling reality. God is dead; and radically immanent reality is made the substitute ground of existence. Ultimately, even denial of transcendence is prohibited, and the whole of existential concern is swallowed up in the ideological diversion. The ideologue elite organize on the pattern of a priesthood of the militantly faithful like monastic orders which alternate discipline and strict asceticism with ritual sadism and orgiastic debauchery. Their success is dependent upon inculcation of dogma by all means, from missionizing and propaganda to gross coercion and ruthless liquidation of opposition—techniques implemented with systematic vengeance through state institutions when a monopoly of power is gained in any society. They regard man as infinitely malleable and are prepared to destroy those individuals who prove to be less than susceptible of their truth. Destructiveness extends through all the spheres of existence from the spiritual to the intellectual, to the emotional and physical, from the social to the personal. Through psychological mass management the single person ceases to exist and becomes a manipulatable cipher whose continued biological subsistence is justified solely by the criterion of conformity and contribution to socially proclaimed objectives. And, finally, the doctrine propagated as truth and made the basis of the establishment of the new reality is itself a premeditated swindle which springs not from

---

[3] For Plato's distinction between *doxa* and *episteme*, see the *Republic*, 476b, ff. Cf. the discussion of *scotosis* in Bernard J. F. Lonergan, *Insight: A Study of Human Understanding* (2nd ed.; London: Longmans, Green, 1958), 191. For a discussion of ideology as predicated upon a conscious swindle and of the *system* as the thought form of speculative gnosticism, see Eric Voegelin, *Wissenschaft, Politik und Gnosis* (Munich: Kösel, 1959), 38ff, 55ff. The terminology derives ultimately from Democritus: "Fr. 6. Of knowledge there are two types: the one genuine, the other obscure (*skotios*)." Cf. Philip Wheelwright (ed.), *The Presocratics* (New York: Odyssey Press, Inc., 1966), 182, 303. Cf. the New Testament usage, Matt. 4:16; John 1:5; 8:12; 12:35. For *diversion* in Pascal, see *Pensées*, Nos. 139 *et seq.*, 166, 168; cf. Nos. 100 *et seq.*

the nobility of humanitarian sentiment, but from the insatiable lust for power of megalomaniacs insanely jealous that they are, in fact, themselves not God.[4]

This aspect of Dostoevsky's apocalypse does not make of him a black prophet or otherwise distinguish him essentially from the ancient apocalyptists: the hope and the faith held out to readers is identical with that held out to readers of Daniel and Revelation. Nor is he either more or less "pessimistic" than were they: the reigns of the Antichrists in history have always been bleak affairs.[5] Projecting his vision from its origins in the sixteenth century toward the climax at the end of history, Dostoevsky affirms that indescribable humiliation and suffering will be the lot of man, but at the End faith will be rewarded. In common with the biblical apocalyptists he shows faith to have intrinsic rewards in the present: man without God ceases to be human and in the absence of faith becomes either a maniac or a suicide. The Legend was written in the depth of crisis, with the contours of the next phase just becoming visible. In it Dostoevsky diagnoses the crisis, shows the etiology and nature of the disease, and prescribes the cure. Like the apocalyptists of old, his message has permanent relevance as an exhortation to faith and righteousness which sustains hope that the community of the persevering may yet curb the ravages of the rebellious; and failing that, it contains assurance that they too shall enjoy the blessedness of the saints. Whether man rebels or perseveres in faith, he cannot avoid death and the Last Judgment of the God of history; and under the aspect of eternity the victory belongs to the faithful. Such, then, is the substance of Dostoevsky's political apocalypse.

As the foregoing paragraphs have made clear, there is not to be read into the Legend any endorsement of the Inquisitor's enterprise

---

4 For the dream world of the gnostic-ideologue as the "second reality," in Robert Musil's phrase, see Voegelin, *Wissenschaft, Politik und Gnosis*, 46. Cf. Robert Musil, *Der Mann ohne Eigenschaften* (Hamburg: Rowohlt, 1952), 1084ff and *passim*.

5 See H. H. Rowley, *The Relevance of Apocalyptic: A Study of Jewish and Christian Apocalypses from Daniel to the Revelation* (2nd ed.; London: Lutterworth, 1947), 36, 163–64.

as either simply inevitable or in any way noble. Nor is there any attempt to polarize the political and the spiritual and to show the impossibility of satisfactorily ordering political existence while simultaneously realizing the promise of Christian existence. To find this to be the meaning of the Legend is to identify Dostoevsky ultimately with the Inquisitor, and such an interpretation is untenable. It falls by the same critique with which the Inquisitor is refuted. In addition, one can observe that only the claims of the spirit are absolute. Because the life of the spirit is possible only in concrete, individual human persons, these absolute claims can only be self-imposed. This means, as a consequence, the claims of institutions on men are not absolute, and the concrete political order of a society can pretend to no more than a limited and provisional function in directing the lives of its people. Political existence is not the whole of human existence; and for institutionalized order to arrogate plenary authority over the lives of men to itself is a totalitarian derailment whether committed by a church, a party, or a government. Moreveor, there are in principle no permanent solutions to the problem of how satisfactorily to represent order. There is only the perennial task of modifying and adapting traditional patterns and contents of institutionalization to the needs of concrete men in particular societies with full attention to their essential humanity, the abiding truth of being, and the peculiar pragmatic exigencies of historical existence under changing conditions in the world.

That the teachings of Jesus run counter to the necessities of political existence is well noted. But it is difficult to suppose Dostoevsky discontent on principle with the Pauline compromises of institutional Christianity. Nor would he embrace the Inquisitor's proposal that because of its difficulty the life of the spirit be abdicated to the modern ideologue as the only other available alternative. This is, of course, not the best of possible worlds; but it is the one we have. Dostoevsky was, as he claimed to be, a realist; and since the time of Plato, politics has explicitly been understood to be the art of the possible. Dostoevsky knew, inimical though it is to institutional rigidities, that the life of the spirit must find a place at the core of political order or suffer destruction through perversion. He was, therefore, concerned to find a solution to the problem of institutionalization that was both possible and at least moderately satisfactory.

The spiritual and the political do not as such polarize in the Legend. Still it is evident that the brutal tension of the defection from the order of being—represented apocalyptically as the final battle between Christ and the Antichrist, ethically and metaphysically as the irreconcilable demands of good and evil and of being and nothingness in human existence—does effect a polarity through radical dissociation of the power of spirit and the will of self. This existential split, while untenable because it perverts the nature of man, nonetheless always is a concrete possibility because of the fact of the freedom of the human person. With the actual occurrence of such a breach as a political phenomenon, the complex of issues emerges which can be termed the problem of the sources of order in society when the truth of being has for any reason been eclipsed or destroyed as a socially effective ordering center. Out of the broad range of ensuing political pathology, Dostoevsky selected for particular attention, because of its centrality, the phenomenon of secular power in its diseased manifestation. The Legend is in this aspect a tract for the times, a veritable handbook for political practice in the twentieth century. The perpetuating of political institutions as effective devices for preserving peace and insuring the multifold activities essential to the continuation of existence in the wake of the collapse or revolutionary destruction of the old order is achieved through the exercise of raw power. To the mystery of freedom in Christ, the Inquisitor opposes the mystery of power socially articulated. The truth of the Inquisitor's insight in this respect is perhaps the principal source of strength to his whole position: when all other alternatives are exhausted, there can be erected through brute force under color of just authority a political shelter capable of sustaining life, one which overcomes factional strife and brings a semblance of order out of potentially disastrous social chaos.

But like all he says, even this is only a half-truth. The exercise of power is, of course, characteristic of every political structure. Institutionalized coercion has an indispensable place in every society, and it is universally considered to be an acceptable means of main-

taining the force of the laws wherever less stringent means fail. Three
levels of the problem of political order and power can be distinguished in a discussion of the Legend. First, insofar as the Legend is
apocalypse, it expresses the bequest from the ancient apocalyptists
of the sharp contrast between empires as pure power constellations
without ulterior significance and the community of the faithful as
the carrier of meaning in history. The full consequences of this
legacy—leading ultimately to the conception of history as divisible
into the sacred and the profane, and of reality as articulated into
the *civitas Dei* and the *civitas terrena*, among much else—need not be
explored here. But two related conclusions drawn from the consideration of power at this level may be mentioned: the inference
that the substance of politics is power; the inference that the life
of the spirit is radically other-worldly and can be institutionalized
only in politically sterile sectarian or monastic communities, whose
persistence as enclaves in society is to be condoned solely on condition they in no way disturb the secular order. Both of these conclusions are invalidated by Dostoevsky's analysis. To trace their careers
in modern political thought would require another book. But it is
pertinent to observe that here the limits of apocalypse in the Legend
are reached, and the separation of the form from the content of Dostoevsky's meaning occurs. For it is precisely the integration of spirit
into the political order as its central constitutive factor which most
concerns him. Dostoevsky is, therefore, by this token, not himself an
apocalyptist in the decisive sense; but the Inquisitor, by the same
measure, is shown to be precisely an apocalyptist. Like the ancient
apocalyptists he has embraced as true the assertion that spirit and
secular power radically polarize; but in direct contrast to them, he
has rejected spirit and embraced power. Dostoevsky shows this to be
the essence of political apocalypse as a modern phenomenon: it is
the inversion of biblical apocalypse. The privatization of noetic reason and the life of the spirit—reflected in the Inquisitor's doctrine
and also present in modern Western democracies since the time of
Spinoza and Locke—is symptomatic of the apocalyptist mentality.

The second level of the problem derives also from apocalyptic
thought. It poses the issue of the hypostatization of power under-

stood to be a derailment. The inference that the substance of politics is power is the position symbolized by the Inquisitor. Insofar as he represents an appeal to religious enthusiasm, he also absorbs elements of the content of the inference that the spiritual life is politically irrelevant. The result is that the Inquisitor's city is a pure power configuration disguised by sectarian trappings. It is designed to foster no more than the biological subsistence of its citizenry while gratifying its ruler's lust for dominion. His ideology purposely obscures the nature of the enterprise (as he confesses to Christ) which he knows to rest on a swindle and ascribes to it great and noble purposes. The senselessness of the lust for power after power without justification beyond itself must be concealed through "miracle, mystery and authority"—that is, through the dogmas and rituals of the state. The totalitarian state is depicted as a prison whose rulers can rest content only when all of mankind has been entrapped within its walls. From the crisis of a society whose traditional order falters and collapses there comes the apotheosis of power, the secular hell of a totalitarian system. The assertion of the gnostic intellectual, under the pretext of a bold new realism, that power is the sovereign principle of politics is the dogmatic equivalent, at the level of *doctrine*, and of physical and psychological terror, at the level of political praxis. The act involves a willful perversion of being through illicit hypostatization of power. The pathological use of an intellectual doctrine deliberately to obscure reality and to conceal the true explanation of action (rather than to illumine reality and reveal the reasons for action) Dostoevsky recognized as the essence of ideology. He characterizes the teaching of the Inquisitor as systematically elaborated obfuscation. To claim not only that power is the substance of politics, but to attempt also to exercise plenary power in existence is the substance of metaphysical rebellion: a defection from the will of God in idolatry of self. It was, therefore, rightly understood by the ancient apocalyptists as the derailment of human existence, a symbol of the rule of Antichrist.

The third level of the problem is recognition of power as the attribute which permits the persistence of every existent. Dostoevsky's analysis here is divorced from apocalypse. Anthropologically seen, power is traceable to the lower range of man's nature as posited together with the brute fact of existence itself. Politically seen, power functions to insure the maintenance of regulated peace within a society as the essential precondition both to continued individual existence as well as the flowering of human life made possible only by political society. This is because man is by nature a political, living being in that his synthetic nature is distinguished by rationality, freedom, the power to discern good and evil, and to communicate discursively through speech and linguistic signs. In its external dimension, political power secures existence against destruction by enemies. Since Machiavelli it has been clear that power relations define the field of pragmatic political action with respect to the issues of hegemony and subjection. In this sphere civilizational merit plays at best a secondary role. A superior power can vanquish an inferior power regardless of respective intrinsic worth on the scale of civilizational attainment. Hence, power is irrational. And so far from being an autonomous factor in politics, it must ever be coordinated with some end as a means. If by perversion it is itself mistaken for the end of action in an absolute sense, then it can only serve the unregulated gratification of the base passions of which it is naturally the ally and servant: it becomes the *libido dominandi* and, if institutionalized, becomes despotism and rule by terror. Without content in itself, power is subordinate to the objectives of a political entity and can as well serve imperial expansion as the establishment and preservation of social justice and domestic peace.

While these formulations do not exhaust the subject, at least the central issue has been clarified. If existence is to be more than mere brute existence, then power must be subordinate to reason and spirit and be the servant of the range in man's existence distinctive of his humanity. This pragmatic political task requires attentiveness to the continuing problems of maintaining the master-slave relationship between spirit and power and of constantly gauging with accuracy the level and forms of power essential to the preservation of society's existence. Power is, therefore, neither the supreme good nor sovereign principle of politics, nor even much of a "problem" in political theory. Rather it is one among other important factors to be considered in arriving at specific political decisions through the exercise of informed common sense. That Dostoevsky rejected as symptomatic of disorder the radical existential split between the power of the spirit and the power of the self is clear from his analysis of reality. The split implies rebellion. Only in the wake of such rebellion can power be hypostatized as the central feature of politics. The portrayal of the ideology of the Inquisitor as a mere camouflage of simple lust for power, combined with Dostoevsky's perception that the *libido dominandi* comes down to no more than vacuous nonsense—in which, however, men can resolutely persist—may well be regarded as the ultimate tribute to the wisdom of the modern ideologue.

It may finally be mentioned that there is no indication of new revelation in the Legend. Dostoevsky is no prophet of the wave of the future, of some post-Christian faith for a mankind for whom the biblical God is dead. He recognized disbelief and rebellion as maladies of the spirit—not symptoms of a coming radical new revelation which might somehow reconcile in principle the Inquisitor and Christ considered as opposites. His faith is biblical, as the evidence shows; and virtually everything said in the Legend is illuminative of biblical religion. To be sure, Dostoevsky maintains the openness of the soul which is the precondition of faith, the attentiveness to the silent voices of grace, to the hope for renewed revelation by God. This attitude is indispensable to the life of the spirit and as characteristic of the Old Testament prophets as of Christians in every age. The Legend stands squarely in this tradition. Confronted with the overwhelming tendency of the age to rebel and deny, neither Dostoevsky nor his Christ joins the movement to head it—as Belinsky had anticipated they would. Nor does he impose upon the process of history any sort of inevitably unfolding dialectic which dogmatically asserts the reconciliation in principle of the *coincidentia oppositorum* of good and evil through a new synthesis. Had he done so, then he would himself have become a gnostic apocalyptist, just as was the Inquisitor, and as did Hegel.[6] This is true both because: the

---

[6] For the identification of Hegel as a speculative gnostic, see Voegelin, *Wissenschaft, Politik und Gnosis,* 51–56, 90ff; "On Hegel—A Study in Sorcery," *Studium Generale,* XXIV (1971), 335–68; cf. Thomas J. J. Altizer, *The Gospel of Christian Atheism* (Philadelphia: Westminster Press, 1966).

historical dialectic is a dogmatic assumption incapable of being critically and empirically established as descriptive of the process of history; and the dualism of "sacred and profane" posits two realities thereby raising the implication that yet a third reality can emerge through synthesis. This is, however, to misconceive and misrepresent existence. There is but one reality, and all that *is* participates in being and derives its "reality" from that fact. Hence, the "profane" is only the less-than-perfectly-sacred reality that is in essence nonetheless sacred and good. The only admissible "dualism" is being and nonbeing or (alternatively) nothingness.

Like the ideologues, the sectarians were for Dostoevsky both indicative of the dangers of religious enthusiasm to the traditional order of Russian society and symptomatic of the thirst for spiritual rebirth that he perceived at all levels of society. He hoped to capture the fire of these movements so as to revitalize the disintegrating order of tsarist-Orthodox Russia. Neither ideology nor sectarianism did he regard as offering a valid solution to the problem at hand; rather both promised disaster. In this judgment he was not wrong. Unlike Nietzsche, Dostoevsky was not so impressed by the mass movements of his time that he supposed them capable of driving God out of existence. He took his stand instead with the Suffering Servant of Deutero-Isaiah who knew whence revelation comes, to maintain attunement to the truth of transcendent Being through faith and proclaim His Word even though his was a solitary voice crying in the wilderness of man's rebellion. To proclaim the death of God and accept it as a piece of scientific information, he could only have regarded as the apocalypse of a pseudomillenarian sectarian, at best spiritual obtuseness, at worst monotonous blasphemy. In this respect, it may be said Dostoevsky was both the prophet and judge of our age.

Dostoevsky having begun as a rebel, the Legend performs a cathartic function. The justification for rebellion—the idealism and conviction of sensitive men and women whose sense of justice and truth is outraged by the hypocrisy, callousness, and inhumanity of existence —can be effectively countered only in the same way Dostoevsky purged his own rebellion, namely by drawing out unflinchingly all the consequences of rebellion when translated into the concrete action of individuals and societies. This is the tormenting theme of passion and suffering taken on the pilgrimage from *Crime and Punishment* to *The Brothers Karamazov*. To it he devoted the greatest moment of his art, a noble affirmation of the divinity in man.

INDEX